CARIBBEAN
SPACES

D1563500

CARIBBEAN SPACES

ESCAPES FROM TWILIGHT ZONES

CAROLE BOYCE DAVIES

UNIVERSITY OF ILLINOIS PRESS
Urbana, Chicago, and Springfield

Library of Congress Cataloging-in-Publication Data
Boyce Davies, Carole, author.
Caribbean spaces : escapes from twilight zones / Carole Boyce
Davies.
pages   cm
Includes bibliographical references and index.
ISBN 978-0-252-03802-0 (hardback)—ISBN 978-0-252-07953-5
(paperback)
1. Blacks—Caribbean Area—Migrations. 2. Blacks—Caribbean
Area—Ethnic identity. 3. Human geography—Caribbean Area. I.
Title.
F2191.B55B69   2013
305.8960729—dc23   2013010202

For the next generation:
Ilori Waithe, Joseph Boyce III,
Christian and Chace Boyce,
and Ila Rose Flanagan

Remembering: Joseph Anthony Boyce Sr. (1938–2011)—
"Big Brother Joey"—who joined the elders
in that famous family photograph
and
Rihanna's emblematic Gran Gran Dolly,
Clara Braithwaite (1940–2012), who is also captured
in the meaning of this work. I was happy even
in her grandmother's passing to learn that RiRi
had a "gran gran" available in New York.

Asymmetric infinity, on the other hand, implies an enfolding and unfolding of cultures beyond tamed vision, or totalitarian caprice and loss of revolutionary soul, it implies unseen yet real natures whose life is indefatigable . . . and whose therapeutic horizons-in-depth lie beyond logical fate that frames canvases of existence.

—Wilson Harris, "The Schizophrenic Sea,"
in *The Womb of Space: The Cross-Cultural Imagination*

CONTENTS

ACKNOWLEDGMENTS

A few of these essays have appeared in different form, updated with new content for this collection: A portion of "Connecting Stories: My Grandmother's Violin," was published as "Secrets of My Mother's Sweetness," in *Caribbean Erotic* (2010), edited by Opal Palmer Adisa and Donna Weir Soley (now with two additional sections); "Women, Labor, and the Transnational: From Work to Work," was published as "Caribbean Women, Domestic Labor, and the Politics of Transnational Migration," in *Women's Labor and the Global Economy* (2007), edited by Sharon Harley; "Haiti, I Can See Your Halo," was a plenary address published in the *Journal of the African Literature Association* (Spring 2011); and "'Changing Locations': Literary Pathways of Caribbean Migration" appeared as "Triply Diasporized: Literary Pathways of Caribbean Migration," in *The Routledge Companion to Caribbean Literature* (2011). A portion of chapter 4 appeared as "Transformational Discourses, Afro-Diasporic Culture, and the Literary Imagination," *Macalester International* 3.20 (1996): http://digitalcommons.macalester.edu/macintl/vol3/iss1/20.

Thank you to Marcia Douglas for use of the poem "Voice Lesson," which first appeared in *Claiming Voice*, a student poetry booklet compiled by Douglas for the author's Black Women Writers course in 1994. The poem "Leaving" appeared initially in volume 1 of *Moving beyond Boundaries* (1994), edited by the author. My friend Abena Busia is acknowledged here as well for reminding me about the film "Twilight City" and for critical affirmation. When I showed her the book's cover, she offered the opening line from her sister Akosua's novel: "There is no blue like the blue of the Caribbean Sea."

Thank you to Brian and Dalia Davies Flanagan for providing a beautiful pre-wedding location in a villa in St. Lucia where this manuscript was a companion; a lovely corner in their apartment, significantly in Brooklyn, for work on the final draft; and above all for the gift of a first granddaughter, Ila Rose.

My colleague Kenneth McClane deserves my unwavering gratitude for affirming this book from the start and helping me maintain my sense of a creative/intellectual self in the midst of then swelling contradictions surrounding Cornell's redesigning of its Africana Studies and Research Center. And, ironically still, Cornell University is acknowledged for providing the research location again in upstate New York that brought back to actuality how twilight zones work and what was needed to finish this manuscript. Thank you especially to librarian Sharon Powers and Africana Library director Eric Acree for providing the actual research environment and support that a scholar like me values. You have made my research time so pleasant.

Opal Palmer Adisa, Merle Collins, and Kamau Brathwaite encouraged me to write the family and personal narratives included here. Much love and Nuff Respect! I want to specially recognize the editors at the University of Illinois Press for professional elegance. I am also indebted to the unnamed reviewers who offered insightful readings, wonderful suggestions, and the kind of critical affirmation which allowed me to go forward with this book.

Wonderful graduate students at Cornell, such as Courtney Knapp, Alyssa Clutterbuck, Kavita Singh, Ryann Alexander, Jessica Alarcon, Keshia Hicks, Ayanna Parris, and Patricia Abraham, and bright undergraduate students, including Tia Hicks, Elizabeth Rust, Rocelio Rocio, and many others, have always brought fresh insights, references, and their own creative, political, and intellectual work that inspires and must always be recognized as the lights of hope in sometimes otherwise dismally regressive academic settings.

Kadija Sesay and Michael La Rose in London provided helpful connections for photographs by Armet Francis about the early Caribbean experience in London. Photographers Noelle Theard, Jean Willy Gerdes, Carl Juste (Miami), my dear friend Charles (Chuck) Martin (New York), and master artist LeRoy Clarke in Trinidad gave kind permissions for the inclusion of their work. Thank you to Babacar M'bow of Multitudes Gallery in Miami for help with photographs as well and for the choice of the art for the cover. My nephew Joseph A. Boyce Jr. provided urgent technical computor support at a critical point and is offered my deep love and respect. Thank you to Cuban artist Alejandro Mendoza for use of "The Border", from his *Locations* series, the artwork that is featured on the cover of this book.

CARIBBEAN
SPACES

CARIBBEAN SPACES

Reflective Essays/
Creative-Theoretical Circulations

"Caribbean Spaces" is my way of describing plural island geographies, the surrounding continental locations as well as Caribbean sociocultural and geopolitical locations in countries in North, South, and Central America. A Caribbean diaspora, we can now assert, has also been created in countries via various waves of migration to particular areas that became Caribbean Space. These are social and cultural places (spaces) that extend the understanding of the Caribbean beyond "small space," fragmented identifications. The claiming of Caribbean Space captures ontologically ways of being in the world. It assumes movement as it makes and remakes the critical elements of Caribbean geography: landscape and seascape, sky and sun, but also music, food, and style.

Caribbean diaspora spaces, in the continental context, refer to those locations in which there are distinctly identified re-creations of Caribbean communities following migration. Essential ingredients include a sizable demographic shift in the population to this given location and the development of Caribbean business communities: travel agencies and barrel-shipping agencies, locs and braid hairdressers, botanicas, assorted businesses, restaurants, bakeries, and shops dedicated solely to the preparing or selling of Caribbean food products—fresh produce and ground provisions, roti and patty shops. Entertainment in the form of excursions, dances, Caribbean block parties, parang, concerts, fetes, and other similar activities contributes to the re-creation of Caribbean culture in diaspora. These extend the notion of Caribbean Space as a larger ontological referent as they attempt to reproduce a decolonized set of arrangements. But there is more: Caribbean record shops, music producers, and related networks for the production of shows; communications media ranging from newspapers in London, New York, or Miami; blogs and e-journals, newsletters, party fliers and cards, radio and television stations; soccer and cricket clubs and matches; language diversity, including Creole, patois, Spanglish, and specific Caribbean forms of Spanish; and a public or street-oriented culture manifested in "liming" and its associated stories and boasts, street banter and calling out, loud talking, conspicuous (sometimes ridiculous) clothing styles, and public male-female flirtation and promises. A certain intergenerational camaraderie and socializing, particularly in relations that have to do with the care of children and the elderly, shopping for foods and their preparation, beach outings, and other transgenerational family celebrations with food, music, and dance also create Caribbean space.

Caribbean Spaces then are locations that preserve certain versions of Caribbean culture as they provide community support in migration. A product of diaspora, one can call it, Caribbean spaces are clearly marked by their own self-identification: in London not only Brixton but also Ladbroke Grove and Portobello Road; Powis Square, where there is a Carnival Village and the launching site for the Notting Hill Carnival, and Finsbury Park and the cultural space created in the area around New Beacon Books; Brooklyn, which hosts the Labor Day Parade annually, and Harlem, with its early history of Caribbean businesses, bookstores, and creative expressions and still an island salad bar; Miami, with its complexity of neighborhoods—Little Haiti, Little Havana, and Lauderhill, the 441 strip in North Miami; the North Side of Chicago, around Rogers Park; the Baltimore–Washington, D.C., corridor; Hartford, Connecticut; Toronto, Canada, with its Caribana festival . . . Amsterdam . . . Paris . . . we could go on. Indeed, noting the public celebrations of Carnivals in diaspora is one way of recognizing Caribbean space.

Zones of family interaction also reveal Caribbean space: weddings and funerals, the migrations of children and adults in consistent ways in both directions; the care of elderly and its implications in geographically divided community and family contexts; long-maintained childhood and neighborhood friendships and other fictive kin relationships; the development of generations in communities and a variety of intermarriages—cross-Caribbean/cross-Americas—and other ethnic communities; and the purchasing of property and other residential markers, such as the planting of ackee, banana, mango, and June plum trees in Miami.

Caribbean island spaces provide a certain set of well-documented cultural interactions and neighborliness in community, an assumption of reciprocity, a set of cultural formations produced by waves of migration to the Caribbean from India, Africa, Europe, North and South Americas, northern Africa, the Middle East. History ensures some distinct markers on land, in and on the bodies of the people, in and around the created communities. A certain geography of interconnection in archipelagoes ensures the repetition that Antonio Benitez-Rojo identifies as well as the consistent politics of creolization as articulated by scholars and writers such as Kamau Brathwaite and Edouard Glissant. And the reach into continental locations such as Guyana, Venezuela, Belize, and the United States ensures the set of spatial extensions already identified. But following Alejo Carpentier, one can also think of a Caribbean Mediterranean (83), in which the sea is basically enclosed by land spaces that make up the Caribbean. Wilson Harris had also described a "pre-Columbian bridge of myth that runs through the Americas and with which Pym achieves uncanny, however unconscious, synchronicity in the womb of cultural space" (24). The sense or desire, perhaps, of that mythic yet actual sea bridge arching into the Caribbean and moving into the Americas is one, in my view, still worth seeing or feeling.

Archipelagization provides one entry point, as it carries the marks of history but also the possibilities of consistent transformation, resistance, and re-creation. And there are several archipelagoes in the Caribbean, each with relational patterns of repetition and difference. The histories of these archipelagoes are also as seasoning places for enslaved Africans, the launching points of colonial conquest of the Americas and the creation of departments of colonial powers overseas. A laboratory of sorts was developed by colonial powers on islands used to create new plants and hybrid people. Thus, a contemporary celebration of a "Spice Island," with all its sensual evocations, sits on top of a historical reality that the island was used to develop various types of spices, evocative then of colonial botanical experimentation. The evidence is there in any walk through botanical gardens anywhere. Landscapes in Indian Ocean archipelagoes with similar patterns of sugar cane plantations, assorted tropical products, and "creole festival culture" confirm this as they also provide interesting parallels. *Archipelagoes of Sound: Transnational Caribbeanities, Women, and Music* (2012) is a nicely conceptualized contribution by Ifeona Fulani that in its introduction uses Benitez-Rojo for the framing of a launching point for a "meta-archipelago that flows outward sonically implying boundless, dynamic movement" (2).

Still, Caribbean people embrace and indigenize their landscapes, as Sylvia Wynter describes it: growing their "ground provisions," herbs, vegetables, and plants; populating the landscape also with their duppies, jumbies, and other spirits; carnivalizing all locations consistently, creating housing sometimes precariously on hilly terrain or in densely populated urban environments that later become desired locations overlooking seascapes; living on fault lines sometimes; and, in periods of difficulty, at times creating new identities. Still, pharmaceutical experimentations, as in the Puerto Rican context, or the blatant uses of Caribbean locations as military bases, as in, say, Guantánamo or Vieques, are newer colonizations of contemporary economic globalization that bring forward the ongoing contradictions for people trying to navigate where they are in the world's priorities, which often do not include them.

And although Carnivals are sites for "taking space," Caribbean women's bodies are sexualized both in home and in diasporic contexts. In the latter context, the movement out of the original cultural and geographic locations with their histories renders a displacement into large urban cities around the world where we are now under a variety of uninformed gazes. Bodies writhing on the paved roads or bottoms bent over in front of policemen's genitals mimic a kind of historical distortion that invites a range of readings. And men with cameras placed between the legs and at the crotches of dancing women in Carnival or those photographing only buttocks create pornographic videos of Carnivals, often without any remuneration to the individuals so used.

M. Nourbese Philip has captured the dynamics of external and internal space in her essay "Dis Place: The Space Between," in which body space mimes colonial dominant-subordinate relations, as the owners of these bodies attempt to claim a certain personal power. For Nourbese, what is defined as empty space actually hides an understanding of how "inner space," in terms of black women's bodies, produces "outer space" at the economic, demographic level. The space between black women's legs easily transforms into place, she asserts.

Still, in the larger geographical context of the Americas, Wilson Harris, in his introduction to *The Womb of Space,* had described a desired movement of an "intuitive self . . . endlessly into flexible patterns, arcs or bridges of community" (xviii). Although he had limited his study to selected works, Harris was actually reaching for a "cross-cultural exploration rarely undertaken by readers or critics" (xix). His definition of a womb of space then is actually a "womb of cultural space" (17), which still demands an ongoing mediation between all structured systems. Wonderful phrases such as "ambiguities of freedom," "meaningful distortions," an "asymmetry within the infinity and genius of art" capture some of his intent (17). But he was also, it seems to me, claiming "a womb of evolutionary space" and a variety of "concentric horizons"(29) that have now become more visible.

Zora Neale Hurston's desire to pursue similar horizons was further clarified during a visit to the Cape Canaveral, Florida, launching point for NASA, the National Aeronautics and Space Administration of the United States. I noted a caption that in many ways summarized Hurston's view of the world and makes her, as she wanted, a bona fide "Welcome to Our State Floridian": "In our time we have learned that the human horizon is infinite." And, ironically, it was this search for the horizon where Zora began her quest and where "Jump at the Sun" still resonates. Along the way, she saw and did beautiful things, including travel throughout the United States, the Caribbean, and Central America, and thus found a way to embrace Caribbean Spaces in ways that are worth emulating. That she wrote *Their Eyes Were Watching God* (1938) in Haiti is still worth underscoring.

An interesting other use of space conceptually is the notion of "problem-spaces," as advanced by David Scott (*Conscripts of Modernity*) to account for discontinuous theoretical though temporal spaces, in which actual unfolding conditions produce alternative meanings. Here we have a different understanding of space, but more as a theoretical conjuncture that moves beyond flattened or perhaps unicentric historical meanings to offer new analyses, in which anticipated outcomes give way to new formations. An overview of a variety of approaches to Caribbean culture, using metaphors of space and place, forests and floral metaphors at times, is provided by Marsha Pearce on caribbeanculturalstudies.com. Here Pearce searches for meaning that gets at the uniqueness of a Caribbean cultural studies model, citing Norman Girvan's insistence that the term *Caribbean* is also an imposition or ordering on a diverse and complicated land- and seascape.

For McKittrick and Woods, the unknowable always has to be factored into discourses of space and place, particularly when race sometimes creates uneven geographies. What is often read as empty space hides a range of yet to be discovered or understood realities. There is a wonderful essay by Thomas F. Carter called "Absence Makes the State Grow Stronger" (2011), in which he describes the use or avoidance of certain spaces assigned to state power that, even when not populated, signify loudly or become, in his words, "materially and spatially manifest." He was describing the Plaza of the Revolution in Cuba with the intent of looking at the use of public and private spaces and further revolutionary space. His expressed desire was to take the logic of "small space" and find ways to extend it beyond its meaning, beyond its local understanding, to thereby examine other small spaces that have that kind of global reach, but also to examine what he calls the "body-space dialectic" (60). I was quite excited to see "Caribbean Spaces,

Transatlantic Spirit: Violence and Spiritual Reimaginings in the Caribbean"
(Prater) as the title of an essay but discovered that it was the attempt of a
panel discussion to capture the ways in which spirit challenges spatial limitations but included one essay on Michelle Cliff with a note on what the
larger intent had been.

Caribbean Spaces: Escapes from Twilight Zones intends to identify a series
of passages and locations between the Americas that facilitate movement
as they identify a set of specific traumas. It is not so much interested in the
"archipelagoes of poverty or pain" theses or the foci on crime and security
and the traffic in drugs, the seamy underside of the use of Caribbean space.
Instead, it tries to move beyond the macro "middle passage," between Africa
and the New World, in order to speak about the way we understand cultural
spaces. To do this, it moves between explorations of Caribbean culture in
a variety of locations (spaces) to a larger imagined geographical Caribbean
space, broadening its meanings at every turn. It also attempts a move between
the autobiographical and the conceptual, the experiential and the theoretical,
in order to disrupt the logic of exclusionary academic discourse that often
denies the personal.

Recent scientific discoveries on space as infinite and ever expanding provide a larger conceptual framework to think about Caribbean space as also
ever expanding. In critical theory, this is matched by the theorizing of "ever-
becoming" space (Massey), which advances toward openness and therefore
provides the possibility of understandings of space as relational, concentric,
or overlapping. This moves us also away from the conquest-of-space narrative
that is at the heart of colonial projects. Thankfully, humans can never conquer
space. The scholarship on postmodern geographies has been important in
reasserting the relevance of space over the overarching temporal logic that
underlies the range of philosophical traditions, including Marxism. In each
case, space is not only location itself but how social, political, and cultural life
informs and reshapes geography. For Soja, even the various "posts" carry a
particular temporality that obscures the spatial. In "Toward a Spatialized On-
tology" (*Postmodern Geographies* 129–30), he outlines a series of arguments
for a spatiotemporal dialectic that leads him in the end to find other spaces.
This provides the discursive openings for thinking about Caribbean Space/s.
Cianci, Patey, and Sullam cite the notion of space as defined by Lefebvre as
produced by a range of social and cultural forces, the politics of space that also
accounts for processes of decolonization and globalization. Thus, we can read
space as politicized, gendered, racialized, and therefore also classed.

Because the Caribbean is clearly one of those geopolitical locations impacted by these larger historical developments, reading Caribbean space in

this contemporary period means using different understandings of how this space is contoured beyond assumed fixed geographies, based on a range of theoretical, political, and experiential movements and events of which we are the beneficiaries. Appadurai offers an assessment by way of conclusion to his essay "Disjuncture and Difference in the Global Cultural Economy" that what characterizes the contemporary are both the radical disjunctures and the movements toward sameness, all within a larger imaginary in which "global flows and uncertain landscapes" (2) operate unevenly, sometimes overlapping, all inflected by a range of factors and actors.

This book is written so that my friends who never made it to university or graduate school, or those who are professionals but rarely read academic books but are also intelligent readers, can read with ease. Often, in differently presented work (that is, work presented mostly for academic readers) they become eavesdroppers to these discussions or owners of books with pride that they show to friends but never read beyond the first few pages. So I have developed a deliberate narrative strategy to present this as though I were relaying to them what people talk about in academic communities while also speaking to those same academic audiences. In terms of documentation format, I have used parenthetical citations of authors whose works are listed in the bibliography instead of extensive footnoting. There is also a deliberate navigation between the autobiographical and the research-based analyses and discussion using deliberate reflective breaks.

Thirteen chapters are included. The first chapter sets up the discussion of "twilight zones." Chapter 2 is a reflective piece, "Reimagining the Caribbean: Seeing, Reading, Thinking." Chapter 3 is autobiographical, describing how I came to consciousness as a Caribbean American subject. The idea of "spirit scapes" is pursued in chapter 4, which also brings together Brazil and the Caribbean in a more analytical essay based on fieldwork in Brazil. It is followed by "Middle Passages: Movable Borders and Ocean-Air Space Mobility." Chapter 6, a research-based chapter on Caribbean domestic labor, provides some concrete examples of women and Caribbean migration and has been updated for inclusion here. "Connecting Stories: My Grandmother's Violin" is a reflective piece that touches on issues of sexuality in the Caribbean context but also provides some extended family history. It is the counterpoint to the experiential chapter 12, "My Father Died a Second Time." Literary examples of issues of migration are captured in chapter 8, "'Changing Locations': Literary Pathways of Caribbean Migration." The iconic meaning of Haiti in African diaspora symbology runs up against the difficulties of contemporary Haiti in chapter 9, "'Haiti, I Can See Your Halo!': Living on Fault Lines." Chapter 10, "Caribbean GPS: Compasses of Racialization," and chapter 11, "Circulations:

Caribbean Political Activism," engage some of the political realities of living as a Caribbean person in the United States, as well as some of the political responses that a variety of Caribbean political activists have pursued. Finally, chapter 13 returns to the "twilight" theme but this time focusing on the logic of "escape routes," arguing that the paradigm of the North as being the only place of freedom can be contested with this contemporary framing of the South and the Caribbean as also carrying that significance of freedom and escape, which is the overarching theme of this book.

Caribbean Intellectual Space

Intellectual material that allows us to study the Caribbean on its own terms and from our best thinkers has grown in waves from the early 1950s and '60s decolonization initiatives. Although there was some earlier work before then, this decolonization period is a fair marker of a new body of scholarly inquiry. Some stellar examples include the contributions of Frantz Fanon, a Martinican who went to France and became a psychiatrist but in the process encountered the French variety of racism. He wrote *Black Skin, White Masks* (1952) and perhaps the more well-known *The Wretched of the Earth (Les damnés de la terre)* (1963), which initially had the interesting subtitle *A Negro Psychoanalyst's Study of the Problems of Racism and Colonialism in the World Today.*

George Lamming, from Barbados, who spent a number of years (1946–50) in Trinidad, went to England as a writer and there became a friend of Claudia Jones, a major subject of my research and wrote novels and a book of essays called *The Pleasures of Exile* (1960). From different angles, he and a cohort of writers, perhaps the most well known being V. S. Naipaul, accounted for Caribbean realities in wider geographic colonial spaces and contexts. In the 1980s, another Martinican, scholar Edouard Glissant, wrote *Le discours antillais* (1981), *Caribbean Discourse* (trans. 1989), which offered definitions that contemporary students and scholars like. He was articulating a poetics for the Caribbean, which he defined more extensively in his *Poetics of Relation* (1997), moving from the specifics of the Francophone Caribbean to arrive at general discussions of the entire Caribbean or what is Caribbeanness, in conversation with the architectural and cultural theory called postmodernism. In a similar way, another writer, this time from Cuba, Antonio Benitez-Rojo, wrote *The Repeating Island: The Caribbean and the Postmodern Perspective* (trans. 1992), which conceptualized the Caribbean as a series of repetitions with difference. But before them, the work of Kamau Brathwaite, historian and poet from Barbados who had lived in London and worked in Ghana and studied Caribbean creole cultures, developed much of the basis for discussions of creole cultures and creolization. Brathwaite has developed more recently a theory called "tidalectics," which defines how we exist with the rhythms of the ocean, and has contributed as well the idea that "unity is submarine."

The historical, political, and economic writings of Eric Williams and C. L. R. James, both of Trinidad, in the Anglophone Caribbean, have already set the context for understanding the Caribbean in relation to the development of European capitalist enterprises. But before them, a variety of political actors, such as Hubert Harrison from St. Croix and Marcus Garvey from Jamaica, had made major contributions to Pan-Africanism that resonated subsequently in the music of reggae through the legendary Bob Marley and Peter Tosh in the 1960s and into the present. And the work in development economics of Arthur Lewis, from St. Lucia, guaranteed him a place in history and a Nobel Prize.

A great deal of thinking has come through the creative. Derek Walcott, also from St. Lucia and another Nobelist, continues to demonstrate that the "sea is history," moving himself, during a more mobile time in his life, in the 1950s, between St. Lucia and Trinidad, recognizing along the way the logic of a vocal twilight. Perhaps Antiguan Jamaica Kincaid's entire body of work can be identified for its struggles with autobiography as with Caribbean identity, or the reader may like Barbadian American Paule Marshall's books or the young adult–targeted work of Rosa Guy from Trinidad, or find Michelle Cliff critical to definitions of space. More recently, Edwidge Danticat, as a Haitian American writer, in almost all her work has accounted for the movement between Haiti and North America, though *The Farming of Bones* (1999) is situated in the difficult history between the Dominican Republic and Haiti on the same island. A fascinating story titled "Ghosts" identifies the harsh conditions of Bel Air in Haiti in which hardworking people are sometimes caught in the machinations of crime as executed by gangsters she refers to as "ghosts," people who are no longer operating with expected norms of humanity, As a result, North America becomes an urgent possibility, for, as one brother says safely from Canada, "Home is not always a place you have trouble leaving" (2).

From Puerto Rico and the Dominican Republic, a number of writers, such as Mayra Santos-Febres and Angie Cruz, provide the expansion of our understanding of the Spanish-speaking Caribbean on some of these questions. Santos-Febres's *Sirena Selena: Vestida de Pena* (2009) also captures the transgressive, though painful, life of a Puerto Rican transvestite, "dressed in sorrow," which the subtitle captures.

A number of critical texts have more recently continued a process of writing theoretically about the Caribbean. These include Michael Dash's work *The Other America: Caribbean Literature in a New World Context* (1998) and Silvio Torres-Saliant's *Caribbean Poetics: Towards an Aesthetic of West Indian Literature* (1997). And although there has been a growing body of work in migration studies, no work, as far as this author is concerned, has addressed, in a developed way, the Caribbean/American and simultaneously taken the movement south to Brazil as well as this one does.

In beginning to think through this subject, I found a guiding text in David Harvey's *Spaces of Hope* (2000), which pursues issues of spatiality but expresses them in an experiential, though analytical, way. The scholarship on space and place provides a whole area of scholarly inquiry in the fields of geography and urban planning that offer useful definitions of the geopolitics of space and place. Edward Soja's *Postmodern Geographies: The Reassertion of Space in Critical Social Theory* (1989) offers perspectives on what he calls "the making of geography," privileging geography over history and suggesting that there are hidden geographical texts, particularly how "relations of power and discipline are inscribed into the apparently innocent spatiality of social life; how human geographies become filled with politics and ideology" (6). In this way, diaspora becomes another way of thinking of alternative geographies, as McKittrick and Woods show in their discussion of black populations in New Orleans following Hurricane Katrina, particularly in the section of their introduction subtitled "Submarine Roots: Towards a Reconstruction of the Global Community" (2007).

David Scott's *Refashioning Futures: Criticism after Postcoloniality* (1999) and *Conscripts of Modernity: The Tragedy of Colonial Enlightenment* (2004) provide an interesting set of insights that scholars find useful. Of equal importance is his creation of Caribbean intellectual space in the journal called *Small Axe,* with echoes of Bob Marley's "if you are the big tree, we are the small axe." Thomas Glave, a Jamerican who has boldly claimed Caribbean space that challenges oppression of all sorts, therefore resists homophobia as a normalized Caribbean prejudice. His edited collection *Our Caribbean: A Gathering of Lesbian and Gay Writing from the Antilles* (2008), definitely about the assumption of space, includes a series of Caribbean essays and short stories that challenge prescribed boundaries of the imagination of the possible. What Glave wants is that we move toward a more expansive sense of ourselves and a more advanced and noble imagination that has been our history in other areas, from Bob Marley to Marcus Garvey, in the Jamaican scene. Capturing the erotic between women specifically in ways that evoke the earlier biomythography of Audre Lorde, *Zami: A New Spelling of My Name* (1982), Omise'eke Natasha Tinsley in *Thiefing Sugar* (2010) interrogates a range of sexualities in the Caribbean often unaccounted for or existing just outside the vision of most scholars, but clearly in evidence in the literature itself.

Historians and political scientists of the Caribbean have provided wonderful background work on the Caribbean useful for any contextualizing of early and current developments. From Eric Williams, as we have pointed out, we have his magnum opus, *Capitalism and Slavery,* but also *From Columbus to Castro: The History of the Caribbean, 1492–1969* (1970/1989). Franklin Knight in *The Caribbean: The Genesis of a Fragmented Nationalism* (2012) and the earlier work edited with Colin Palmer, *The Modern Caribbean* (1989), continuously updates historical understandings of the Caribbean, as has Hilary Beckles, who, with Verene Shepherd, has written *Caribbean Freedom: Economy and Society from Emancipation to the Present* (1996) and *Freedoms Won: Caribbean Emancipations, Ethnicities, and Nationhood* (2007).

An interesting sociohistorical approach is provided by Mimi Sheller's *Consuming the Caribbean: From Arawaks to Zombies* (2003), which describes in its introduction "the exclusion of the Caribbean from the imagined timespace of Western modernity" in "popular culture and the media, but also within academic discourse" (1). Yet this conceptual exclusion accompanies a simultaneous consumption of the "natural environment, commodities, human bodies, and cultures of the Caribbean" (3). Finding interesting parallels between the way the Caribbean is imagined in terms of island space is Elizabeth DeLoughrey's *Routes and Roots: Navigating Caribbean and Pacific Island Literatures* (2010). Perhaps the most popular recognizable assumptions of Wilson Harris's "bridge which arches" between the Americas come from hip-hop artists, creating a genre that brings together consistently the urban culture created by migration and the interaction of Caribbean, African American, and Latin American contemporary cultures. And new forms continue to emerge all the time.

Caribbean Spaces: Escapes from Twilight Zones combines autobiographical essays with scholarly essays and accounts for the Americas in this larger context as it reimagines Caribbean space. It also argues that just as the North has iconic significance as a destination of escape, so do the far South and the Caribbean and Latin America, with movements in both directions.

Twilight zones in the way that I am using it here refers to the spaces of transformation from one condition to another, one location to another, one reality to another, and the sometimes newly created emotional, physical, and conceptual space that then becomes another identified location. Twilight zones can therefore be scary spaces of loss but also of gain. One echo and prior use of *twilight* is, of course, Derek Walcott's "What the Twilight Says: An Overture" (1971). In my rereading, his invocation of twilight had more to do with the impending dusk and movements into sensual darkness. Additionally, in this much younger Derek, all the complications of racial and cultural hybridity that occupied him permeate this sense of twilight. A more recent revision of his reading is his 1992 Nobel presentation, "The Antilles: Fragments of Epic Memory." Here, Walcott relocates his vision to Felicity, a village in Trinidad on the edge of the Caroni plain. In this essay, he paints a picture of the dramatization of Ramleela of the Hindu epic the *Ramayana*, in a landscape on which was superimposed Indian festival culture. "Felicity," with all its resonances and with all its history in Anglo-Saxon coloniality, but not without engagement with its African and Indian diaspora memory, actors, and mythologies, provides a landscape as peopled by a series of actors, dramatizing a variety of fragments of various epics. But above all, it captures the re-creation and joy in this process that mark the Caribbean.

Thus, for him, "visual surprise is natural in the Caribbean; it comes with the landscape, and faced with its beauty, the sigh of History dissolves." Like Zora Neale Hurston, for whom Eatonville, Florida, was as much an escape as was the Bahamas, he believes, "We make too much of that long groan which underlines the past." Thus, Felicity, a name that invokes happiness, becomes his metaphor of a new Caribbean creation. For him, "It is such a love that reassembles our African and Asiatic fragments. . . . This gathering of broken pieces is the care and pain of the Antilles, and if the pieces are disparate, ill-fitting, they contain more pain than their original sculpture, those icons and sacred vessels taken for granted in their ancestral places. Antillean art is this restoration of our shattered histories, our shards of vocabulary, our archipelago becoming a synonym for pieces broken off from the original continent."

At home in the Caribbean as a young man, Derek Walcott was able to navigate Trinidad with ease, as his own St. Lucia. Along the way, he was able to capture that epic recognition of the "sea as history" in the meaning of the Caribbean but also its ongoing new histories, as Wilson Harris would also refer to "the womb of sea and space" (31) and Kamau Brathwaite to the idea that "the unity is submarine." Walcott offers a powerful line: "Caribbean genius is condemned to contradict itself," which almost becomes a self-description.

In the present, though, he captures another living contradiction of people and space remaining caught between the constructed world of the "tourist brochures," where "the Caribbean is a blue pool into which the republic dangles the extended foot of Florida as inflated rubber islands bob and drinks with umbrellas float towards her on a raft. This is how the islands from the shame of necessity sell themselves."

So *twilight* also captures the space of difficulty, of poverty, in which some are trapped, as it also refers to aspects of contemporary urban landscapes like London, living between the "unstable present and the fragile past" as expressed in the film "Twilight City" (1989). According to reviewer Kodwo Eshun (2004), this filmic essay presents a poetics of globalization (7) as it "seeks to evoke the psychogeographical landscape of living through the de- and re-territorialization of culture" (8). An allied narrativization of a deteriorating urban landscape, this time in the Caribbean itself, is presented by Edwidge Danticat in her story "Ghosts." Pascal, the story's protagonist, caught in the clutches of the one-armed gang leader as the story ends, after being erroneously arrested and then released under the auspices of his now resident ghost, imagines a radio program of lost limbs: "He would open with a discussion of how many people in Bel Air had lost limbs. Then he would go from limbs to souls, to the number of people who had lost family—siblings, parents, children—and friends. These were the real ghosts, he would say, the phantom limbs, phantom minds, phantom loves that haunt us, because they were used, then abandoned, because they were desolate, because they were violent, because they were merciless, because they were out of choices, because they did not want to be driven away, because they were poor" (10).

Caribbean Spaces: Escapes from Twilight Zones offers more deliberate continuities with the Americas and so plays on "Underground Railroad" imaginaries and histories. But it similarly pieces the fragments together as a mosaic or quilt. Here escape routes refer to a set of passages that pursue liberation in different directions. In the way that I use it, the term *escape routes* refers to movements of freedom not only toward the North, but also from the North to the South, therefore also from the Caribbean to the United States, but also its reverse, from the United States to the Caribbean. If we follow Harris's logic, then, the Americas, because of the "New World" histories of genocide, enslavement, and colonialism, were sites of escape in a variety of directions. Thus, it is no accident that tourist destinations follow those same north-south routes, seeking also escape, movement away from northern constrictions, or that descendants of indigenous people assume the Americas as "ever evolving" space in which man-made borders should be transgressed. Caribbean Spaces are not so much idealized locations as spaces of possibility.

When I recently learned in a casual television factoid that Jamaican Olympian Usain Bolt covers at least ten feet with each stride, given the configurations of body, space, movement, and speed he possesses, it made me realize anew that all human endeavors of excellence have been about taking space, from basketball athleticism at the level of its highest performance to intellectual thought, the place of myth, and the challenges of received geography and history. It is significant that Wilson Harris titled his 1983 work *The Womb of Space,* as he was clearly also working on taking us toward an understanding of Caribbean Space as carrying much larger meaning, mythic possibilities and actual geographical locations where the cross-cultural imagination can flourish, emotional space in which we give ourselves the room to be brilliant.

Caribbean island—showing view of island taken from sea. Photograph by the author.

Haiti village at sunrise. Courtesy of Jean Willy Gerdes.

Botanica plaza in Little Haiti, Miami. Courtesy of Jean Willy Gerdes.

Guadeloupean woman shopping in Caribbean produce store (Route 441 Caribbean Shops, North Miami). Photograph by the author.

Botanica Twa Zom Fo in Little Haiti, North Miami. Courtesy of Jean Willy Gerdes.

Cigar factory in Little Havana, Miami. Courtesy of Jean Willy Gerdes.

Little Havana welcome sign in Miami. Courtesy of Jean Willy Gerdes.

1

BETWEEN THE TWILIGHT ZONE
AND THE UNDERGROUND
RAILROAD
"Owagea"

Twilight Zone

Twilight! That space of unreality between night and day, where spirits begin to roam and objects that seem perfectly normal in the daylight assume
strange patterns and shapes, that gap between different realities, that zone
of instability between darkness and light, that time when transformation
happens. Perhaps it was Rod Serling's fault and all those episodes of *Twilight
Zone* I watched in black and white in my youth, I thought, which provided
the pretext or at least a possible explanation. Learning that Serling was from
and imagined the sense of twilight space in Binghamton justified my feelings.
Recreation Park, on Binghamton's West Side, which I passed many times
to visit friends, then had a carousel that no longer functioned and seemed
to invite that sense of mystery. I was not surprised to learn that it served as
inspiration for some *Twilight Zone* episodes. It was not a stretch to conclude
then that the entire Binghamton area, where I lived and worked for a large
chunk of my adult life, was indeed the Twilight Zone. But this was before
the now popular *Twilight* series of movies in which likable vampires move in
and out of human habitations and as usual seduce young women with their
charms. And though they are set in Washington State, they could easily have
been anywhere else, upstate New York for sure.

One rainy night, I find myself lost amid the emptiness and sameness of
the buildings and the depressed grayness in the area around Antique Row on
Clinton Street. Warehouses from a bustling past of economic vitality either
remained empty or hosted quaint antique shops. Making the best of postin-
dustrial depression! Echoes of another time, vibrant in old black-and-white

film footage, are all over the place in beautifully carved building fronts as in aging frame buildings and leftover train tracks. Sometimes cobbled streets peek through the tarred surfaces and create a bumpy ride. Driving off the highway, I take a wrong turn and somehow end up on a back street. Not sure which direction would take me to Main Street, I panic, observing the strange shapes that meander like ghosts. I panic and breathe a sigh of relief only when I finally cross the bridge over the Chenango River, pass the occasional streetlight, and see the Metro Center, perhaps the only new addition to a dying downtown.

TWILIGHT SCRIPT I

A Caribbean girl at heart, caught in upstate New York, attempts to negotiate her way out of the Twilight Zone, repeatedly. Speeding through the hills up over the city behind the Oakdale Mall or driving through winding highways in sleepy upstate towns, life seemed to suspend itself. I could be in the rolling mountains described in *The Legend of Sleepy Hollow.* Hilly terrain, houses that appear as the road bends; absent of human life as I recognize it, barns dated from 1876 are falling apart; occasional deer peer from the side of the road as they contemplate a crossing. People seem to vanish from their proper years only to find out that they had been sleeping all along and the world had moved on.

Flying in and out presented one escape. In pre-9/11 days, I could get onto a flight swiftly and look back at the receding trees as the plane climbed to its preferred height. One could always talk a ground attendant into letting you on the plane in what seemed like five minutes before it took off, and often there was someone else after you. One day, barely making it to the airport on time, I discover that for some reason, maybe bad weather elsewhere, or some other unspoken reason, all flights were indefinitely delayed, pushed back as one waited for the ominous decision—canceled. As I stand near the wall phones (in those days before mobile phones), planning to call my girls to tell them what had happened, deciding if I should wait around or try to fly the next day, I overhear a conversation of another delayed passenger contacting his people at work, or perhaps a girlfriend or wife somewhere: "I'm trying to get a rented car to take me out of here. I cannot spend the night in this rinky-dink town. There's nothing here.' Sorry, ma'am!" He smiled, knowing that I had overheard. Me: "Oh, I'm not from Binghamton!" The thought of being consigned to what others saw as a "rinky-dink" town enveloped my consciousness. I refused to sign over my sense of belonging to this place. It was one of those moments of clarity when all the narratives that one constructs to keep one's life in place fall apart, for in reality, as I reflected: My work is here. My children are here; one of them was born here. My house is here. This is not really a rinky-dink town, I attempt to convince myself. Twilight Zone!

Maybe he was right. Flying in again after years of absence and having been in and out of larger-size airports, in various parts of the world, Link Field, as the airport was named (now Greater Binghamton Airport), seems even smaller, a space that opens suddenly between the trees. The plane, as usual, seems on the verge of overshooting its mark. The runway appears out of a field of grayness and trees stripped of leaves, paths of white-covered ground underneath trees. A few roadways become visible, a glimpse of a winding river, perhaps the Susquehanna, which I heard referred to as the native high-way, maybe the Chenango, as the two meet in Binghamton, with sometimes historic and legendary overflows. A few scattered houses emerge, and then the mound that seems as the plane takes it to be on the side of an extended cliff drop, and the airport now, a beige-looking structure, isolated, weather beaten. A lone ground attendant in a yellow rain suit eyes the plane, a face resigned to a fate of helping people come and go. And I reflect on taxi drivers who proudly claim they have never traveled out of town since "the war," or teachers of my children who had never been to New York City.

Reclaiming one's baggage is always easy, though, as there is never much on the slowly winding belt, sometimes one lonely suitcase that is yours and easily spotted as it comes through the hutch from the other side. Then that meandering drive past some small farms onto Reynolds Road, the mall, Route 17, and then over to Vestal Parkway. That sinking feeling returns of having to leave behind always exciting other locations to return to a sense of (un)reality, where people crouch in the comfortableness of their lack of knowledge of the world.

Twilight Zone! People disappear here! Strange aliens walk around some-times! Carousels sometimes turn aimlessly and reclaim the past with their painted horses—a happier time, perhaps, for a range of European immi-grants. People easily walk into other time zones here. But upstate life for black people is fraught with a sense of permanent danger . . . not of the kind that means you are going to be caught in an accident or the crossfire of some city crime, but another unspecified danger, such as capture, if you were escaping from slavery. So remaining undercover for black people be-comes normalized, as each makes his or her way silently and clandestinely in a maze of whiteness, as in the past not sure if bounty hunters would recapture one back into enslavement.

Living in a zone of unreality, of mystery and unspecified danger, demands awareness and skill. An exhibit on migration to the western New York and northern Pennsylvania region in a local museum showed a series of memorabilia from past upstate scenes. But rounding a corner, a life-size Klan figure startles the unsuspecting. For most black viewers, it is a moment of terror; for many others, it is a dramatic curiosity. So it is easy to see how a perfectly undistinguished professor can make himself distinguished by bringing the KKK as his special guests to campus, mindless of the power imbalance in the classroom, the history of violence and terrorism that accompanies the Klan, the contempt of the community that such behavior represents. One student from the Bronx said it best: "Well, I hang around with a lot of people from my neighborhood who are kind of a bad element, and I could bring them on this campus so you all could experience them, but I didn't think this was that kind of place." Pennsylvania and northern New York for a long while hosted the upstate headquarters of the Klan, the exhibition says.

Professor Klansman appears in front of the class in his freshly laundered white robe and smiles. "Today I am going to teach you about affirmative action . . ." He adjusts his white pointed hood and presents his colleagues to the class. The students are caught in the twilight zone, unable to leave, but one escapes.

TWILIGHT SCRIPT II

Upstate New York provides a landscape of numerous prisons and youth detention centers, often in picturesque communities that one drives by or passes on a rural highway, only to have to take a second look because of a sign marking itself. And only a few miles from Cornell University, on Upper Creek Road, in Ithaca, New York, a house is marked with locational blue and gold signs that identify it as a stop on the Underground Railroad. A sense of the past in the present permeates everything. Contradictory twilight zones of freedom and incarceration coexist.

The sinking feeling that similarly appears as one rounds Great Bend, Pennsylvania, and drives into Binghamton has a basis in history. As the visual markers of the town appear, my sense of resignation always returns. Unlike the students who could, if they choose, do four years and head back to the city, black people who live in upstate New York, like their students for four or five years, are similarly contained. And indeed, one of my colleagues has figured out that state prisons that populate the upstate region, like universities, run on the same principles: shared architecture, furniture, budgets, and sometimes land space.

Harriet Tubman's final home and grave site is in Auburn, New York. A place of freedom for her then is contradictorily now in the same neighborhood as a large upstate prison. A living contradiction in that incarceration is now read as the new enslavement.

SUNNY?

So I head across the parkway and onto the Stair Tract, taking that angled road to the more residential Vestal. Country Club Road, where I live, was named for the site of a former country club. Sometimes the landscape is white, with mounds of snow piled on both sides. Most of the time, it is rainy, a slight and continuous drizzle in place. But other times, it is a rich and vibrant fall, with myriad colors of browns, reds, and golds, competing for the fading sun, and for a moment it is breathtakingly beautiful and challenges the logic of continuing grayness. And the sun is there but just above the clouds.

On another gray day, thinking that the sky was too overcast to really fly, I reluctantly took a flight out of Binghamton. It seemed like bad weather was a permanent condition, but of course I had to go somewhere, and then we took off, and as the plane attained the necessary altitude above the heavy clouds that blanketed the city, the sun burst powerfully into view. The same thing happened once as we were about to drive south. That trepidation about getting on the road in bad weather stayed, but there was light, and clarity, south of Pennsylvania.

Moving out of the twilight can also mean moving into the dark, which sometimes is where the true light exists. The sun is always there, just obliterated under a cloud of dark grayness, ready to be revealed if one could only burst through and penetrate the surface obscurity.

Once a group of students with whom I had worked closely came to me during their senior year and announced that they had decided that when they graduated, they wanted me to leave as well, that they saw upstate New York as not a very safe place for activist intellectuals. Of course, they were not the first class of students who had felt similarly. For many, teaching in historically white institutions is an uphill battle, a struggle of positions. A willingness to challenge a whole history of dominant ideologies, misinformation, and tendencies to maintain the Eurocentric approach to knowledge provides an already-created construct. One is poised, then, if a truthful intellectual, against a mountain of distortions, half-truths, and incompleteness in the educational project. If one is committed to the task of education in a serious way as a professional, especially if critical of normalized racial or gender abuse, it is that which is taken as transgressive, which positions one as always the irritant, perhaps an impediment in a march toward destruction, and minimally as one who consistently raises issues that others, even one's colleagues, would rather silence, avoid, or defer.

I came to Binghamton in the early 1980s, after having just completed a Ph.D. in African literatures at the University of Ibadan, Nigeria, having taught in Trinidad as part of my government service and a one-year position at the University of Mississippi. I remember I wore a red suit one of the days of my interview, not even thinking until later how transgressive that could be taken by others, but clearly going with my energy . . . red comes naturally. At that time, those who came for on-campus interviews stayed in guest rooms in the student union building. I remember the discussion over salary upon being offered the position and that I felt so elated that I did not realize that the salary being proposed was so low that it would install me forever in a pattern of inadequate income throughout my Binghamton career. A few years later, after one of the group of professors who was hired with me left and decided to go to law school instead of suffering a professional poverty salary, I learned that one of our group had negotiated at least ten thousand dollars more than the rest of us (there were about five hired that year).

My position was a joint appointment with the African American Studies Department. I was given an office in the main hallway of the English Department and one on the thirteenth floor where African American Studies was located. I took the latter as my primary office rather than the promise of isolation and solitary existence in the English Department as the then only black faculty member. I was told by some colleagues that there used to be another black faculty member years before. This symbolic choice would mark my entire career, and I would relive it in all other professional locations. More recently at Cornell, I was offered a 100 percent move to English, which the person offering it thought a good option, but it was clearly after I had taken some public political positions in support of the historic Africana Studies Center. Many would have happily accepted this offer, and others had sought similar deals, but I felt that my political history would not support such a contradiction.

Besides, English Departments are very particular locations with specific colonial histories. Ngugi wa Thiong'o and his colleagues were right to assert that they should be abolished in his African context with their origins and intent as fundamental to English colonial structures at the intellectual level. In the United States, they are often "hearts of whiteness." There is always an underlying set of narratives that only the embedded know, which seem outside of the realm of things that interest the black scholar: who is sleeping with whom in the department, who has taken whose wife, who has power, even without major publications of his own, to decide on someone's tenure. But anachronistic to the end, they are unified in their love for and commitment to European hegemony. Parties were specifically timed, from 5:00 to 7:00 p.m., for example. Often I chose to arrive about 6:30 to avoid small talk and curious queries about one's hair or clothing. Often at 6:30, people were leaving the event. It was clear these were unlike Pan-African parties, where an announcement of that sort would mean people would probably show up about 6:00. So I practiced that dance between realities, that negotiation in the twilight.

Department meetings are also twilight spaces, as one has to coexist politely with those who publicly express fear of the loss of Eurocentrism, a colonialist engagement with Britain that remains steadfast, a resistance to new knowledge if it is not Euro-generated. Long debates could center on hiring one African literature specialist to represent an entire continent when there are ongoing assumptions of multiple hires, periods, and genres in other fields. Taking any kind of affirmative positions means being beset by a series of constructions and distortions that fit the convenient given reality.

I remember talking with a colleague and telling her casually that one of the things I would love to do was not come back to those meetings. Often, I would put myself in Caribbean space on those occasions, perhaps on a beautiful beach, water lapping against my body, the sun, greenery, coconut water, a revelry interrupted perhaps only to challenge a normalizing position. My colleague, in her matter-of-fact way, asserted, "Now that you have tenure, you don't have to go back to those meetings." It hit me then that she was right. So I showed up only when there was a vote that counted or when such a depressing experience would not color my entire day.

At one point, a faculty member with a recognized history of mental illness, who could speak no Portuguese, adopted a young black Brazilian girl, about twelve years old, and without the skill to take care of her or understand the child's resistance to this new identity had her put in a home for children with psychotic behavioral problems. The entire department's approach was an aversion of the eyes and an attempt to convince themselves that this was not bizarre. Having just completed a Fulbright professorship in Brazil, and with some Portuguese language skill, I offered to get the child, whom I had met before, out of what must have been a nightmare unfolding. So one day, with the colleague organizing a car and driver, my children and I set out for a two- to three-hour journey to a remote upstate location near Albany to have the little girl released into our care and kept her for a few days in our normal home environment in which she gradually began to feel comfortable as Afro-Caribbean students came to braid her hair and make her feel at home. But after a few days, she was again retrieved legally from our care by the disturbed adopted parent, and I learned later that she again ended up in a series of detention homes. I still wonder, and the occasional student who met her still asks, what became of Claudette? A black Brazilian girl caught in a twilight zone of upstate New York.

THIRTEENTH FLOOR

African American Studies was on the thirteenth floor, as, coincidentally, were all the programs that were not mainstream—Latin American Studies, Judaic Studies, a translation program. The thirteenth floor, in a concession to a certain twilightness, it was often remarked, was a floor omitted in many American buildings. A colleague who demonstrated a pattern of student involvement, committed teaching, and community activism was denied tenure just after I arrived there. Student activism to have him reinstated was unrewarded. Powerlessness permeated everything until a former university classmate appeared and told me categorically that the students needed another committed teacher, and I realized, yes, this was our position as graduate students at Howard. I decided that I would simultaneously build a publication profile that challenged and far exceeded all local expectations. An international profile is more desirable in any case.

Teaching has always been the most rewarding of academic experiences. Following my acceptance of a professional position, I discovered that I was pregnant with my second daughter, Dalia, who accompanied me, in utero, through my first semester at work. The course in African American literature that I developed was demanding, as it should be: a literature and history that students must read, relevant and rewarding discussions to engage. So on the last day of that first class, as we came to the end of the syllabus and finished off the process, I was stunned by a standing ovation from a class of more than fifty students. It became a defining moment for me, confirming the links between student work, demanding curricula, and high teacher involvement regardless. That moment of applause still remains etched into my consciousness, not unlike artists or preachers who identify that moment of intense antiphonal audience response as what energizes. The other parallel intense moments of satisfaction are those when students go on to do wonderful things: enter law schools, complete graduate programs, are committed to social justice in important ways, create magazines, write their own books, take political positions, run for office, become themselves super teachers.

I was talking once with a famous black feminist theorist who is also a friend who identified the "abuse paradigm" as a fitting descriptor of the nature of black women's relationships with these institutions if we are in any way defined as being out of the mainstream in terms of identity, politics, and so on. Institutions use sexualized discourses of "flirtation" or "courtship" in talking about acquiring faculty. Once, after some interest from the University of Michigan in Ann Arbor, I got a note for a colleague at that institution clandestinely passed to me during a conference: "Are you interested in Ann Arbor or just flirting?" Being hired is almost like a marriage contract in which you are the woman and you sign on to obey. The first year or so is described as the "honeymoon phase." But there are also abuse episodes, and once hired, one should expect the occasional beat down. So another colleague and I spent a great deal of time joking about the modes of "living with" or separation and divorce from, without pain, these institutions using that paradigm. Being assigned to committees that are normal for others means at times either existing passively in these spaces or being pushed into radical positions, even if that is not your manner. So if a professor insists on bringing the Ku Klux Klan to campus and others equate that with bringing Angela Davis to campus, one has either to shut up and agree with them, stay silent, or speak and in speaking speak the truth, challenge, clarify, articulate. For the speaker, that means being located in positions counter to the dominant interests, which often have the media to deliver their position and are willing to spin false constructions if it meets their needs.

So teaching engaged, wonderful students is always the saving grace, the reality check in these contexts. Students come from other realities and are more in touch with a world outside the one normalized in universities. They necessarily create a social life that approximates home in the ritual of cooking Caribbean foods in upstate New York, or the attempt to reproduce a Carnival against all odds, or sometimes the desire to challenge the institutional basis of exclusion is actualized.

Parenting in the '80s

Constance Coiner, who disappeared in a flash in the downed TWA Flight 800 on the way to Paris on a trip with her daughter as a reward and celebration for getting tenure, was ironically writing a book on "silent parenting." She had interviewed me and asked me to contribute a piece that I never really wrote. I had a certain resistance to her notion of silent parenting, feeling always that parenting could never be a silent activity from my end or the institution's. One had no choice but to take on both, to engage the two activities with boldness. It is clichéd by now, but black women have consistently worked and raised children. I saw this as no different.

So the other activity that oriented my early academic years was raising children, almost as a married single parent. An M.D. husband who, of course, had to and did always put his work before everything and everybody else never had time to do anything interesting, not even hold an intelligent conversation. I learned that when men do this, a separation is already instituted, and you grow to feel disgust and revulsion for them or that they may have other interests.

But how did I get here? In July, about three months pregnant, I had headed for Binghamton, following the route, I suppose, that some took on the Underground Railroad from Mississippi to New York. After settling in and feeling that everyone would soon notice, I told my chair with embarrassment that I was pregnant, and he to my surprise offered congratulations. At that time, my then husband was studying for his medical exams that would make him eligible to work in the United States. But we still liked each other and were having this baby, scheduled conveniently to be born during the intercession. December came and went with Christmas, the new year came in and still no baby, and the second semester was only three weeks away. Finally, the morning of January 6, I felt a tremendous kick in my stomach and a gush of water, and a few hours later, Dalia appeared to join her then three-year-old sister, Jonelle, who was as ecstatic as she was concerned about defending her right to all the toys, all the love, all the space. But a little sister became a special baby for whom she would perform antics to make laugh if she cried, a coconspirator on trips to London to smuggle as many dolls as possible on the trip, well behaved on the front row of a panel at an MLA (Modern Language Association) convention in New York City in December between Christmas and New Year's, and accompanying presences on myriad adventures—hiking to waterfalls in upstate New York that I described as an equivalent to going to church and spirituality, visiting the Amish in Pennsylvania on the way to Hershey with its chocolate factory, traveling to New York City to see the play *Once upon an Island,* or Brooklyn to see family, perhaps Caribana in Toronto.

The experience of juggling parenting and work was a reality of those years. Rushing from a class, because I could feel my breasts hardening and painful, to find a breast pump in my office is one memory that stands out, but still nevertheless making all necessary meetings in those days before maternity and paternity leave was normalized. I remember going to Black Student

Union and Caribbean Students Association functions with young children and having to rush onto the stage to speak or receive an award without a worry or a look behind because there was assurance that my girls would be okay. Once, after I traveled to a conference and had a student babysitting, another one complained when I returned that she wondered why I had never asked her. It was always like that, unquestioning support. That first conference was an interesting moment, though, as when I returned, my then eighteen-month-old acted as though she did not know me, snuggling in the arms of her father, who had come up that weekend, showing her resentment for my absence and settling back into normalcy only the next morning when she woke up and was assured that I was there. Coming through the years, though, I realized that there would be no such thing as consistent partner support. But I knew how to do single parenting well; I had seen it, lived it, knew how to graciously accept support but that my life would have to be dedicated to raising my children, as my mother advised, with patience. Oddly, the more I did, the less support was ensured. It is an old story with which women are all too familiar.

In the 1980s, though, before men fully assumed more responsibility for parenting, faculty meetings were often held at four P.M., ending at five or five thirty. Luckily, the campus preschool was not hard to get to, and often, closing in on six, my child would be the last one there, and then I would rush in and apologize to the weary, stone-faced teaching assistant for being late and collect preschool child and then baby from a babysitter nearer to my house. A couple of speeding tickets from unforgiving police officers were early warnings to slow down, which I sometimes did not heed. I always felt I was rushing from or to one place to the other and so developed the pattern of cramming numerous activities into one day.

On the plus side, though, I developed a pattern of rising early in the morning when my children were babies. Having been awakened in the wee hours of the morning, I would use those hours before the business of the day started fully to read at least one article or chapter or write something (or both). Once I told a colleague jokingly as we walked from a lecture that I had given at the Commonwealth Institute in London that I had lost my momentum and needed another baby to orient me. She looked at me with a quizzical expression on her face. My work progressed nevertheless, and the responses have always been good.

Somehow, and without any warning, the difficult Reagan years passed. Soon it was my older daughter Jonelle's graduation, which now that I look back became another defining moment. Whereas my marital dissolution was a bittersweet moment of loss of dreams, disappointment, but—joy—this signaled a certain sense of new visions and possibilities. One learns after the fact that close parenting is but a brief phase and there is a whole other range of experiences waiting to happen.

Escapes

The Underground Railroad works both ways: south-north; north-south. Binghamton. I was told that the area going into Johnson City toward the Oakdale Mall was a stop on the Underground Railroad. So too was Ithaca, New York, I learned from a descendant of Harriet Tubman at a Cornell Africana event a number of years ago. Sojourner Truth spent some time in Elmira, New York, I discovered in a museum there, traveled to Rochester to meet allies. Seneca Falls has historic meaning for women's rights. Frederick Douglass too traversed upstate New York. Harriet Jacobs lived in Owego and helped to start an academy for girls there, I was told by a historian. Safe houses and Quaker way stations, still standing as stately homes, were escape landmarks that dotted the landscape in unremarkable ways.

Once I organized a trip for a black women writers class to Auburn, New York, where Harriet Tubman settled, to learn that she ended her years with a husband twenty years her junior. Along the way, we noted signs of prior escape activity everywhere. Indian massacres littered upstate New York and still surprise each time one comes upon a historic marker: "Welcome to Owego, an Indian Village Burned August 19, 1779 by General Clinton's Force enroute to join General Sullivan" (New York State Education Department, 1932). Upstate New York is a contradictory site of massacres, destruction of indigenous people's lives, that left black people sometimes still underground. The famous prison in Auburn, New York, houses, as usual, a large population of African American and Latino prisoners. Universities like Cornell have prison education programs that faculty and graduate students deliver, but Cornell itself was built on Cayuga Indian territory, according to the American Indian Program on campus. There are centers for incarcerated youth in the city in Lansing or off some of the main routes that provide the contradictory meaning of freedom and incarceration. Native people's presence sometimes still marks the landscape, as they remain off the mainstream. Onondaga Nation Territory is a sign on Highway 81 just outside of Syracuse. Taking the exit out of curiosity reveals nothing remarkably different, perhaps a few signs or a museum or school.

"I wonder if you can ever forgive me!" a woman who had wronged me once said in the most inappropriate of times, at a funeral at which taps was being played. Shades of Klanness appear in different forms in the Twilight Zone. We walk into these spaces, sometimes live in them, without questioning their surrounding histories, distant and recent.

Underground Railroad

The Underground Railroad moves in myriad directions. So upstate New York and the iconic North Star is but one of these. Underground and aboveground escape routes have to be found. A number of other like-minded colleagues name ourselves Harriet. Refusing to be captured, escapes are frequent: New York City for plays, conferences, shopping every now and then; Brooklyn for Caribbean foods, parties, Carnivals, reunions with family and friends, visits to hair-braiding salons; sometimes in unusual places, surprise encounters with past boyfriends for whom the desire or practice of polygamy is as instinctive as breathing; Toronto for more family reunions; Baltimore to my mother's house, a babysitting refuge when things were tight or I had to go out of town for another meeting; Washington, D.C., for post-Howard returns or concentrated black intellectual life.

More extended escapes to Brazil, London, or Trinidad, Ghana or Senegal, Ethiopia or South Africa . . . the kind of culturally rewarding trips that make living in upstate New York possible for any extended time. Each escape recreates the person, culturally rejuvenates and allows one to work and prepare the ground for the desire for the next escape.

The legend goes that at least nineteen times, Harriet Tubman went back and forth, defying the odds in conditions way more challenging than we have today. But I learn that this is an arbitrary number, and in some assessments, her journeys are many more. We will never know how many journeys there were, except that Harriet Tubman identified the necessity of movement and the transgression of imposed borders as fundamental and critical. And Africa Road in Vestal has symbolic and historical meaning beyond the emptiness of a street sign. And upstate New York is also a place of waterfalls, natural beauty perched over dangerous gorges. And one always has a choice of the kind of life one leads . . . complacency or challenge.

But besides the iconic North Star, there is another Underground Railroad from north to south. In this view, there are other underground escape spaces. South of south is one of these where the Caribbean operates as a different geographical space and is the given and desired arrival point, another symbolic destination of freedom. Kairi!

Sign marking "Owagea," the original name of what is now Owego, as one crosses the Susquehanna River. Photograph by the author.

2

REIMAGINING THE CARIBBEAN
Seeing, Reading, Thinking

On another of those journeys loaded with personal and epic meaning for me, from Grenada to Carriacou, deliberately recapturing lost personal history, I retrace the journey that Avey makes in Paule Marshall's *Praisesong for the Widow* (1983). On the way, I learn from a feisty Jamaican writer that the turbulence one experiences, and to which Marshall gives epic meaning, is actually the result of volcanic action that is producing another island (affectionately called "Kick 'em Jenny"). In the middle of the Caribbean Sea, I peer into the distance, trying to imagine where this island would come up. But it is a rainy and cloudy day, and in the misty, foamy gray-white distance there are a number of smaller island shapes, and even my "resident seer" for the moment is not sure but had located somewhere in the distance the general area of this new activity. A few baby island forms appear, and I am not sure what I am supposed to see anymore except that the whole seascape is awe inspiring. Around me, formidable, self-possessed, otherwise glamorous colleagues, fellow travelers, are falling into the throes of that seasickness that Marshall describes. In my own preseasickness moments, the entire experience appears as a moment out of some powerful creation myth. The myth collapses into the reality.

The Caribbean, in my vision, is a place of constant new birth, consistent destruction and regeneration, tearing down and making over, an ongoing site of transformation.

A related memory surfaces: As a little girl growing up in Trinidad, my sense of island security shifted radically when it was announced that another island had come up off the east coast of Trinidad. In my otherwise secure dual-island

national identity of Trinidad and Tobago, this new presence had many meanings. In the late 1950s, we had witnessed a time of epic transformation, the
beginning of the end of colonialism, a failed West Indian federation in 1958,
ending the decade with the Cuban Revolution of 1959. Talk of a would-be
three-island link with Grenada seemed to accompany a ridiculous "send them
back home" deportation of illegal "small(er) islanders" narrative. Newspaper
photographs presented what seemed to be a baby ghost island, actually the
result of volcanic activity, a muddy, squelchy, furrowed landmass, like other
newborns covered with the residues of water and grime, giving off a sense
of not being sure where it belonged.

Creation in my understanding, then, is never a once-and-over seven-day
mythic event, but is an ongoing, active creative process. So, certainly, a few
intrepid souls would attempt to claim this new island, plant their own flags,
but as easily as it came up, the would-be island submerged to where it was
before, as if not quite ready to be.

This memory has always remained with me fundamentally. It has taught
me that island space, indeed human land space, is always unstable, fragile,
always in the process of creation, subject to the motion of elements, violent
storms, and natural movements of the earth. But always what remains constant is the possibility of new creation, transformation.

In this meditation, I want to contemplate three frames of engagement in
an exercise of *seeing, reading, imagining,* outside of the parameters we have
been given, outside of the boundaries we assume, outside of the definitions
we take as normative. Here theory and creativity will be allowed to collapse
 and collide.

From naming to the specifics of physical reality, the contemporary Caribbean has been produced through numerous historical processes, ranging
from genocide, enslavement and traffic in human bodies, ecological degradation, and exploitation of natural resources to colonialism, imperialism,
and economic globalization. We already know that the term *West Indian* is
a misnomer produced by Columbian error and reproduced continuously
even by those misnamed themselves, a concept that needs to be consistently
troubled. The gap between tourist constructions or outside media presentations and lived reality also remains.

Caribbean culture, then, has been produced in spite of and often in response to these, as a way of writing oneself out of these various enslavements,
through pathways for the reclaiming of the imagination. The path through
popular education to the creation of a specific Caribbean subjectivity and

a concomitant literary tradition has been well documented by Caribbean scholars. But what of all the other creative pathways? In myriad capacities, we can witness a range of "watchers and seekers" who continue to bring forward particular visions of Caribbean reality, seeking transformed consciousness and transformed worlds.

The necessity of *seeing* is required of the casual viewer as of the serious reader. *Seeing* refers to a way of engaging with Caribbean space, in a dialogue or conversation of the eyes, as opposed to surfing, spectatoring, voyeurism, or detached tourist engagement. In Caribbean context, *seeing* refers to having high-level vision, the ability to see and read, that is, interpret beyond the given, into the past, in the present, and into the future. A "seer" (woman or man) is often employed by those without the training, the gifts, the mental faculties to go beyond the surface, to see what is hidden or yet to be revealed. In a way, then, we all have to become "seer women and men" if we want to pursue the levels of critical engagement that allow us to really see the Caribbean.

By *reading* I refer to pursuing the signs, the codes, the hidden meanings, the silences, erasures, absences. I refer also to a process of active engagement with all textualities (oral, scribal, performative, carnivalesque, literary, scholarly) that emanate from the spaces we call the Caribbean. In other words, our own subjectivities inform how we read, but always we strive to become more informed readers. But *reading* also implies contestation over meaning that exists by the very nature of the process, producing multiple readings, sometimes even by the same reader. I am using *reading* with all its normal implications, its meanings in print-oriented cultures, but also here its meaning in Caribbean folk and obeah traditions. One also engages a *reader* if one is not able to read and understand a particular set of life experiences or chart a certain future pathway. So what if we also become multilayered *readers* ourselves?

By *imagining* I refer to that mental process of liberating the mind and the various senses so that one moves outside of what is given reality, material or concrete, to pursue other realities. The constrained imagination is unable to see other possibilities beyond the given. The liberated imagination engages in transformative processes, trying always to enter that zone of high intensity that high-level artists, performers, or athletes get to in order to create and sometimes to fly.

Without the full exercise of the imagination, then, one remains on the surface, unable to fly, unable to fully understand, to see, read, or engage. The

Caribbean embraces all of these forms of engagement and more, for they are sites of invention and reinvention, of often free-flowing imagination, sites of *krik and krak.*

From Edwidge Danticat's novel *Breath, Eyes, Memory*:

"Krik?" called my grandmother.
"Krak!" answered the boys.
Their voices rang like a chorus, aiding my grandmother's entry into her tale.
(123)

From Merle Collins's poem "Crick Crack":

Crick!
Crack!

But what is the mirage and what reality?
Do we know what is truth and what is truly fiction?

Crick!
Crack!

Much of the early part of this poem speaks well to the question of seeing and hearing, using the antiphonal, engaged quality of Caribbean and African diaspora culture but also the play between what we perceive as reality and what is fiction, the relationships between oral culture and the written tradition. Subsequent verses of the poem take us further into the dynamics of myth, received history, naming, identity, necessary skepticism about given reality.

Mapping and Remapping Caribbean Space

In this meditation, then, I reflect on ways of seeing, to think about ways of reading and imagining Caribbean space. From my point of view, the Caribbean is *space,* is not constraint, but the deliberate taking of space, as dancer Pearl Primus explained her process. My own particular version of seeing the Caribbean comes from being located in a series of contiguous spaces, in the Caribbean landscape and seascape, in the air space above, recrossing the Atlantic Ocean, living in North America, Africa, Europe, and South America. But beyond identifying actual localities, for me, seeing the in-between spaces as possibility, not as barrier or as emptiness, is as critical.

From each location, the Caribbean is something else, takes on different meaning. One important re-viewing came from being in Brazil and having to describe where I was from. A profound shifting of the sense of location had to take place for one who always had a convenient north-south narrative to describe home. Instead, from Brazil Trinidad is the first of the islands as you leave South America, and in this identification, it seemed much more geographically related to South America than otherwise. For a North American questioner, one has to say it is the last of the islands before one reaches Venezuela, and from here it presents a much more distant location. But if one looks carefully at the "Turnabout Map" of the Americas, Trinidad is actually off South America, not the last Caribbean island but the first.

Once in Salvador da Bahia, Brazil, I saw a small Carnival troupe vaguely familiar in terms of style, music, and costuming and was told by a friend that these were people from *Guayana de ingleses*. Chatting with them, I learned that that these were people from Guyana who had come by a land route to northern Brazil. Possible proximities are available if we are able to access the routes that early travelers have taken.

Seeing the Caribbean outside of the North-South axis is perhaps the most difficult to undertake for those occupying what is defined as the "North," already with all the oppositional meanings of the "Global South" in political science formulations. If one remains with that conception of the Caribbean as located somewhere between the North and South America, then one operates from a logic of positioning that seeks only to contain, delimit, circumscribe meaning, and erase a variety of possibilities. The Caribbean in this meaning becomes reducible to any "islands" through which one may cruise from the North, observe with curiosity and detachment, enjoy, and so on. Although this is one possible, albeit limited, vision, clearly it is not all of it. In this vision as well, the Caribbean remains fragmented, unconnected island spaces.

On a plane flight to Trinidad, returning home for a family visit one night, I sat next to a man who identified himself as an American medical doctor. As we talked, I learned from him that he normally docked his boat in Trinidad, as it was the safest spot away from hurricanes and the like and also allowed him the southernmost point from which to use his boat to cruise the islands northward. For me, going home on family business, linked to the care of my mother, I became aware that his was a life outside of my economic reality. Many of us will never have the possibility of seeing all the islands that this man could name that he had already visited. I smiled at his stories that confirm how layered economic realities are and how they also circumscribe vision, mobility, and full possibility.

Perhaps the location in the Americas may offer a more interesting or developed way of reading and seeing the Caribbean. At least in this context, we operate from an other-than-island context but another kind of space in which one sees the various movements through the Caribbean, the Caribbean culture locations operating in Colombia, Cost Rica, Belize, Brazil, Honduras, and a series of other archipelagoes. Here the Caribbean appears for some as a kind of radiating center that throws out a series of rays of culture, food, music, Carnival, dance, and seasoning across the Americas. And there have always been these movements across the Americas that Caribs, Arawaks, Tainos, and other native groups took as part of their navigating of the seascapes and landscapes they inhabited as their natural way of operating in the world. How do indigenous realities combine with a series of other realities or even, as among the Garifuna, produce a kind of "Afro-digenous" reality? This remains an open question.

But there are more ways: A definable Caribbean diaspora exists in Europe, Canada, the United States, Africa, and Australia as other extension points. Learning basic Spanish, one learns that the United States is always referred to as *Norte America*. This can be a shocking and destabilizing reading even for African Americans who have fought for their own identity within the United States of America, but has different meaning in an international sense. A journey to Key West, Florida, reveals a series of connected Caribbean islands (keys) in terms of geography and culture, and Cuba, at the closest connecting point to the United States, is only ninety miles away and seemingly visible in the distance depending on the day, time, and tide. Bimini, Bahamas, is even closer—forty-eight miles away.

In Australia a Caribbean community that calls itself Carib-Oz organizes cultural festivals that include mini Carnivals and steel bands and food. They welcome Caribbean cricket players as part of their recreation of a home landscape. And Marcus Garvey's United Negro Improvement Association once had a chapter there. In Sydney and Melbourne, one can find Caribbean space.

One can, of course, work with each island space in relief and each in relation to the other spaces, its own politics of location, history, geography, and language. But this exercise in mapping for me is, of course, an important pedagogical and theoretical strategy, one of the first places we stop in beginning to think about the Caribbean as we constantly remap, reexamine our understandings of Caribbean space, and in the process become ourselves more informed readers.

A sense of living with tragedy and beauty at the same time permeates the Caribbean. In St. Lucia, the majestic Pitons hover over small and beautiful villages below, always with a sense of impending danger as the beauty is revealed over cliffs with amazing photo ops. Here one learns that Soufrière, which seems a magical name in the Walcott corpus, evokes the smell of sulfur that is palpably in the air as one gets closer and actually enters volcanic space to take a spa-like bath in volcanic mud and heated water; both claimed to have legendary healing properties or rejuvenation. A misty steam rises from one part of the volcano and presents that aura of ongoing creation that I saw in the mist between Carriacou and Grenada.

Recently in Europe, I was reminded that the distance between Jamaica and Trinidad is almost two thousand miles, much farther than the distance from England to Italy, Germany, or Spain. The assumptions of proximity of all islands in the Caribbean or the reduction of the Caribbean to "the islands" is a kind of imperialist reduction and spatial limitation that have implications beyond our everyday understandings. The distance from Trinidad to Brazil is shorter than from Trinidad to Jamaica. And perhaps the largest irony, from Trinidad (English speaking) to Venezuela (Spanish speaking), the distance is only about eleven miles in some understandings, zero aeronautical miles, and there is constant spillover in culture, language, food, people.

My own situated way of seeing the Caribbean comes from my own locations, my migrations, my studies and constant reexamining. I came to know myself as a Caribbean subject in the context of the ending of colonialism. The first big political event, besides hearing my family talk about "the war" and "ration cards" and "Butler," was the end of colonialism and the possibility of a Caribbean *Federation*. As a child in elementary school in the 1950s, we were fed with its promise, as states are wont to feed their ideology through their schools, the media, the family. Miss Lou's song "Federation" was played on the airways repeatedly then, and our schoolteachers prepared us for a federation, and so we all looked forward to a Caribbean unity. Its short-lived reality and its failure were accompanied by a sense of sadness, calypso commentary and banter about Jamaica, but an accompanying and more exhilarating rush of national pride. *Independence* and its promises became the other state narrative that again ran its course through the schools, the airwaves, the family, the politicians, the festivals, the songs, and so on. The failures of national independence are less apparent. Its successes were many compared to the colonialism that had precipitated decolonization struggles.

I come from a generation shaped by a world-class historian as prime minister who gave lectures weekly in what had been dubbed "the University of Woodford Square," and one could hear as background to homework his flatlined voice on the radio on those nights as family listened and responded to his lectures. This political education that I heard with one ear permeated discussions at all levels of family and community. But so did the message of education as a means to transcendence in calypsos as in political speeches.

Basically, my narrative is one that remembers the ushering in of "independence." So it is a memory that recalls the experience of being put out to line the streets in nice uniforms, waving British flags when some member of the royal family showed up, but also later on as girl guides to line the streets, this time with Trinidad and Tobago red, white, and black flags, also when another member of the royal family again visited, perhaps the queen, Princess Margaret, somebody who passed by with a quick wave after we had been in the sun for what seemed like hours.

But from my memory, the meaning of Britain figured not as a desired colonial mother country at all, but as a distant location for the migrations of uncles there in the 1950s who sent presents home of British pounds and books and stamp collections and other items. Britain as reality fast faded into American relations with the Caribbean in terms of business, the prime minister's successful struggle to reclaim the American base that existed at Chaguramas in Trinidad. A growing number of people, including my brother, made the journey to the United States. My own family migration occurred in 1967, in the same time frame as many of the community who were caught in that two-prong desire for movement. Though mine was a migration linked to education, we ended up producing families divided, with branches in either colonial space, that is, Europe and the United States, a kind of replaying of a certain route of the Middle Passage, always with the dream of some return to places of origins. At that time, farewell parties with sad country-and-western or bluesy love songs were standard among the adults, particularly dating couples in which one partner was going away or a member of a close-knit family was leaving to study nursing. Family members crying at airports or at seaports often with a sense of never seeing each other again was not an uncommon sight. But, for my generation, there was always the promise of reunion of friends and family in the United States, as many were planning or making the same journeys.

Years later, doing research in London, I learned from some of the older activists I interviewed that the pre-federation and pre-independence vision of the Caribbean was as a Caribbean nation—not a series of island nations and separate locations but as regionally integrated (politically, economically, and structurally). They saw what evolved then as only a partial success and in some visions a failure. This Caribbean-nation paradigm, it seems, is what continues to elude all Caribbean politicians, as we operate still with at least three or four languages without programs of multiple language studies and still with some quasi-independent nations, semicolonies, as Kamau Brathwaite would describe them. In a sense, then, a writer like Aimé Césaire from Martinique, in his speech later published as *Discourse on Colonialism* (1955), has particular resonance in his condemnation of colonialism, but it reveals him as also caught in a contradiction marked by the inability to imagine a Caribbean nation.

The Caribbean for those writing out of the British or French experience, such as the *Négritude* poets, and even Claude McKay's exploration of the meaning of living in the United States, comes out of a particular set of historical locations. Still, the exercise of locating oneself in history, in geography, in politics, the remapping of the terms of our existence, is central to any explorations of the meaning of the Caribbean, whether one is located in the United States or in the Caribbean. The fact is that the United States has historically operated since 1823 in a colonial relation with the Caribbean, from the Monroe Doctrine onward, the Platt Amendment of 1903, minus all the trappings of the former colonizers, but with all the power of its media, military, and markets. At the same time, as close as the Caribbean is to North America, there has been scant attention to really seeing, or knowing, the Caribbean, outside of tourist contexts, destination weddings, business opportunities, or quick military invasions, and sometimes the conjunctions between these are also in place, as they came together in Grenada.

Understanding Caribbean space must come out of lived realities, experience, social conditions, political history, and a careful examining of the meaning of these experiences in time and space. Still, there is always a need for another set of imaginings about the Caribbean from each generation of thinkers coming of age in each historical period. The need for fresh vision, not always accepting what is but moving into the future and locating ourselves more solidly in history, allows for a certain social transformation.

To claim as a given our presences and thereby to engage some themes that have occupied our thinkers over the century and thereby to offer some positions on the issue of space is where I am in this framework. In *Out of the Kumbla: Caribbean Women and Literature* (1990), Elaine Savory Fido and I said, by way of introduction, that we had departed from "constricting and restricting spaces . . . taking control of and above all locating ourselves at a different vantage point from which to view the landscape" (19). Nourbese Philip's (Tobago) "Dis Place: The Space Between," a fascinating engagement with a kind of gendered spatial reading of the Caribbean, is worth recalling again. Much has happened since then in terms of the development of Caribbean feminist discourses, Caribbean women's literature, and the study of Caribbean gendered social relations. We are therefore able to move deliberately to ideas and meanings of birth, migration, the gendered oceanic voyage, navigating city spaces, historical spaces, contradictory spaces, finding safe spaces to the performative, body and space.

Kamau Brathwaite's (Barbados) notion of the Caribbean as *tidalectics* captures well the sense of movement, as do a range of Caribbean thinkers who have spent quite a bit of time thinking through some of these movements in terms of archipelagization, repetition, and other geopolitical spatial configurations as we reimagine Caribbean space. With a similar intent, Ngugi wa Thiong'o's theorizing of globalectics "combines the global and the dialectical to describe a mutually affecting dialogue or multi-logue, in the phenomena of nature in a global space that's rapidly transcending that of the artificially bounded, as nation and region." And significantly participating in the larger discourse of expanded spatial frameworks, he adds, "The global is that which humans in spaceships or on the international space station see" (8).

As we look for and recognize Caribbean spaces, particularly when they exist outside of the accepted Caribbean-island and nation-state designations, we can also imagine a different reading in which the logic and meaning of smaller spaces can be read alongside a more expansive, larger, global Caribbean. Thus, since Florida became the twenty-seventh state and the last state east of the Mississippi River to enter the United States of America as a state, only in 1845, one has to see the significance of Florida as an alternative imaginative and physical destination for Africans escaping enslavement.

A Carnival in Miami on the street, or the launching of that Carnival in a stadium in Miami Gardens, is also the re-creation of Caribbean space that is also a movable space. Caribbean food, music, body performance, spatial creation, and visual elements of costuming are also some of these, as is the appearance of certain sounds and patterns of colors. And there are also community re-creations like Little Havana that seem to freeze Cuba into particular nostalgic pre-1959 frameworks but in which there is always movement, as is a more diffused Little Haiti landscape with botanicas next to churches marked "Église" in Harlem as in Miami. Women cross the streets with heads tied casually, wearing white cotton dresses as though they are walking in island space to see a neighbor next door.

Reimagining Caribbean space within and outside of assumed U.S. domestic spaces, beyond island separations, language geographies, but also in diaspora contexts, provides us the means to see and read and imagine more innovative and creative Caribbean realities.

> And yet the Caribbean is more than that; it can also be regarded as a cultural sea without boundaries, as a paradoxical fractal form extending infinitely through a finite world.
>
> (Antonio Benitez Rojo, *The Repeating Island*, 270)

Labor Day parade, Brooklyn, New York. Courtesy of
Charles Martin.

Carnival character in Brooklyn street scene. Courtesy of Charles Martin.

Grenada Day in a Brooklyn park showing "moko jumbie" stilt walker, 2010. Photograph by the author.

3

CARIBBEAN/AMERICAN
The Portable Black Self
in Community

This story really begins in 1968. Martin Luther King was killed during my freshman year in university. I stood as a quiet participant amid the outpouring of grief by fellow students, glued to television sets in the lobby of the dormitory, unable to come to terms with the meaning of this violence and reliving the perpetual and senseless destruction of black political leaders. It was in a university in Eastern Shore, Maryland, in a close-knit community of African American students from the D.C./Maryland/North East Corridor that I came to a full understanding of myself as a black political subject in the U.S. racial context in the middle of the Black Power movement. King's passing in many ways captured the transition to a youth movement through which one could actually make tangible political claims beyond the meaning of civil rights.

In Trinidad, before traveling to university in the United States, my teenage years had gone happily by, as a member of a group of six close friends. We visited each other back and forth, played mas' in the annual Carnival, came to awareness of sexuality, and attended a round of parties. Every now and then, one of our group would report that she was being pressured by her boyfriend to have sex, and a few did, one becoming pregnant. I remember my mother telling me then that I should never shun or reject my friend because of her condition. And we have remained fast friends. But I was going to university, and for me a baby was not an option. So I played the kissing and touching games very carefully, only going so far, even with the most passionate encounters or pleadings by boyfriends to relent. I remember talking with my pastor about this once, and he used my inquiry about sexuality to direct a sermon targeted to church youth. I discovered that my discussion earned perpetual respect from him, and at later occasions when I returned home for visits, he would always express a certain respect for my questioning him on this issue and articulated this on many occasions in subsequent years.

Political awareness had remained on the periphery in Trinidad, part of a giant backdrop that included family conversations and sporadic news events. But I had watched my stepfather order from abroad a book by Dr. Martin Luther King, possibly *Strength to Love* (1963), and I would listen to him as he read and reread aloud passages from the great man's text whenever he had a free moment, shaking his legs from side to side as he read. Still, the popular political education of a scholar/prime minister (Eric E. Williams) framed my basic consciousness as I came of age. But my teenage round of parties, and the excitement of meeting boyfriends and following the latest U.S. fashion crazes, movies, and music, avidly, as well as preparing for exams and getting ready to leave high school dominated. The media images of students marching against segregation played like an old black-and-white movie, though it was happening at that very moment. Instead, movies of U.S. black soul culture and music were places where one could get fashion and style ideas and see performed popular songs and dances.

I also did not connect before even then that my brother whom we had sent off with sweet sorrow to college in the United States on an A.M.E. (African Methodist Episcopal) church scholarship to, of all places, Little Rock in 1959 was landing in the middle of U.S. racial desegregation activity. I was about ten or eleven then, and my big brother whom I had adored and idealized was going abroad, realizing the dreams of many in our neighborhood. The joy of witnessing my big brother's success overshadowed any fears or concerns we had for him as a family. After the normal tears at the airport upon departure, his letters home remained strangely silent about all of that experience, and instead we got wonderful black-and-white (sometimes color) photographs of him and friends in college, new girlfriends, a future wife, dormitories, and classroom buildings, which I showed off to my friends in high school. I had tried in subsequent years to have him fill in much of the space between, but there were still many silences that had not been, nor will ever now be, broken. As I watched in December, 2011, with disbelief my brother lying silent and cold in a funeral home in Baltimore and in a church the next day, his mouth fixed as though he is just about to say something else, I realize that we never got to talk in depth as adults about what he went through personally in that period.

But in 1967, it was my turn to travel to the United States, and entering university as a freshman, I quickly became distinguished as one of those Caribbean students who did exceptionally well: always aced tests, was always well prepared for class, always running to and from classroom buildings, never having the time to hang around and socialize too much, not knowing how to play bid whist, for example. Still, 1968 would mark the turning point of my generation in the United States. It would be followed by three more years of marches, attempts to integrate the little racist town of Princess Anne that kept our movements circumscribed and segregated. We could go to the drugstore, the Greyhound station, the five-and-dime store, the post office, the supermarket, the Somerset Bank, perhaps over to Deal Island or the part of town reserved for the black community to an off-campus Omega party, but that was it. We bought our food at the Kampus Korner or the Hawk's Nest, went to the black Metropolitan Methodist Church, and perhaps went to Salisbury (about fifteen miles away) to shop or to a day at Ocean City, about an hour away. But our movements were circumscribed. At first there were still restaurants and guesthouses with signs outside that said "Colored," and the only formal hotel in town was off-limits to black people as patrons.

Significantly, classmates, some even with the last name Tubman, came from now familiar locations, Chestertown, Potomac, Brandy Wine, Maryland . . . places that I would learn only later had historical importance. Cambridge, Maryland, was one of those iconic places, the launching point from which Harriet Tubman escaped and returned to as part of her campaign of liberating the enslaved. Frederick Douglass had been enslaved and escaped from Maryland. H. Rap Brown, then a fiery activist in the Black Power period, also hailed from Cambridge.

After 1968, then, an unconscious decision was made, collectively it seems, that our university town had to accept our presence and at least provide a modicum of equality. Wasn't this what King had died for? But what had also died was the entire logic of "passive resistance." And with the dawn of the "Black Power" era, with students all over the country and the world, it seems, activism and self-conscious black pride defined this period. Our student government and the Black Student Organization (yes, in a historically black institution) demanded that we be accorded all the rights of the University of Maryland system, and we took over the administration building on more than one occasion, demanded our president be replaced by someone vital and more progressive. The most dramatic of these actions occurred when it was decided that if the town did not want us, then we would go into town as an entire student body and withdraw all our money from the one small

Somerset Bank. My roommate and long-standing high school friend and I joined the march in columns of two with a plan to go into the bank and in an orderly fashion simply fill out a withdrawal form and withdraw our money. As we turned into the main street, our procession was met by state troopers armed to the teeth, dogs at their sides. The student marshals yelled orders to us to not to speak to them, not to look at them, to keep our eyes forward and simply proceed. It was only later when we got back to campus that I realized the terror we were under. For months later, we endured the jokes that the Trinidadian home girls had marched with eyes brimming with tears of fear. But it had made us part of the community forever.

So my black and conscious self came of age in the United States in the midst of Black Power activity. It was a black self, constructed in full identification with U.S. African American struggles but with a conscious link to other black struggles internationally. Student activism and life as a student in a historically black college would shape my identity from this point. In retrospect, we had an enviable window on black culture, as mandatory student assemblies for freshman and sophomore classes included concerts by Duke Ellington, Lionel Hampton, Geoffrey Holder, and a number of classical performers who made the college-tour circuit at the invitation of various presidents. Homecoming celebrations featured pop groups like the Chilites or the Spinners, and we learned to "slow drag" African American style with guys who came cool and full of dance moves out of places like Detroit. But in this period, life became a round of meetings, rallies, sit-ins, takeovers, marches that colored my sense of a black student self all the way through and into graduate school.

It was absolutely important too that the major Black Power proponent was an attractive, politically confident Trinidadian in the person of Stokely Carmichael (later renamed Kwame Toure) who was at the forefront of groups like SNCC (Student Nonviolent Coordinating Committee) and the Black Panther Party. In many ways, it was Stokely who provided the guiding identitarian position for a black student from the Caribbean at this point in history, and therefore made activist participation perfectly logical and doable.

My own involvement in what would become my profession would take off at this point and intersect with my politics. I had spent my freshman and sophomore years listening to many stories about the legendary Mary Fair Burks, who was away completing her Ph.D. at Columbia University. The story was that she was the most deadly of professors—failed you in a minute, then invited you to her home for "tea and sympathy." It was with great trepidation that I entered her Romantic Literature and Victorian Literature classes one semester and American literature another semester. I found her challenging, but amazingly knowledgeable, and more like the strict teachers that I was used to in the Caribbean who nevertheless loved their students but did not cut them any slack. Of course, I aced her classes too. In that subsequent class in American literature, she created a teaching approach that took African American literature into the performative—skits and poetic monologues and one-woman shows, with texts from Phyllis Wheatley to Langston Hughes. It was also the same Mary Fair Burks who opened the magic of Broadway to us, taking a group of black students from a Maryland historically black college by bus on a four-hour drive, for the first time to a Broadway play. Her approach to education continues to inform my teaching. Above all, Mary Fair Burks was an always well-groomed, made-up, and wigged post-seventy-year-old in black high-heeled boots and black midcalf skirts. She demanded respect and knowledge and "gave us the space to be brilliant" if we wanted to be. Much later, I learned from Paula Giddings, in *When and Where I Enter* (1984), that Mary Fair Burks had been in another period of her life one of those people who worked on civil rights and school desegregation projects. Years later when I went back to campus for homecoming, I visited her in her immaculate home, her living room dominated by a baby grand piano. I told her then how much it meant to have had her as a teacher and how it had shaped my professional choices. She subsequently asked me to write a letter for her, as she was planning to go abroad to the Middle East to teach, postretirement.

Still, as I completed my senior year with its round of parties, sexual experimentation, plans for the future, I knew I was headed to at least law school or secondarily a career in international relations. I remember announcing this to the head of the English Department, and seeing his face, crestfallen, as I, perhaps his best student in that class, announced to him, insensitively, that I was never going to be a teacher, as I was going to law school, so why would I do a graduate degree in English?

Pledging Body and Soul

Perhaps no experience characterizes entry into a certain version of Afro-U.S. identity than joining a black sorority. The one of my choice then stood out because most of the members were black women of a darker hue than the other popular sorority, but, more important, held consistently the campus average for highest G.P.A. among "Greek letter" organizations and, not only that, had members visibly active in student leadership.

I remember after I made the decision to "go on line," and actually went through the pledging experience, that this constituted perhaps the clearest induction into the African American cultural experience. From ribbing from by "big sisters" over accent, bringing my Caribbean style to participation in a Greek step show where my line name was "the Foreign One," I became part of a group of sisters with a long history linked to women's suffrage rights as to club-women politics. We learned songs together, lived together in very close quarters during "hell week," ate the same things, went on errands for big sisters, learned steps, sewed our outfits, learned to put Delta words to gospel songs like "We are climbing . . . Delta's ladder . . . We are climbing . . . Delta's ladder . . . ducks of DST . . . every rung gets . . . higher, higher, . . . every rung gets . . . higher, higher . . . every rung gets higher . . . ducks of DST." Renditions of "Crimson and Cream" to the tune of "Come Ye Disconsolate" based on an arrangement from gospel groups provided an initiation into a way of being black in the United States in a concrete way. When I started pledging, once I remember being told that we would have to each find a tune and put Delta words to it. I had heard the popular folk song "Yellow Bird" one day on the radio and used it to make a song. It elicited comments of "Cute!" and the like, but, of course, it was corny and could not be used, except in play. My sisters, meanwhile, were going for the depth of pain and experience that resided in black gospel, and not being a heavily religious person in that way, I had to enter that consciousness and try to reach the pain and joy of black life in North America in order to enter that experience fully. The links to rhythm and blues, particular rhythms that reappeared in the music of the period, are honed in the gospel tradition. But so does a sometimes surprising witnessing of the steps and stomps that one learned as part of the black Greek experience and the chants and songs that go back past the immediate history and connect with similar rhythms in other parts of the black world. Listening to a retrospective concert on the music of Curtis Mayfield, "Here but I Am Gone" at the Lincoln Center in July 2012, opened up floods of recognition but also of memories of a period in which everybody felt we would transcend whatever pains had led up to that period of struggle and consciousness.

In the twilightness of Binghamton, upstate New York, a sorority affiliation provided grounding with the larger African American community during years of raising children. There was always a group of sisters, however short-lived the encounters. But, importantly, one had a ready organization to support the designing of an implementation of community projects, such as a

Saturday school in the Black Experience or a project on Women and Physical Abuse, the latter two in which my mother happily participated whenever she visited. This remains one of my most significant Afro-U.S. identifications: community-service projects together, weddings; lamenting the deaths of one young sister in Baltimore and another who became a popular principal in Detroit; attending national conventions with thousands of other women with similar purpose and vision, all dressed in red or white.

As Caribbean/American, one has a variety of choices as one lives some form of the African American experience in the United States. One of them can be the identification, creation, and definition of small or large enclave-like communities with no serious relationship to the larger African American community, except perhaps through work, church, or occasional meetings. This, perhaps the most comfortable of routes for the immigrant, allows him or her to build his own type of cultural and social community in the face of the dominating American ideologies. Another option is to work in terms of "communities of struggle," those communities and relationships that see themselves as consciously allied for the advancement of the entire black population globally. This is the model created by Caribbean Pan-Africanists before me.

It clarifies the example of Kwame Toure, who remains one of the most important icons of my generation of Afro-Caribbean students in the United States. But once when Stokely came to speak on campus, I attended a reception for him at a colleague's house afterward. I finally got enough nerve and close enough to tell him that I was from Trinidad, expecting that we would share that identity. He responded loudly, "Trinidad, that place that would not let me in!" as he proceeded to tell the story of Trinidad barring his entry to those in his immediate listening circle. He was referring to the decision by the same Eric Williams–led People's National movement government that in the height of Black Power did not want such a leading icon of that movement to enter Trinidad, even if it was his birthplace. The Trinidadian activists have since corrected that wrong, welcoming him home before his passing and creating a lecture annually in the Emancipation period. But for Stokely then, it was a sore that would not yet heal. And as a young professor, I understood.

A few years later, though, Stokely visited again, and not wanting to repeat that encounter, I stayed politely away. As I sat in the audience, one of the student handlers came to tell me that Stokely had instructed, "There is a sister from Trinidad who teaches here. If she is out there, tell her to come back here!" I was ushered to the room where he waited to find him sitting alone with campus security at the door. He told me he wanted me to sit with him and keep him company before the lecture, and as we chatted amicably, he told me that there was a phrase they would use during times of active movement work: "Who would protect us from the protectors!" I believe my presence then added to his sense of security for several reasons.

His presentation was in its usual electrifying manner, a demonstrable ability to field questions with dexterity and knowledge even from activist Zionist members of the Jewish Student Union who challenged him on his support of the Palestinians. Still, he had a certain vulnerability even with all that public demonstration of power that I would imagine all of the activist men who took assertive positions had. It made one want to get even closer to protect, to share, to understand, to learn, to fulfill at least one fantasy that almost all of my generation shared for daring iconic figures like Malcolm X and definitely Stokely.

Brooklyn

The Greyhound bus to New York from Maryland was the necessary conduit to a variety of overlapping locations and portable identities. One drove through Dover, Delaware, with its DuPont funk, New Jersey and all those chemical emissions, over a series of impressive bridges to arrive in the busy center of New York City. Once upon arriving late in the night at Port Authority with my friend Pam, as we waited for our ride, we witnessed with shock a black man beating up a blonde woman we assumed was a prostitute, she cursing and calling him racist names, he demanding loyalty. Port Authority was always a place that challenged any comfortable assumptions of identity.

My conscious Brooklyn experience did not really start until the summer of 1970, though I would visit back and forth a few times before that. And it was Nostrand Avenue, Fulton Street, Flatbush, and all the cross-streets in between that would reinstate or allow a Caribbean American identity to flourish in the United States. The availability of foods in markets, the chance encounters with people one knew back home, the bakeries with breads and puddings, the record shops, the music.

The Labor Day parade ushered in a range of relationships. The first year there, I met an ex-boyfriend who had left Trinidad before me and had gone to St. Croix with plans to get to the United States, as was not unusual then. We knew we would meet somehow, and though we had lost contact for at least three years, and though he was now married, we embarked on a hot summer affair, even going to the point of being godparents together for the child of one of our friends. I remember visiting his home with a group of friends one Christmas night, and after he offered us the usual round of drinks and snacks, he left with us to go on a night of liming to other places, while his wife, a nurse, stayed at home. Polygamy is as natural as breathing air for Caribbean men, as is the boldness of having an affair under the eyes of the wife for Caribbean women. I lived this experience for a year or so, worked, spent long holidays, and then went back to college, as a student who did no wrong.

Brooklyn also meant family and community connections. My mother, my aunt, and their friends worked as nursing assistants and licensed practical nurses (LPNs), caring for elderly white women, while they maintained apartments in Brooklyn and spent most of their time on those jobs. Weekends would be a time of hearing those stories, "poets in the kitchen" style, which Paule Marshall identified, and the various dramas associated with making a life in the United States. Listening to it all with one ear were people like me who were in college or university and had a relationship of respect from those women who knew that we were going to do better. Still, challenges came from many elders of our community who were well read and wanted to know what they were really teaching us in those schools. "Do they tell you about Garvey?" some would ask and proceed to provide their brand of community education. In *Unbought and Unbossed* (1970), Shirley Chisholm captures some of this as well in building up to her run for Congress and the presidency, all part of the political background of the time.

The "Caribbean community," again another monolithic construction for what is really a series of Caribbean communities that re-creates themselves with memories of home, determined to create their own centers in an otherwise alienating North American landscape. In my view, they carnivalize North America, defy its assumptions of a certain given order. And Brooklyn, like Brixton, or Toronto, becomes an extension of the Caribbean into North American space. And for someone like me, a student navigating both experiences, it provided a certain set of ingredients that I could take with me wherever I went. In many ways, Brooklyn also became home. I still get pangs of nostalgia whenever I drive through the streets of Brooklyn. Family and friends still reside there. This too clarifies that for those who migrate, a series of homes redefine belonging.

Black Consciousness, Washington, D.C.

Washington, D.C., and Howard University were all I imagined they would be. It was the midseventies, and black youth were active. Social and political consciousness and organizing were still in vogue. An elegant Stokely presented to overflowing audiences at Howard, to adoring young women who would have willingly been prone but were beginning to question the political location of women in the context of Afrocentric men who were asserting African traditions such as polygamy to which all should acquiesce. Walter Rodney lectured and was challenged by campus activists and classmates on the fine points of Marxism, which they felt he was not engaging fully. Stevie Wonder performed and Patti La Belle in the days when she was with the Blue Belles and later on LaBelle; Earth, Wind & Fire; Count Ossie and the Mystic Revelations of Rastafari who would begin his presentation, "So this is Washington, the belly of the beast!" to loud acclaim from the audience. Bob Marley presented to an overflowing crowd in the RFK Stadium and at the Blues Alley in Georgetown to an audience where the smell of ganja hovered over the hall and where people openly passed blunts around.

I lived on a short residential street behind Columbia Road, then a neighborhood with Latino culture on its edges. Across from my friend Carolyn's apartment was a movie theater where we learned routinely that the Immigration and Naturalization Service would close the doors and let out only those with appropriate papers and arrest all those who remained inside. Of course, this was destined to run this theater out of business, and the last time I saw it, it housed some sort of bargain-goods store. But Columbia Road then was the enclave of a number of African American and Caribbean students. We routinely hosted parties, and I was always making a pot of rice and peas for these events. There was a Cuban restaurant in the Adams Morgan area, good for black beans and rice dinners, and we frequented a range of types of Latin American dry-goods stores that sold *bacalau*, art shops, and even a Claudia Jones Left bookstore before I understood her significance.

Having shared the number-one graduating position with one other person and after getting admitted to both Columbia University and American University, I decided on the latter to pursue the Master's in International Relations I had planned. But American University's international relations M.A. then was populated by career diplomats, many in their fifties who had already had a tour of diplomatic duty and were fluent in European languages and could speak from experience about some of the issues we were reading. I was an Afro-puffed young black girl who felt totally out of place, the only black student in that unit. I made a political decision instead to go to the more exciting Howard University's African Studies Program for the second semester. It was immediately fulfilling. I learned the fundamentals of African Studies methodologies for fieldwork and research from P. Chike Onwuachi, the then head of African Studies who was critical in developing the concept of the "African World." But then there was a clear sense of separation between

an African Studies Program and an African American Studies Department
. . . one doing the United States, the other Africa. My work brought them
together, as I ended up having advisers from both units on my thesis committee. Stephen Henderson, author of *Understanding the New Black Poetry*
(1973), came to the African Studies Program building for the first time for
my M.A. thesis defense he admitted. Leon Damas, of *Négritude* fame, then
an African Studies professor, was my primary thesis adviser.

On Howard's campus, I routinely saw people like Sterling Brown, Haki
Madhubuti, John O. Killens. A physically diminutive but powerfully present Dorothy Porter ran the Moorland-Spingarn Research Library and surprised many by getting married again later in life, in her seventies, it seems.
One of the things that happened in a place like Howard was that one was
exposed, almost routinely, to a panoply of black intellectual figures as either
teachers, lecturers, visitors, or other members of the campus community,
often without knowing their value outside of the institutional context until
much later. All of those names identified are pretty well-known writers in
the black U.S. canon, but one also had exposure on a day-to-day basis to C.
L. R. James, with his tall, lean presence and Stetson hat and open trench coat,
as a normal feature of campus life. Poet Ethelbert Miller worked upstairs in
the African American Studies Library in the same Founders Library where
I worked as a library assistant, and was fast becoming the famous poet that
he is today, and I believe I saw him every single day of the week. Caribbean
male students hung out on the steps of Founders Library between classes to
talk and curse about politics and home and everything else.

I sat in on C. L. R. James's Pan-Africanism course routinely on the invitation of a fellow-student boyfriend, and there I saw Sylvia Wynter for the first
time when she visited campus—a sophisticated black woman scholar in her
prime, speaking to James's class at his invitation. Through her I realized the
possibility of being a Caribbean woman scholar.

From Leon Damas, I heard the stories of encounters with Langston Hughes
and life in Paris. I remember seeing once what I thought was a white man
who seemed overly comfortable with the campus and asked the librarian who
was that man who was so often greeted warmly on campus, only to be told,
"Why that's Sterling Brown!" My African American literature courses were
taught by Arthur P. Davis, editor of *Cavalcade,* then the preeminent source
for African American literature before the field became the staple that it is
in the academy. Arthur P. knew everything there was to know about every
writer in the canon at the time and taught his course in a conversational
tone, expressing direct and personal knowledge of all the writers and their

works. Stephen Henderson, who specialized in poetry, taught in African American Studies on the third floor of Founders Library. I remember going to see Stephen Henderson one day only to see him sweating and very anxious. I learned subsequently that Ted Joans had done a poetry reading about freedom and in the process had started to take off his clothing.

I had perhaps the most special mentoring relationship with Leon Damas, one of the founders of the *Négritude* movement in Paris who taught in the African Studies Program in the 1970s, my thesis adviser. He often invited us to his home for dinner with his wife in a lovely apartment in southwest D.C., surrounded by all the memorabilia and photographs of him one now sees in books. I would also run into him in the corridors of the Library of Congress and no doubt established myself to him as a scholar by that very fact. When I received a Commonwealth Scholarship to go to Nigeria to study African literature, I began to make my plans for travel but was still tight on money. At what would seem a time congested with travel arrangements, Damas gave me a project, weeks, it seems, before I was to leave for Africa. I had to catalog for him all the M.A. theses and Ph.D. dissertations that had been done in the African Studies Program at Howard. I completed the project in between a great deal of anxiety over traveling and preparing. In those precomputer days, I typed the list and turned it in to Professor Damas. He in turn handed me a check for five hundred dollars, way beyond what I thought the work was worth and no doubt because he wanted to give me something to help my journey but did not want to simply hand it to me and instead found a mutually beneficial project that I could easily do. I remain forever grateful for his generosity. Tears still mist in my eyes when I recall that experience because that would be the last time I would see him. When I returned to the United States after gaining my Ph.D. in Nigeria, but also pregnant with my first daughter, I learned that he was gravely ill and in that same week that he had passed. He was so excited over my success and I wanted to share all my experiences with him, but I never saw him again. It was Damas who instilled in me, though, that anyone doing African or Caribbean studies is incompletely informed unless he or she is knowledgeable about Brazil.

West Africa

I arrived in the chaos that was the Lagos Airport after a long flight that stopped first in Liberia and then made its way to Nigeria. I was told that someone from the Ministry of Education in Nigeria would meet me. So when I saw a well-dressed, official-looking young man waving at me, I assumed

he was the person. He was not, but was one of the young men who had created employment for themselves facilitating entry of visitors into Nigeria,
past military officers and into the city. There was no romance of arrival into
Africa for the first time for me, though I am sure the walk from the plane
and into the building should have generated some of those feelings. I have
absolutely no memory of any such emotions. I do remember, though, that
the young man helped me through a chaotic process and put me in a taxi for
a hotel once I got through the crowd in my cute outfit and matching Sam-
sonite luggage, and I paid him, I learned later, handsomely for his services
in American dollars. But it was absolutely worth whatever was paid, as I had
no idea what else to do. The next day, I headed for the airport, arrived in
Ibadan, and took a taxi again to what was going to be my residence in the
Tafawa Balewa graduate hall. I learned later what I did quite casually was an
amazing taking of risks and that the Trinidad High Commission is normally
informed of one's arrival in order to present the necessary meeting protocols
and conduits. But nobody had told me this . . . so I arrived unescorted from
graduate school in Howard University, after reassuring my anxious family
at the JFK Airport in New York that the whole process was totally managed.
Without planning it, I had performed an act of amazing bravery, according
to all who heard how I had arrived. For some reason, even today I tend to
not wait around for or expect the niceties and protocols that sometimes come
normally with rank or status.

From the start, though, Nigeria was an exciting and heady time, of new
friends, parties, and a range of new social encounters and experiences. It was
not unusual to be asked to dinner by a faculty member, only to learn that he
had more than a passing interest. Still, it was easy to see and meet African
writers like Amos Tutuola or Chinua Achebe directly, to be part of an intellectual community that had claimed its own space, and to work with people
who were the leaders of the then budding field of African literary criticism
as developed by Africans themselves. Ironically, some of these scholars are
now professors in American universities.

Going into town and into the markets was always one of those experiences of sight, smell, and sound. I would go into the markets to have my
hair braided, sitting on low stools with my head in the lap of women with
strong female body odors who could deliver an amazing style of cornrow for
what is now small change. One could buy anything in the Mokola market.
Approaching the entrances, calls of "Customer!" ushered one directly into a
community of laughing women who wanted you to buy or try something else
or braid your hair for what seems now like pennies. Still, one could search

for equivalent Caribbean food products like plantains and make selections from the sometimes scarcely available vegetables and fruits.

Once I went to a Fela concert at his Kalakuta republic and still have a photograph of him playing on his trumpet or saxophone and eyeing me, then an attractive twenty-four-year-old, as he performed. I was with a group from the Trinidad High Commission, and we were seated in the front row. Lagos and Ikoyi served as our refuge during holidays for me and the other Trinidadian students and also created some lifelong friendships. A community of "West Indian wives" of Nigerian men also became part of the social framework with a variety of social events and visits to their homes. A few of them were women who had left the Caribbean to study nursing (yes, that group of the farewells to England when I was a child!), married Nigerians in London or Canada, and then accompanied husbands to Africa as wives. One of them who was my brother's childhood girlfriend who came from Enugu once to meet me; two of the Ibadan wives were my mother's contemporaries. We were told stories of some finding out there were prior wives in polygamous contexts, mothers-in-law who did not speak to them until they bore a child, the classic results of delayed pregnancies as captured by the Ghanaian playwright Ama Ata Aidoo in *Dilemma of a Ghost* (1965). Several created their own "underground railroads" to escape disastrous marriages and controlling and abusive men, and many warned us, "Don't marry these guys. Finish your degree and go home." I followed their advice only partially, marrying one from Sierra Leone, who fascinated me with family stories that established a Caribbean connection.

Suddenly, it was my wedding day, and I felt like I was floating on the ceiling of the church, looking down at myself walking down the aisle. Looking back, marriage for me seemed to protect against what I was repeatedly warned about: that one could not get a Ph.D. if a woman in a Nigerian university without using "bottom power," as it was referred to there. There was as well the particular assumption of the availability of young women in a range of situations, and several undergraduates accommodated the culture of receiving gifts from wealthy men. Those were the days when money flowed in Nigeria and people came into the banks with briefcases filled with naira to conduct business. Military coups were also part of the experience and meant a kind of hunkering down and military music on the radio as the government changed hands, as happened during the coup that ousted General Gowon. Foreign students were told to stay in their rooms and lay low. Nigerian students chatted in groups or remained almost as shocked at the death of Murtala Muhammad at a subsequent coup event as did Maryland students at the death of Martin Luther King Jr. Soldiers whipped traffic offenders on the streets, and it was standard that all business transactions were accompanied by a "dash," or a small tip, to ensure that whatever it was happened.

Once I went to a local police station to request a certificate of good character in order to apply for a position in the diplomatic service and was sent to speak to the *oga,* or big man, to tell him what I wanted, as the policemen who were the desk clerks could not understand the request. The police chief understood, of course, and was pleased to meet a young woman from the Caribbean, and he took my particulars, including my address. A few days later, one of the hall maids came to my door, her face written with anxiety, and announced that a big man had come to see me. It was the same local police chief in khaki uniform, holding the accompanying short cane, with waiting policemen who escorted him and remained in the corridor as he entered my small room. Before long I realized that this was a social visit with a desire for a date.

In the end, married and pregnant, I defended my degree, after waiting six months for an external examiner to show up from London, as was the university protocol. Fortunately for me, a Caribbean scholar named J. D. Elder had come to Nigeria at the same time to do research on the Yoruba antecedents of Caribbean culture and served on my committee and facilitated the kind of work I wanted to do on Caribbean and African literatures and cultures.

Living in West Africa for three years allowed a series of interesting journeys, though. Travels by road to Cotonou, Lome, Accra, Abidjan were exciting opportunities for students in that period. I traveled once with an African American woman, and at the northern Ghana border with Côte d'Ivoire, her American passport was recognizable; my Trinidad and Tobago passport presented a challenge for border guards who had never seen such a passport nor understood where such a place was but who were more curious than hostile. After trying all sorts of explanations with my limited French, I finally started throwing out cultural cues and eventually said: "Bob Marley!" An amazing point of recognition occurred immediately: "Ah, les Antilles!" was their response, and excited about seeing someone from a part of the world they had never met, they began calling over others to see and meet us and marveling at my crossing their border as almost a favor to their "diaspora literacy."

On another occasion, I traveled through northern Nigeria with a Nigerian male friend who was then a veterinary student. We slept wherever we could and got as far as Niger with a plan to go to Mali, which had to be abandoned in Niamey. It was way too hot and too difficult then to traverse the desert by road, and we were too young and crazy then to know better. Reason prevailed and instead a return via Dakar was selected. But along the way, we rode on camels and saw from the inside some of the areas traveled only by locals or itinerant traders. But both of these journeys provided amazing opportunities to see some of the internal and less traveled African locations and experiences that perhaps now are commonplace for travel shows like those on television such as the Travel or Discovery Channel or Anthony Bourdain's *No Reservations.*

Portable Identity

I once wrote a solicited essay for a publication of the Modern Language Association (*PMLA*) about my theoretical excursions and definition of "migratory subjectivity." I was describing then that my *Black Women, Writing, and Identity: Migrations of the Subject* (1994) came out of my experience of navigating a range of communities and that "personal experience" for me in scholarship is about taking individual experience out of the statistics into real life. I am never more startled than when some casual experience that I relate about my mother and her experience of working in New York is identified as a statistical reality for those doing political economy or the sociology of migration—for example, the work of Saskia Sassen, *The Global City* (2001) or *Deciphering the Global* (2007), or Patricia Pesar's *Caribbean Circuits* (1996). I was talking once with Monica Jardine, with whom I have cowritten a few essays on the subject and who was beginning work then on Caribbean migration, about my mother and her frequent journeys back and forth, which I know bothered my brother, only to have her say at each turn that for those Caribbean women who migrated to the United States in their fifties, her experience has been documented as, in fact, part of a pattern of activities. The research revealed that their generation never planned to settle in the United States permanently but saw their presence as helping advance another generation, while they maintained critical connections at home—church, community, and family relationships and friendships. And this would be consistently so for all kinds of other related experiences. The idea of one's personal experience being part of history is something that many fail to fully understand.

As the daughter of such an experience, I am very conscious of the implications of my various identities, honed in the Caribbean and in the United

States. I have lived in Nigeria, in Brazil. I have returned to live and work in Trinidad as well, as an adult. I have experienced the U.S. South; Washington, D.C., the nation's capital; Miami; New York; Chicago, right across from Lake Michigan. In each of these locations, I have taken some aspects of my portable Caribbean identity with me, and that identity has consistently overlapped with my black woman identity, my identity as a black faculty member in major universities, my community experiences, my experiences as a mother, consumer, traveler, and so on. The sense of being "in transit" consistently marks my experience. One of my childhood girlfriends told me recently that she felt the same even before leaving the Caribbean and as a young woman would drive with a guy she was dating in Trinidad to hang out in the airport and watch people come and go, as it gave her a sense of the possibility of going somewhere beyond given expectations, accessing elsewhere.

Clearly, the range of political positions, identitarian locations that one occupies, is informed by a series of concrete experiences. The time and context of entry into the United States inform the way one navigates U.S. culture. These can allow not so much full absorption as an option but preferably a range of mobilities in different communities. But it also presents a clear loss of possible commensurate status at home. Being in the United States during the Black Power period meant that one had to have a credible position on issues of African American rights to full participation in the society they helped create. One could not (and I still believe cannot) just reap the benefits of the African American civil rights struggle, but instead one had to actively participate in social transformation. But it does not mean an obliteration of any other identities one would hold, for indeed this was the time when a range of "Third World" cultural forms were becoming part of the steady experience of African Americans, particularly at the level of popular culture.

At a lecture in Binghamton a number of years ago, Clayborne Carson, who was working on a book on Martin Luther King Jr. and was presenting a lecture, "Malcolm X and Martin Luther King," indicated that Malcolm X, unlike King, was never a member of "the black community." When pressed on this issue by a number of student questioners, his response was that Malcolm X never participated in "the black church," never joined "the black fraternities," or any other identified black community mainstays and markers. This was a shocking assertion to many who saw Malcolm X as one of the most clarifying representations of being African American in the United States. But Malcolm X also had Caribbean background in one line of his family and was formed in part through his father's activism and both parents' participation in the Garvey movement (Carew; Marable), and perhaps this is what disqualified

Malcolm in his eyes from membership in "the black community," as Carson defined it then. But this is precisely what makes Malcolm X, in my view, fully African American as well. A narrow reading of black identity reveals that there is still, in some visions, a stereotyped "black community" and not a range of black communities. For me, a monolithic black community has tactical political agency for political gains, but it is composed nonetheless of a series of overlapping, intersecting black communities, which is not so much *disintegration,* as Eugene Robinson (2010) calls it. What seems to be happening instead is the creation of a series of intersections. Disintegration seems to presuppose a certain unity without conflict. Instead, we know that these communities overlap, collide, confront, alter, and are altered by each other and a range of other ethnic communities. Far from being invisible, these, then, are active presences. A sense of a portable self, able to cross over and deal positively with a range of communities, for me, identifies the desirable subject position in contemporary times.

4

SPIRIT SCAPES
From Brazil to the Caribbean

On the way from São Paulo to Natal, the navigational symbol for the airplane on the video screen in the cabin points almost as if it were heading for Africa. I imagine that if we kept going, we could see ourselves recrossing the Atlantic as many of the dispersed Africans did, mythologizing a return journey and thereby making theirs the actual technology of flight. Many of our artists and writers continue this process imaginatively, aesthetically, or make these journeys in actuality. Transatlantic journeys seem to have tangible possibility from this launching point of Natal. The shoulder points of the continents themselves seem to reach for certain reconciliation. One is able to visualize the continental drift as well as its opposite.

Caribbean Space, another angle of seeing the world. Again contemplating the map, the giant shoulder of South America reaches toward Africa. Recognizing that one is at the closest point here to the continent gives me some sort of creative recognition of possible connections and triggers the imagination further. But as the plane turns leftward toward a landing in Natal, the defining Caribbean archipelagos as well as the continental Caribbean reveal themselves. One sees the real possibility of continuing from this point in Brazil over land or sea to the Caribbean, to the Guyanas, Venezuela, and finally Trinidad—the first island one encounters as one leaves South America. It is easy to see why the north coast of Brazil is sometimes seen as its Caribbean coast, for a range of Caribbean cultures combine here in terms of landscape, the history and culture of sugar-cane production, but also people, music, the products of various migrations. It is easy to flip the paradigm of North-South dominance and reading of the world from this angle of vision.

Caribbean Space indeed . . . the spaces of connection, and the consistent filling in of empty spaces. I always want to be in the Caribbean, as I always want to be in Brazil.

Thinking about Caribbean space and Caribbean identity means engaging a series of movements. It means first of all coming to terms with how much both the relatively new Caribbean nation-states and the Caribbean diaspora have been fundamental sites of the creation of Caribbean cultural identities and the extent to which global economic and political forces have also shaped these experiences.

The Caribbean has in common with Brazil an already-identified history, including the destruction of the full presence of indigenous peoples, the wretchedness of enslavement on sugar plantations, colonialism, and the struggles for self-possession and independence but also for re-creation.

When my friend, an Afro-Brazilian activist from Bahia, died at the relatively young age of forty-eight, a turtle appeared in our backyard and refused to be dislodged. Sometimes it would walk over and flop into the pool and swim hurriedly back and forth. Other times it would find a cool place to rest in a shaded area. Consistent removal at pool-cleaning time would deposit him on grass surrounding the pool into which he would eventually flop himself back. Not surprisingly, many saw this as some kind of spiritual message, for Lino was a powerful man who believed deeply in his Afro-Brazilian spiritual tradition, *Candomblé*, as he also believed in the need for a more rapid advancement of Afro-Brazilians into full emancipation. And significantly, his last partner reminded me that he always saw our house in Miami as a reference or layover point in his journeys outside of Brazil. The turtle is totemic for a range of Caribbean and Brazilian spiritualities. LeRoy Clarke, for example, keeps several turtles in his yard, and turtles often appear as dominating figures in his art. And I was told on witnessing a giant turtle living in a colleague's backyard north of Brasília that turtles absorb a lot of negative energy. So one day, also not surprisingly, our turtle disappeared just as magically as he had arrived.

Connecting Paradigms

Candomblé—the Afro-Brazilian sociocultural, religious, interpretative belief system—presents for me an important convergence of the transformational in Afro-diasporic culture as it is expressed through questions of memory and reelaboration. While in this belief system the individual is always endowed with the energy of a particular *orisha* (deity), through preparation and participation, the transformational is intensely manifested. In some individuals, this can be seen primarily in the moving of the body and its corporeality to another level. It is a movement away from the daily circle of life, work, and struggle to one of emotional and spiritual possibilities. In my reading, it is also a movement to a level of history, diaspora memory, return, and reconstruction.

Diaspora memory, in this context, recalls Africa as generating source. It is also, simultaneously, located in the memory of the crossing as well as in the deliberate reinterpretation of "remembered" cultural forms in a new space and in new conditions. Thus, in *Candomblé,* as African *orishas* are recalled to practical existence, they are also given space to move outward, from the past, into a realm of present and future existence.

The significance of manifestation and possession is not only in the re-appearance of an African entity with particular identifiable characteristics that cross lines of gender, place, corporeality, spatiality, and temporality, but also in that it allows the individual person to occupy a different location in relation to his or her larger community. The individual physically becomes something else, somebody else, momentarily escapes the mundane, the "real," the normal, and, with the sanction of the community, exists in different space and time and history. The community in its turn also participates in this process as it witnesses. In fact, it is not uncommon for members of the witnessing community to move also to that level of transformation. I am using *witnessing* here in the sense in which it is conveyed in African American religious practices. Although there is a particular level of spectatorship and performance in place as well, there is also a recognizable witnessing, because of the antiphonal, interactive nature of the process, to an alternative way of being, away from practical definitions of limiting existence.

The public versions of a *Candomblé* ritual begin with drumming and the initiated participants entering and making a circular parade around the center of the space they are using for that ritual, and where the *ashe* of the house is said to be buried. Progressively, through drumming and the sound of the *agogo,* chants, and a variety of other ritual experiences, some participants become other-endowed. Once the *orishas* manifest themselves and that preliminary level is completed, the spiritually embodied participants leave the public space and return vested in—literally dressed in—the clothing and ritual accoutrements as well as the behavioral attributes of the entities manifested. The body of the person carrying the manifestation is visibly present but not as its original self. One therefore witnesses *shango* or *yansan* or *nana* at the same time that one witnesses the force of transformation in the individual. It is important to note that various versions of the same entity often occupy the same space.

A variety of Afro-Brazilian scholars identified *Candomblé* as a source of resistance to the hegemony of European culture in Brazil. Julio Braga, a scholar-practitioner, in "Candomblé: Força e resistência," states that *Candomblé* is a system of preservation, of balance and knowledge that always attains a level of harmony of the human with nature through the interaction with the sacred world without losing the sense of confronting the adversities of life in society as we search for freedom and social harmony.

It is interesting that although *Candomblé* is specific to Brazil, a variety of other versions of the same exist throughout the African diaspora, ranging from Lucumi in Cuba and Shango or Orisha in Trinidad to Santeria in Puerto Rico and New York City, all operating at the level of both "spirit work" and community work. And Macumba in Rio and certain other areas of Brazil echoes Mamcumba, also a spiritual/ritual tradition in pre-Islamic Senegambian villages, at times challenging the incursions of Islam. LeRoy Clarke in Trinidad refers to his artistic work as the practice of *obeah,* another spiritual-therapeutic stream in the Caribbean.

Quilombismo—or *marronnage*—is the second transformative Afro-diasporic pattern I want to identify as a connecting possibility. In 1995 Brazil celebrated the three-hundredth anniversary of Zumbi of Palmares. Palmares remains the longest-lived maroon settlement, or *quilombo,* that existed as an alternative space in resistance to slavery. Palmares was also a site of transformation, an elsewhere, a location that demonstrated by its very existence that there was a practical possibility of "another world" outside of the given definitions of reality at that time. Yet, according to Abdias do Nascimento in "O Quilombismo: Uma Alternativa Politica Afro-Brasileira," Palmares was just one of innumerable isolated black communities that would be identified as *quilombos* today that gave enslaved people a tangible possibility of freedom. Benedita da Silva in her life story (1997) also identifies a *quilombo* led by a woman, Rainha Tereza, in the eighteenth century, near the Bolivian border, that was destroyed in 1770.

Throughout the Americas, there were similar "other worlds," such as that created by the Maroons of Jamaica or the black Seminoles in and around Fort Mose in Florida following the Stono Rebellion. The extent of these elsewhere communities is yet to be fully documented. But the knowledge of the ones in existence provides us with the knowledge of escape southward as just as significant emotionally and physically as escape to the North. And because slavery ended in the English-speaking Caribbean some fifty years before the

United States, and the Haitian Revolution had happened, the Caribbean also had earlier meanings of a place where one could be free.

The use of African or Native American religions, medicines, and therapies was as central to the Maroon communities as were the very forces of resistance and transformation that ran through them. Do Nascimento identified sixteen principles that are generated from the historical idea of *quilombismo* that can be used to create a different pattern of life. These offer an alternative paradigm—one that stresses democracy and egalitarianism in the areas of gender, politics, economics, race, and general ways of being in community.

Liberatory movements, the third connecting paradigm I want to identify here, is represented in the series of liberatory movements undertaken by such freedom fighters as Harriet Tubman (ca. 1819–1913) in the United States, who has become iconic because she mastered or knew intimately all the routes to freedom and then led others through them. Her entire self-identification presents a deliberate sense of journeying to an elsewhere, at times occupying the wild space in between, but definitely always existing maroon-like outside of the most incredible level of oppression, which was slavery in the Americas.

The concept of "migratory subjectivity," which I identified in an earlier work, *Black Women, Writing, and Identity: Migrations of the Subject,* is for me still relevant to contemporary discussions of globalization. I offer there a paradigm of the deliberate and directed migration for liberation to other worlds as opposed to aimless wandering or its opposite, containment, within dominant discourses. Thereby is created another set of movements outside of the terms of the politico-economic systems in place.

For me, then, these worlds and movements exist at the heart of what I see as an alternative global geography and engagement—the transformational, the imaginative in Afro-diasporic culture: first, the level of the personal, psychic transformation that also moves within a community and has implications for resistance; second, the creation of an alternative physical, political space, outside of the terms of the dominant society; and third, the deliberate journeying outside of the boundaries of restriction and oppression. These patterns, in my opinion, are related to the spirit of creative and imaginative space, which can sometimes become the impetus of the literary imagination.

I grew up in an extended family in which "spirit work" was not an unusual experience. My now deceased aunt Olive provided the model of a spiritual woman who held her annual feast, which in my memory and with knowledge gained since then was a time of feeding the ancestors. Other rituals like herbal "bush" baths and the use of incense to purify with smoke persons and houses are recognizable when I see them again in *Candomblé* houses and other ritual contexts. I realize, though, that it was not quite the Yoruba-based *orisha* events that my aunt practiced but something else, maybe a combination of learned or differently sourced spiritual practices. Tantie Olive was also the person who would claim to have a spiritual visitation, via a dream of a neighbor perhaps, that she would test the next day by walking down the street to chat with that person and to learn that they had connected somehow that night in some other world. Tantie Olive, who kept all her surnames, was also community activist and a leader in women's organizations and local politics. I was able to recognize spirit work when I saw it in Brazil.

*   *   *

Salvador da Bahia has been called by its African descendant exponents *"uma nação africana chamada Baía,"* "an African nation called Bahia," a summarizing and repeated theme sometimes used for Carnival. But Salvador da Bahia is also for me recognizably culturally Caribbean in a certain kind of way. One can buy coconut water and cassava bread on the streets or a range of herbs in the markets, get a bush bath from one of the practitioners, feel a recognizable Carnival rhythm and vibe, or be mistaken for a native Bahian by another Brazilian visiting from another part of the country.

Lino de Almeida, whom I mentioned earlier, represented well many of the aspects of Salvador da Bahia that provided those connections and was a go-to person for many cultural workers but also demonstrated his ability to navigate Caribbean and American spaces with dexterity. He was also the kind who was never afraid to challenge oppression publicly, whether he was in the United States or at home. A popular radio disc jockey, he was the primary conduit for reggae music on the airwaves in Brazil and had welcomed Bob Marley to Bahia and created the cultural space Praça de Reggae, where a final celebration in his honor was held. Part of the Salvador leadership of the Movimento Negro Unificado (United Black Movement), he led some of the particular moves for empowerment of Afro-Brazilians we see being realized today and was always sure to capture it brilliantly and rhetorically for an inside or outside audience. A legendary womanizer as well, he was also contradictorily a wonderful friend and protector of women from injustice or danger, although this seems contradictory. I gather at his funeral, a woman shouted, "He was macho, but he adored women!" He was identified also as one who would never run away from a fight. In one notorious example, he got into a physical fight with a local Bahian who, although opportunistically engaged to an African American, was pursuing some newly arrived visiting African American women to their discomfort. He appealed to the man to stop, and the rest is history. A spirited sense of activism in speech, in style, in engagement marked Lino with a certain confidence and grace that one sees in men who believe deeply in these positions, from Malcolm X to Stokely Carmichael.

My first encounter with Brazil came through a four-week educational tour through São Paulo, Minas Gerais (Ouro Preto), Salvador da Bahia, and Rio de Janeiro. Each location offered a different angle of seeing a magnificent landscape. And in Bahia, a handsome Rastafarian activist in union work captured my attention and became a traveling companion through the streets of Salvador and many other surrounding locations. I returned several times after that, each time arriving in Rio de Janeiro or São Paulo first, and then I would make my way to Bahia. An amazing rush of excitement accompanied each visit, as I could see the city line, common landmarks, and the ocean and its littoral as we landed. Once on the ground, meeting always welcoming friends, a drive through a canopied bamboo tunnel outside the airport led to a turn along the route that bordered the Atlantic and accompanied one's journey into the city.

Once while living and teaching at the University of Brasilia, I deliberately took an overnight coach to Bahia, determined to see the landscape unfold from another angle. And it was a rich and wonderful journey, with stops along the way as the sun set and an early-morning arrival in Bahia at dawn. One could also extend this vision via a ferry to the island called Itaparica, where Yoruba *egungun* festivals are known to create another sense of mystery. Or one could go by ferry and road to Morro de São Paulo or over to Cachoeira to see the Irmandade da Boa Morte festivities, stopping in a small, rural sugar-cane town named Santo Amaro, the birthplace of singers Caetano Veloso and Maria Bethania. Cachoeira provided for me, and I suspect many others, a recognition of African ancestral culture residing in the Americas. A clarifying family story surfaces.

*   *   *

My very spiritual aunt Olive relayed to me on more than one occasion that on the night I was born, she had a vision of a woman with big skirts dancing spiritedly. When I decided to accept a scholarship and travel to Africa, she saw this as fulfillment of this guiding presence, which in her consciousness she had seen years before. Throughout my visits to Africa, I always sought to connect that story somehow but never could. I never saw the women with big skirts in Africa. But arriving at the house of the Irmandade da Boa Morte, there was an instant recognition, for here were the women with the big skirts, particularly evident when they dressed to dance the *samba de roda*, which she had described without ever seeing them. Significantly, they are identified as the oldest African sisterhood in the New World. A certain diasporic Caribbean recognition and connection in the Americas happened for me in a small town in northeastern Brazil.

* * *

After the spectacular landscape of Rio de Janeiro, Salvador da Bahia is a two-level magical place, full of *ashe* and one of the primary sites for the fuller relational understanding of the Caribbean. It was able to conserve, in a variety of hidden locations, a set of creative and spiritual processes but also a pace and a musicality that infused itself in so many ways. In front of a Catholic church, a number of people could shower themselves with popcorn, an element used in dedication to Saint Lazarus or Shakpana in Candomblé, a saint or *orisha* identified as a healer. Some would take away leaves and petals from flowers in the church to vitalize baths at home and encourage you to do the same. Petitions of various sorts accompanied candles, dolls, photographs, and other items in the foyer of the church. And sitting at a roadside bar, sharing a beer, one could also see *Candomblé* initiates, dressed in big floral skirts and head wraps, white lace blouses from another era or overlapping community, walking the streets with rectangular trays of popcorn as they engaged the community, performing obligations.

But my activist Afro-Brazilian friends' love for Bahia is as infectious as it is critical . . . critical of folklorization, respectful still of culture. For them, therefore, there was a continuum between enslavement in the traditional time frame that did not end in Brazil until 1888 and the oppression that was to be only continued by other means through economic racism, which also had to be counted equally.

I imagined that those encountering Abdias do Nascimento, through the decades, would certainly have felt the combination of political and spiritual energy of spirit work. Abdias, who lived through the twentieth century and into the twenty-first century, leaving this earthly realm in 2011, living close to a century, maintained a passion about the full emancipation of black Brazilian people until his death and was the architect of the philosophy called *quilhombismo,* which took its logic from the oldest Maroon community—Palmares—as a model for developing transformed communities away from oppression but with a particular aesthetic of creativity that remained outside of enslavement and could contribute philosophically to a sense of being in the world, embracing various communities without oppressing them. He also saw continuity with other black communities in the Americas (North, Central, the Caribbean, and South America).

This philosophy would inform subsequent groups of activists, including the activist and creative group Quilhombhoje, out of São Paulo but with a reach that embraced writers resident in Rio de Janeiro and Minas Gerais and throughout the larger Afro-Brazilian community. The Quilhombhoje aesthetic community would then live out the meaning of Abdias do Nascimento's work and take it to another generation, bringing into it some of the traditional forms of knowledge coming out of *Candomblé* and the philosophical positions, like *Ashe,* Yoruba derived but clearly reinterpreted and transformed in the Americas.

Perhaps the core of spirit work resides in *ashe* (sometimes rendered as *àshé*), which has been described as "the most important religio-aesthetic phenomenon to survive transatlantic slavery almost intact" (Abiodun). Indeed, *àshé* is still one of those African diasporic theoretical concepts, though with different spellings based on location, and though in Afro-American or Afro-Caribbean English may be understood as "spirit" or perhaps popularly as "soul," that has currency among large portions of the population and remains unaccounted for, unnamed or misnamed, or ignored in intellectual discourses. My work in Black artistic and religious communities in Brazil, the Caribbean, New York, and London, as well as my earlier study in Nigeria, has provided the opportunity to reappraise this concept. A preliminary recognition is that it is a concept that clearly had and has migratory capability. Indeed, it was the strength of the meaning of *àxé,* its spelling in Afro-Brazilian ritual discourse, that has provided the impetus for understanding this form that operates as de Almeida and do Nascimento would want it, outside of the "logic of oppression."

As a cultural definition, *àxé* moves across two large discursive fields: that of spirituality and that of creativity, with its meanings and associations of what it is to be human in the world. Philosophical questions of existence, the power to be, dynamic force in all things are embedded in its meaning. Thus, LeRoy Clarke, Trinidadian master artist, who refers to his creative process as working obeah, operates at that same intersection of the spiritual and the creative. In *Candomblé, àxé* functions as the spiritual security of this space, representing a well of energy of all the *orishas* from which one may draw. Objects like plants, metals, stones become sacred and are entered under the central post of the *terreiro,* or religious and environmental preserve, also called *ile àxé* (home of *àxé*). A number of ritual offerings of sacred plants, blood of sacrifice used in a variety of ceremonies, and a variety of ritual acts known only to initiates consistently revitalize the functioning of the *àxé.*

Àshé is also sometimes used synonymously with *medicine, charm, protection.* Robert Farris Thompson in *Flash of the Spirit* (1984) links *àshé* directly with the presence of the *orishas* (the traditional divinities of Yoruba) and defines it as "the power-to-make-things-happen," with the *orishas* as embodiments of *àshé.*

The importance of *àshé* in this particular articulation is as it relates directly to creativity, to cultural production. Margaret Thompson Drewal identifies what she calls a direct correlation between the dynamic qualities of both dance and oral performance and power known among the Yoruba as *àsé.* Beier had earlier correlated *àsé* with the power of the word, "a mysterious force" that provides "that quality in a man's personality which makes his words—once uttered—come true." For the Yoruba, a person with *àsé* (*alásé*)—a person with authority—is one with "innate metaphysical power who by virtue of this power maintains an awesome control over spiritual realms and, by extension, over social ones" (203). *Àsé,* then, is a kind of "voiced power," a "manifest power" that bridges the areas of spirituality and creativity.

Perhaps even more useful is Rowland Abiodun in "Understanding Yoruba Art and Aesthetics: The Concept of *Àsé*" (1994), which identifies its enigmatic and affective nature, speaking particularly to its meaning as "creative power in the verbal and visual arts." Making a link between Yoruba culture and similar manifestations in African American culture, he feels *àsé* palpably in churches, under the rubric of "the spirit," "the holy ghost," or simply "power." And in more secular contexts, in literary and oral traditions such as "signifying," "playing the dozens," "reading," "toasting," "loud-talking," "dissin,'" "snapping," and "rap," there are reverberations of the structure and affective aspects of *àsé* in varying degrees (71).

Àshé then migrates transatlantically across the poles identified separately as secular/sacred or profane/religious in a variety of subsequent articulations ranging from the religious to popular culture. Additionally, its various spellings capture its applications in different language and cultural contexts. The power of the word is central to *àshé,* as through voice one is able to make *àshé* come to life. Thus, it simultaneously has a relationship with antiphony or call and response and what Abiodun identifies as *iluti* (which also means "teachability," "good hearing," "communicability"), that other ubiquitous aesthetic principle in African diaspora cultures.

Through this logic of antiphony and call and response, both art and *àshé* have efficacy. Thus, summarizing with Juana Elbein dos Santos in a 1992 lecture in Salvador da Bahia, *àshé* is one of the most important principles of energy in the world. Without *àshé*, nothing can happen. However, the core of the individual must be developed by "this possibility of realization," and *àshé* can be weakened or increased and has permanent recycling capability, to the extent that one is conscious and able to take the appropriate steps to accomplish this.

As indicated above, *spirit* is one of the equivalent English-language correlates for *àshé*. Robert Farris Thompson would use this logic in his *Flash of the Spirit*, as would Houston Baker in *Workings of the Spirit: The Poetics of Afro-American Women's Writing* (1993) and Joseph M. Murphy in *Working the Spirit: Ceremonies of the African Diaspora* (1995). In Baker's literary text and Murphy's more religious one, the emphasis is clearly on "spirit work," and in particular the more active-process verb *working*, rather than a passive reception process. Although Murphy's definition of *spirit* remains vague, he sees "spirit" as fluid in diaspora traditions (182). But, importantly, he sees it as in the definitions of *àshé* as something to be "worked," that is, "manufactured by human action"—"worked" from more a basic spiritual force into the special force or "personality" (180), and thus linked to community: "Though the spirit 'is' everywhere, the most valued encounter between humans and spirits occurs within the ceremonial confines of community action" (182).

In further "working the spirit," Houston Baker's reference takes it more in the direction of creativity, outlandish fabrication, boundlessness, through a powerful medium that passes it on: "In Afro-American discourse, the spirit may assume various guises. For the classically successful, performance is contingent upon the ability to fabricate outrageously, to improvise and embroider in outlandish fashion" (75–76).

Baker's definition, which ends logically at the doorstep of the "conjurer," language more familiar in the U.S. South, then arrives at a meeting point very much in the area of the definitions of *àshé* as identified in the Afro-Brazilian context with which we started. Its link to community work is clearly also significant in this formulation. Community work, aimed essentially at maintaining well-being and continuity (seeing to the mental and physical health of the community), then becomes a way in which *àshé* operates, in its power-to-be meanings.

Another clear articulation, similarly making a link to creativity, resides in Audre Lorde's "The Uses of the Erotic: The Erotic as Power" (1984) when she says, "The erotic is a resource within each of us that lies in a deeply female and spiritual plane, firmly rooted in the power of our unexpressed or unrecognized feeling" (53). Lorde identifies the "erotic" as "a well of replenishing, and provocative force to the woman who does not fear its revelation" (54). Lorde's specific link here is with energy, creativity, power, and joy, "whether it is dancing, building a bookcase. Writing a poem, examining an idea . . . when released from its intense and constrained pellet, it flows through and colors my life with a kind of energy that heightens and sensitizes and strengthens all my experiences" (57).

*   *   *

Poesia de negro e àxé	Black poetry is ashe
Poesia de negro e àxé	Black poetry is ashe
E àxé	It is ashe
Àxé babá eu digo	Ashe papa I say
Eu digo àxé Nagô	I say ashe Nago
Quando entro nesta roda	When I enter this circle
Incomodo, sim senhor	It is to disturb you, yes sir
Olha o tambo(r)	Listen to the drum
Olha o tambo(r)	Listen to the drum
A poesia negra	Black poetry
Tem a força de um quilombo	Has the force of a quilombo
	(my translation)

This chant used in Rio and São Paulo poetry circles, originating from the group Quilombhoje, is a convenient way of bridging to the meaning of *àshé* in the context of *Candomblé* and *quilombismo* as aesthetic and philosophical concepts. In this chant, the assertion is that black poetry is *àshé,* that is, it carries that power to create/power to make happen/to transform that is embedded in *àshé;* it moves across the poles of the spiritual, the artistic/aesthetic, and the community in an activist-creative sense. The movement of the chant identifies its source as *àshé* Nago, that is, of Yoruba derivation. It also links itself with the logic of the drum, another Afro-diasporic metonymic referent that similarly stands always outside of the confines of Western domination. In the final move, the chant takes it through *àshé* and its equivalences with energy and vital force, into the full and proper realm of resistance in Afro-Brazilian culture—the *quilombo.*

By this, then, this particular school of poetry in Brazil dedicated itself to what one of the members of the Quilhombhoje collective, Esmeralda Ribiero, calls "literary activism," a kind of creativity and community and political work that asserts its location on the side of resistance to the overwhelming racial and class oppression that exists in Brazil under the cover of the logic of "racial democracy." The group Quilombhoje, literally *quilombo hoje* (a Maroon community today), was created in 1980, "with the aim of discussing and deepening the Afro-Brazilian experience in literature." Its purpose is a kind of community and diaspora literacy—spreading of the habit of reading and the diffusing of knowledge and information studies, research on the black cultural experience in Brazil, allowing Afro-Brazilians to become active agents through writing, black cultural resistance, and activism. Through this it has published, so far, close to thirty Black Notebooks—*Cadernos Negros*—which are anthologies of poetry, short stories, essays. Additionally, many of the principal members have now published volumes of their own work. One of their techniques used was the poetry circle—*rodas de poemas*—in which participants, encouraged by chants and music, were able to get up and read or recite their own poems or another's. The aim of this process was not to allow the circle to break or die. The activities of this group, then, have made a tremendous contribution in bridging with scholars and other writers from other parts of the African diaspora and have increased the consciousness of Afro-Brazilians on their racial identity, as it has developed a tendency toward creativity, stimulating productions in other areas. Additionally, because of these activities, other related activities have developed, organized by universities and organizations interested in racial issues and creativity in Brazil. Some of their work has now appeared in anthologies in Germany, France, England, and the United States.

The selection of the *quilombo* as a political principle has direct implications for the kind of resistance poetics that Afro-Brazilian poets in this context want to articulate. A related kind of gesture would be articulated, for example, by the politically and aesthetically aware Harlem Writers Guild in the 1950s, Africobra and similar Afro-U.S. artistic and literary groups in the 1960s and '70s in the sense of a collective that defines an agenda and then seeks to institute it through art and politics. Using African iconography and symbolism and reinterpreting them in the particular New World experience, groups of this sort operate on the logic of alternative space, that is, a *quilombo*-like existence either practically or symbolically.

Several Afro-Brazilian scholars have identified *Candomblé* and *quilombismo* as two of the principal areas through which the African population in Brazil has been able to articulate itself, resist dominance, and maintain a very healthy African-based cultural, religious tradition. Indeed, Abdias do Nascimento in "O Quilombismo: Uma Alternativa Political Afro-Brasileira" (1994), which I identified above, had set out some specific principles of *quilombismo* that provide a model for the "democratic exercise of power in a stable political system." For example, "*Quilombist* economics," he asserts, "maintain a harmonious relationship with fauna, flora, mineral wealth, and the environment as a whole" (66). Additionally, *quilombismo* pertains to all the Americas and Africa as well, it being an experience known in a variety of societies in the Americas, named in different ways as maroon communities, *marronnage* (French), *cimarones, palenques* (Spanish), *cumbes,* and so on, and with some direct relationships logically with African anticolonial and antiapartheid struggles. Do Nascimento identifies sixteen principles and proposals of *quilombismo* that I summarize as follows: (1): a social and political movement; (2) a just and free, egalitarian society; (3) the promotion of happiness at being human; (4) collective ownership of land; (5) the right to work and benefit from one's labor; (6) maternal and child care; (7) education at all levels to include Afro-Brazilian history, African culture and civilizations, and their political systems; (8) creative development of arts within the social and educational system and larger society; (9) the removal of hierarchical structures in culture, formal religion—equal respect for all cultures; (10) the prohibition of bureaucratic state apparatuses that interfere with the vertical mobilization of the masses in terms of communication—rather, a dialectic relationship within members of the society and its institutions, keeping always a progressive and dynamic orientation as desired; (11) antiracist, anticapitalist in orientation; (12) balance in terms of women's representation at the administrative/governmental and judiciary levels, in private institutions, and in public service; (13) the transformation of relationships of production by nonviolent means; (14) the organization of an economic and financial institution to safeguard and maintain and expand the *quilombist* struggle and stop the interference of paternalistic controllers of economic power; (15) a defense of human existence against environmental pollution and favoring instead all forms of improving the environment in order to secure a healthy life of the individual, the creatures of the sea, the plants, forests, and all the manifestations of nature; and (16) Brazil's attempts to concretize the objectives of the 1965 U.N. International Convention to Eliminate All Forms of Racial Discrimination in Society.

It is important to put on record again that many of the *quilombos* encouraged participation from other ethnic groups based on these people's unwillingness to submit to the oppressive practices of the states in which they lived as well as their desire thereby to create something new as they worked for the advancement and protection of their new space. *Quilombismo* operates, then, outside of the logic of oppression and domination. It poses itself as the real and practical possibility of an "elsewhere" that is fundamentally at the heart of Afro-diaspora creativity. Additionally, it functions practically as a way of liberating the imagination by its existence practically and conceptually.

Another relationship between *quilombo* and *Candomblé* has been developed by Brazilian scholars who indicate that the space that a *Candomblé* community maintains, the *terreiro*, or sacred yard, technically functions as an in-city *quilombo*. Muniz Sodré in *O terreiro e a cidade: A forma social Afro-brasileiro* (2002) identifies the *terreiro* as a conservation of space in which there is a sharing in relationships, in *àshé*, in an arrangement differently engendered than in the dominant European models of society. This description of the *terreiro* as an environmental conservatory, a "system of preservation" that always attains a level of harmony between man and nature, the spiritual and the material, without losing sight of confronting the day-to-day adversities and difficulties of life, is yet still a safe space in which one's African culture can be practiced. A range of other scholars such as Cury and Carneiro (1990) have identified these systems and spaces as antihomophobic and female oriented. Thus, Lino de Almeida, in "Religion, Culture, and Revolution in the African Diaspora (Analysis of the Brazilian Process)" (1999), would say finally that in spite of all the levels of domination and oppression, Afro-Brazilians have kept alive and dynamic the consciousness of their culture, resisting, importantly, the onslaught of Catholicism, the official religion of the dominant class in Brazil that attempted to give direction to all social life and exercise absolute control over the Brazilian educational and social structure.

The annual Carnival and festival traditions are loaded with the resonances and iconography that are directly traceable to some of these philosophical and creative epistemologies. *Blocos-Afro* such as Ile Aiye and Olodum carry these histories in their names, patterns, rituals, musical rhythms, Carnival themes, relationship to community, activism. Each of the *blocos* begin their Carnival parading with a ritual offering to *exu-elegbara* and a series of other offerings that are designed to open the pathway and protect the passage through the Carnival. Ile Aiye's in particular maintained as its spiritual mother Mae Hilda, a *mae de santo* who functioned as a kind of spiritual guide and organizing presence. Both Ile Aiye and Olodum have created an active community presence, in terms of education, art, music, dance, working with homeless children, and creating employment.

Afoxés like Filhos de Gandhi and Filhas de Oxum provide an even closer integration of the questions of spirituality. Generally involved in community work, the *afoxé* has a more direct link with practices of *Candomblé* in terms of rituals, intent, music. The *afoxés* are Carnival groups with a more spiritual and political intent than *Blocos Afro,* which are more recent responses to racial hierarchies even in Carnival and therefore more directly reference the African presence in Brazil. Thus, while the orientation was much more spiritual and measured, a large group like Filhos de Gandhi can have close to a million black men parading, sometimes with infant sons, dressed in white with blue accessories in a more a cultural or familial experience.

Filhas de oxum, an all-women's *afoxé* with which I worked, had an active community program of feeding the community one day a week and was otherwise involved in issues of poverty in the surrounding neighborhood. Rosangela Guimares, its leader, I discovered, often used her own money to provide food if funds were not available, much as I saw my aunt do in Trinidad. While the honoring of the *orisha oxum,* the goddess of fresh waters, was its central purpose, in presentation it became almost a mobile version of the *terreiro.* Its final dispatch occurred after Carnival in a smaller community, Piata, away from the center of the city, and from there paraded through the surrounding streets to Lake Abaete, a lake of white sand and warm water, which was traditionally a place of washerwomen in Bahia with a number of ritual associations with *oxum.* The dispatch included offerings of flowers, food to *oxum,* and ritual bathing of large numbers of the community who came for blessings, purification, and witnessing. I participated in these events and had before then never seen Carnival used in this way but understood more clearly the links that are often made between Carnival and spirituality in the Caribbean by writers like Earl Lovelace or singers like Ella Andall who sings chants to *orishas,* or even calypsonians like Hollis Liverpool or David Rudder who can perform similarly lyrically. David Rudder has been very conscious of the links between Salvador Bahia and Trinidad as expressed in his song "Bahia Girl" (1986), which made the connection through Yoruba ancestry and the cultural home, Ilé Ifẹ̀.

Besides Carnival, a large stream of popular tourist art and other formal art dedicated to the representation of various *orishas* and aspects of *Candomblé* are visible. It has also informed what has become traditional Brazilian folk dance. Culinary habits—*Candomblé* food and the like—are part of the traditional Bahian diet and the day-to-day existence; fetishes and offerings are ever present. Herbal medicine, natural therapy that grew out of the knowledge of herbs in *Candomblé,* is commonly marketed.

In latter days, however, criticism has come from many in the Movimento Negro that there is a tendency among groups, such as Olodum, toward the commercial, which borders on actually selling out to larger capitalist interests even as they employ traditional symbology. Another criticism is that there is often a tendency toward a folklorizing of Afro-Brazilian cultural elements that is actually a state touristic orientation, which therefore downplays the resistance aspects of the *quilombismo* and Afro-Brazilian traditions. This is certainly true at a certain level, as it is true of the ways that hip-hop, for example, is marketed in U.S. culture. Yet, in my view, there is a simultaneous re-creation and resistance that consistently escape total domination.

A number of community groups like Geledes in São Paulo, Criolla in Rio de Janeiro, and Projeto Axe in Bahia have active involvement in political, community development work in which the logic of resistance and social transformation informs their various actions. Projeto Axe for a while was very successful in reducing the population of street children, housing them, educating them, and providing alternatives through a broad base of social workers, psychologists, teachers, and volunteers of various sorts committed to working with children. Geledes was also very instrumental in allowing hip-hop to have a space in Afro-Brazilian culture and was definite at the origins about not supporting misogynistic streams of hip-hop culture in the Brazilian corpus. As such, Afro-Brazilian hip-hop tended to maintain its initial orientation of social and political criticism, particularly its critique of social conditions, racism, poverty, favela life, and so on.

Perhaps the poetry of Afro-Brazilians, as I indicated during the earlier discussion of *quilombhoje,* is the place to bring this discussion to a close, for it is there that one sees in its most radical articulations an explicit and direct commitment to using the creative for political purposes. The writers who identify with the philosophy of *quilombhoje,* even though not part of the collective, tend to be people who define themselves as community workers and are often as well linked in various ways to *Candomblé* as they are linked to activist work. An early collection of poetry edited by Paulo Colina was titled *Axé: Antologia Contemporânea da Poesia Negra Brasileira* (1982), which, according to its editor, included works of poets who wanted their work to attack the conscience of those who have usurped the dignity of a people, to use symbols of Afro-Brazilian culture in order to retrieve a fundamental human dignity (preface, 8).

Miriam Alves, one of the most well known of contemporary Afro-Brazilian writers, the author of about eight books of poetry and stories and the compiler and editor of *Enfim Nós/Finally Us: Contemporary Black Brazilian Women Writers* (1995), is a *Candomblé* practitioner who has been involved since her childhood and, having ascended through the various levels, is close to opening her own house. She has spoken deliberately of how the iconography of *Candomblé* resonates in her work. The energy of Oya—the warrior woman—

resonates in her poetic style, her language, her creativity. Conceptually as well, she is committed to engaging the theoretics of Afro-Brazilian belief systems. Her recently finished manuscript "Mulheres Negras Escritoras Brasileiras: A Magia da Força Ancestral Escre-Vindo" is divided into two parts, a conceptual and theoretical section and a section that uses the Yoruba *oriki* (praise poem) format and the particulars of *Ófô,* which she identifies as a poetic form within the corpus of the *oriki.* The rest of the text is made up of several *orikis,* including some that honor the elements, their colors, use shape, art. Via this conception, she is able to take apart the word *to write* in Portuguese, *escrever,* and make of it *escre* and *vindo*—which she calls "writing-seeing."

According to Miriam, since the *orishas* are responsible for her creativity and her power as a poet and a woman, then her creativity has to acknowledge them. This particular work goes the furthest in expressing the principles of Afro-Brazilian *axé* and represents a deepening of Miriam's own work and thinking. Thus, in her presence, creativity and power come together in a significant way.

The conjunction of creativity and spirituality is evident in the practicing Mae Beata de Yemanja in Novo Iguazu, a *mae de santo* in a peripheral city outside of Rio de Janeiro. In the midst of a conversation, she pulled out a folder with poems and read some of them for me and indicated that several other *maes do santos* write poetry.

The meaning of that conjunction resonated powerfully in my own work then, which was focused on the question of women, creativity, and power. The significance of a figure who through ritual and creative power is one of the important conduits of *axé* to the community cannot be understated. In particular, it returns us to the history of *oriki* and Ifa divination in Yorubaland as poetic texts and as philosophical texts. Still, in most cases, as with Mae Beata, the relations of "community work" and "spirit work" coalesce in her "Comunidade de Terreiro Ile Omiojuaro," which is subtitled "Projeto Açao e Viver," "projeto com crianças, adolescentes e mulheres de Miguel Couto-Baixada Fluminense—contra a miséria e pela cidadania" ("Project Action and Life," "project with children, adolescents and women of Miguel Couto against misery and for citizens' rights"). Mae Beata de Yemanja's *terreiro* work with children, with women, with the community is explicitly identified.

In a similar way, Ile Axe Apo Afonja, one of the oldest *terreiros* in Bahia, also runs a formal school on its grounds in São Gonçalo, and the youth are actively involved in the ritual processes either as witnesses or as participants. These *terreiros* work with the mental and physical health of the community, and above all are spaces of ecological conservation, healthy and lush with greenery in neighborhoods that seem otherwise dry and less resourced.

It is not so much that the creative content of the poetry is about Afro-Brazilian religions or its practices, although it often is, as in, say, Esmeralda Ribeiro's "A Rainha Ayo," but that the process of creativity and performativity—*àshé*—becomes embedded in the very formulation of the work and similarly traverses the poles of spirituality, creativity, and community action.

In a similar way, Sônia Fátima da Conceição's poem "Invasão" embeds itself conceptually in Afro-Brazilian spirituality as it gestures to the mask of Christianity that is often employed. In her choice of Holy Eucharist/holy blood images, she is able to capture as well the dual meaning of blood in terms of the revitalization of *àshé* but also as it relates to revolution. Her title, "Invasão," refers to invasion, as it refers to infusion and incursion. That she selects *atabaques* rather than *tamboures,* for example, indicates a specific referencing of the three drums used in *Candomblé* ritual. The choice of the animal for sacrifice, "the goat," identifies itself with a specific line of *orishas* to whom goats would be sacrificed. When I met her, Sônia worked as a social worker in São Paulo, concerned primarily with the issues of urban problems, including the lives of street children. Her work creatively here seems to have as its primary purpose the identification and retrieval of a necessary energy. It asks for a kind of spiritual reworking of the terms of existence, a bringing of this energy to the cities for the processes of reenergization and transformation.

We have already indicated that singers like Ella Andall in Trinidad maintain an active energy with *orisha* music that infuses the popular presentations and brings it into the mainstream. One finds almost an identical recognition and related connections in the poetry of Eintou Pearl Springer, who also practices a similar literary activism as one finds in the work of artists like Miriam Alves who came out of Quilhombhoje.

With an ability to organize ideas in a range of genre—poetry, fiction, playwriting and dramatic production, essay—Eintou is perhaps the only poet in Trinidad and Tobago who spans the creative arts in this way, a friend and colleague to calypsonians, composers, artists, musicians, drummers, intellectuals, dancers, and *orisha* adherents. A performance poet, she is conscious of the production of poetry for the people, the text that lives outside of books, the true meaning then of the poet and of poetry as having their genesis in orality. For her the black woman in the Caribbean as in the diaspora is a "survivor": "I survive / through the strength / a mih culture / beat out / in the skin of the drum / beat out / in the steel of the pan / sung / in the calypsonian's song." Her very productive life has come through and recalls that same history of state terrorism in enslavement, colonialism, and neo-colonial continuance, summed up in "On Reparation": "Don't look into my eyes / You may sense / the sadness / of my decimated tribes / 150 million / uprooted from their land" and "Don't pry between my thighs / you may see the / screaming mass / of those who died." But again, she sees a role for that same black woman: "Don't walk into my space / I may just hit out blindly / at the suffering of my race / Move aside, make way for me / grappling here with my destiny / Be wary of these eyes / I'm about to soothe the sadness / of my decimated tribes."

"The Caribbean Sea" appears too but always with its link to history. Its beauty and its inviting features camouflage a history of "Carib warriors / swimming, fighting / jumping to their death / preferring the kiss / of their welcoming sea / to the shame and the horror / of shackles and whips." But it is also an audible sea that "moans / over the bodies / of slaves / fed to sharks / It has wept for centuries / and its rage and fury / has left terrible marks . . . a sea / real sea / blue and warm / awaiting still / new Caribbean dawn." The same theme is picked up in "I Want to Know," written for the children of Upaven primary school in Wiltshire, England . . . an excursion through a history before 1492, through enslavement, indenture, Caribbean cultural creation, in which she lets the voices of the children carry the poem: "I want to know of people / living in our midst / whose history has been linked / to mine / through many centuries" (31).

In many ways, Eintou has kept the faith in the children to produce new worlds of transcendence, and this particular poem, perhaps more than many others, carries it forward: "I want to know / and know and know / and help bring about / respect and understanding / and sharing / in this land / Land of steelband and calypso / beaches sea and sky, / within your isles, / like paradise, / a great-proud history / lies."

Poems that attempt to capture *àshé* in a spiritually strong way are "The Yard" (for Iya *l'orisha* Melvina Rodney), which recounts the active presence of *orisha* in Trinidad; another poem, "Focussed," is seemingly for children of the African diaspora of a "common mother" searching for a "sense of history, sense of self; /proud of all that went before; / reaching, reaching for the light; / reaching, reaching, for our right."

On her own active involvement in the Black Power movement in Trinidad, Eintou in "I Have Had No Youth: Reflections on 1970" recounts the impetus for struggle, the actions taken at the time, the continued motivations, the active figures, the chances taken, the creative fires, the dreams and desires to

build pride in youth, a strong country, all seemingly ended without fulfillment: "Now dreams are dust, / betrayed, / by leaders, / undeserving, / of our
trust." Still, the poet's hope prevails. "The Healing" and "The Path" offer ways
forward—*a healing, a purging, an exorcism* are operative words . . . invoking
"new leaders, new griots, new priests, for a new beginning" (99). Therefore,
the final poem, "Emancipation," continuing with this theme, asks for "unfet-
tered minds," new seeds, a mixture of the old with the new, "moving beyond
passages of pain," "spawning generations." The operative words in this poem
are *new birth, change, creation, emancipation,* equated with past strengths
and present and future beginnings. Her recent work to ensure the Carnival
origins in Canboulay are staged as the opening to Carnival, as street theater
provides another cultural link that is maintained for a new generation.

Advancements for Afro-Brazilians and Afro-Caribbeans have moved
steadily though both creativity and political power. Separations often because of language were maintained over time, but many more connections
are made now. When David Rudder sang "Bahia Girl," which incorporated
resonances of samba and calypso, generated in part from an African spiritual
historical place, Ile Ife, it provided one way of extending those creative geographical connections, which I want to articulate and maintain in thinking
about Caribbean space. For Abdias do Nascimento, interviewed by Henry
Louis Gates Jr. shortly before he died in 2011, there remains still something
scandalous and disgraceful in the fact that despite years of struggle, there are
glaring disparities in the ways that Brazilians of African descent are treated.
But through it all, creativity is what connects and provides space for the spirit
of transformation to live.

5

MIDDLE PASSAGES

Movable Borders
and Ocean-Air Space Mobility

The Middle Passage, which has attained iconic significance in African diaspora discourses, is a loaded concept. It references the transportation of numerous Africans across the Atlantic; difficult and pain-filled journeys across ocean space; dismemberment referring to the separation from their families and kin groups; the economic trade and exchange in goods in which Africans were the capital, commodities, or source of exchange and garnering of wealth for others; deterritorialization, the separation from one's own native geography or familiar landmarks and the parallel disenfranchisement of Africans in new locations; the necessary constitution of new identities in passage and on and after arrival.

The evidence resides, according to political economists like Joseph Inikori who study Atlantic economies, in the ways population demographics in the Americas and in African locations changed before and after the fifteenth century but also in the transformation of these landscapes by the introduction of different economic, agricultural, and cultural practices and performances.

But the Middle Passage has also become a historical marker in space and time, for some an aesthetic, for many an evocative body memory in terms of confinement to limited spaces, but absolutely a break between different ways of being in the world. For Caribbeans of Indian descent, the *Kala Pani* has similar evocative meaning—aesthetically, politically, and historically. Joy Mahabir and Mariam Pirbhai (2013) advance this aspect of the discussion of Caribbean space substantially as they account for Indo-Caribbean women's writing within frameworks like "transnational realities" and "diasporic subjectivities" as these relate to "Indo-Caribbean localities." For the editors, "the transoceanic journey signifies the momentous catalyst for migration which not only radically impacted individual destinies but also irreversibly remapped colonial and postcolonial cartographies" (1).

Geography and Empire

The issue of geography and empire can best be understood as a series of mapping exercises in which various land spaces are acquired and located within an orbit of control. In this context, the opposition between land space and ocean space becomes negligible, as both are sites or routes of conquest. Travel for Western economic and governmental state entities meant land grabbing. Navigation became conquest and domination as set by the Columbus navigational paradigm as opposed to simply curious "discovering" someplace new, adventure travel, or even touristic exchanges. In this model, the vision of land from the sea was translated into opportunities for control. A recent Hollywood fascination with "pirates of the Caribbean" provide reminders of how the Caribbean was navigated by outside entities. Now visits to the Caribbean include locals who point out familiar landmarks that were used as pirate movie settings—in St. Lucia and St. Vincent, for example—and how some people were able to find work on the sets or supporting industries like costume making. Earl Lovelace's *Is Just a Movie* (2012) clarifies.

Basic background knowledge of imperialism's history of border transgression is useful to contextualize some of these processes. An assumption of unlimited space and movement and the development of technologies to do this led to the development of triangular trade routes. The economics of slavery and colonialism provided the means for the advancement of European modernity. These prefigure contemporary notions of globalization as therefore always already economic, but also ones that assumed space and the widening of existing European borders. Thus, today commentators can identify the ways that corporate globalization amassed in the twentieth century fortunes similar to those amassed during the slaveholding era.

* * *

I walk around the streets of Bristol, England, deliberately in the summer of 2011 after attending a conference in Oxford on transatlantic activism. I want to get the feel of a city that was a major trading depot. I post on Facebook some photographs, my findings that indicate that streets and buildings still carry the names of slave traders, that in the Shad museum one can purchase books that document or question some of the names given to streets like White Ladies Lane and Black Boy Street, that the economic life of the city of Bristol was based on the fact that it was the launching point of more than one thousand slaving journeys that enriched the city and the larger British economy, that one can go on a tour of these historical sites today. A casual walk through contemporary Bristol reveals that present business holdings derived from the wealth amassed via the enslavement of Africans still drive the city's economy. Bristol is worth visiting if only to confirm that this happened.

An earlier visit to Liverpool a few years before had produced a similar response, and in each case I was caught by the starkness of older warehouses and docks now used as museums and the sense that these used to be sites for vibrant commercial expeditions in the transatlantic traffic in human bodies. Now they are relics of that past enterprise. But the money earned has now a different mobility for wealthy families and national treasuries. Liverpool has a huge museum devoted to this topic, and one can also purchase the memorabilia from those earlier trafficking pasts. British port cities have some difficult histories, loaded with emotions that range from the shock of recognition or anger when approached by African descendants in the Americas.

Advances in technologies of domination along with ocean transportation allowed countries like France, England, Portugal, and Spain to amass huge financial fortunes. The evidence of this major engine of Western capitalism still resides in cities like Liverpool and Bristol in England or Nantes in France and in various other locations that facilitated Europe's advancement and prepared the resources and structures for modern capitalism. There have been several readings of imperialism as practiced by the old imperialist nations that created colonies around the world to advance their interests. And I personally witnessed a building in the Docklands area of London that still carried company insignia in the 1990s that said "The Royal West Indian Company." But there was also a Dutch West India Company, French West India Company, Danish West India Company, chartered companies, and business enterprises dedicated to colonization, overseas trade, and a range of explorations that accompanied the rise of European states. Many of these have suspicious datings, locating them squarely within the heyday of enslavement and the traffic in bodies.

A newer argument, though, indicates that the United States assumed a more contemporary or modern version of imperialism through economic globalization ensured by the role of its armed forces, which extended the space for U.S. business monopolies. The developments of new technologies of communication, through satellites and aerial drones, provide the means for the surveillance of several countries outside the borders of the continental United States. This relates to the Caribbean, which is defined explicitly as its "backyard" and thus within its orbit of control, managed militarily by SOUTHCOM or Southern Command, based in Florida.

There is another interesting reading that sees the extending beyond the boundaries of the thirteen initial colonies into Louisiana, Florida, Texas, California, Arizona, and Hawaii as a preliminary version of imperialist conquest. Thus, in each of these states, there is a sense of that past colonial relationship in either the nature of its population and their assumed movement over an earlier and natural nonbordered terrain or a set of cultural practices that do not always assume full membership. Sometimes there are visible signs and markers that tell this story.

Michael Hardt and Antonio Negri in *Empire* (2000) assert, "The passage to Empire emerges from the twilight of modern sovereignty. In contrast to imperialism, Empire establishes no territorial center of power and does not rely on fixed boundaries or barriers. It is a *decentered* and *deterritorializing* apparatus of rule that progressively incorporates the entire global realm within its open expanding frontiers" (xii). But this modern form of empire has, it seems, come with a cost, as a decade later the Wallersteinian scenario of the closing days of empire seemed more the reality, as we witness the unraveling of the economic might of U.S. and European capitalism. Immanuel Wallerstein, who was a faculty colleague at Binghamton University (1980s and 1990s), had consistently argued that there was an imminent collapse of the world economic system. Back then his predictions seemed like fascinating academic theorizing. But his various pronouncements have come to light in the difficulties that plague contemporary capitalism, as witnessed by the various bank collapses and Wall Street deceptions and the failing economies of many countries in the eurozone and the capitalist economies, which have, on the one side, the hollowness of a shell game and, on the other, the rapid amassing of fortunes by the 1 percent, as the discourse of the 2012 Occupy Wall Street protesters revealed.

As it relates to the Caribbean, it is perhaps easiest to read U.S. imperialism in its regional sense in terms of its relationship with its created colonies, particularly in the Caribbean, since the Caribbean experiments would be replicated in different versions and locations. Essentially, then, one witnesses the movability of land borders out into the ocean. The flexible borders of the United States include the assumption of a completely open ocean and air space. Under this new order, then, the airwaves, and airspace, become the open space of imperial control. Media like CNN become doubled signs of information and control. Transgressing other nation-state borders of lesser-militarized countries and less technologically advanced countries is therefore assumed from a variety of angles, as manifested in targeted drone-attack possibilities anywhere.

Caribbean feminist scholar Claudia Jones, in an essay titled "American Imperialism and the British West Indies" (1958), during the heyday of the development of this process, had taken an analytical, anti-imperialist position, clear about U.S. corporate interests in the Caribbean as they related to or were distinct from British versions. Indeed, Jones had earlier noted a remapping of the older colonial boundaries in the interest of the United States. She felt that the new Caribbean countries that were leaving a federation and moving to independence were going to be heavily mortgaged to U.S. corporate interests.

The location of Puerto Rico in its relation to the United States becomes representative of these relations. The Puerto Rican experiment provides an interesting comparison, as it operates as the model of most direct U.S. control with only minor benefits to the local population. Kelvin Santiago's *Subject Peoples* (1994) describes the nature of the Puerto Rican colonial relationship to the United States. The more recent struggle over Vieques from 2002 to 2009, the earlier medical experiments on Puerto Ricans, and the whole nature of the U.S. corporate experiment in Puerto Rico typify this relationship. All other Caribbean countries either experience incorporation into an American zone of economic domination or have to face the wrath of the United States, as has Cuba for fifty years. Cuba, like Haiti, is then held out as a possible negative "example" for the rest of the Caribbean. But lack in Cuba is different from lack of material resources in Haiti. I have seen both.

* * *

In 2005 Grenada a rusty Cubana Airline plane still sat on an abandoned Pearl airfield with weeds growing out of it as if a consistent reminder of what is and is not possible. The abandoned plane, a play spot for children, mirrored the abandoned possibility of true self-determination and change. Unable to fly in the rest of the Caribbean, it became a relic of a failed possibility of connection. In the capital, St. Georges, another historical marker remained in the shell of a bombed-out headquarters of the New Jewel Movement, which stood on a hill overlooking the city, as if to remind again of what was and is possible. Graffiti that celebrated Maurice Bishop and the Grenada revolution still appeared in areas of the country in unusual locations, and the possibilities of cooperative economics persisted in shared communal relations.

* * *

To understand Caribbean space, then, one has to understand the peculiar context of domination existing around U.S. power. The U.S. invasion of Grenada occurred before consultation with the British government, which still maintained colonial overseership, demonstrating U.S. control of regional American space. The mobility assumed via migration can be understood in terms of this varied use of *space*. The interplay of movement, escape, and return that allows agency for Caribbean people also describes some of the particular relationships between the Caribbean and the United States. Thus, Cubans have a particular access to the United States in ways that Haitians do not, again because of the particular politics of relations between these countries. The tension between drives of encapsulation into small places and drives of transcendence permeates Caribbean discourses. The United States in this context functions as a controller of Caribbean space as it tries to maintain its role as the ensurer of the larger global networks. A series of occupations and invasions populate the historical time line of the Caribbean from the Monroe Doctrine to the present. Caribbean culture also constantly navigates between tourist readings and the more substantial meanings of Caribbean identity, whether they have to do with Carnival, literature, or politics. The logic of "tourist culture" that at times permeates the inhabitants, the politicians, and so on, in many ways, camouflages more serious issues and forces, in some cases, a trivializing of Caribbean culture for tourist delight.

Yet the Caribbean postcolonial is a difficult formulation in the presence of multiple existing colonialisms. Puerto Rico, Martinique, Curaçao, and St. Maarten divided between two colonizers are the most visible of the numerous colonies that still exist. On the British side alone, a visit to the Institute for Commonwealth Studies in London reveals a huge map of the world with pinpoints marking still existing colonies, more numerous than the few "self-governing" nations. Jamaica, for example, is still not yet a republic, as its recently elected prime minister, Portia Simpson Miller, reminded in her January 2012 inauguration speech. This was soon followed by a diamond jubilee visit of a more contemporary and young British prince, Harry, this time dancing with and charming a new generation with a newer version of what his predecessors did.

Arriving in Martinique in March 2011, I instantly observe huge graphic celebrations of the recently departed Aimé Césaire (1913–2008), the poet of *Négritude* and former mayor of Fort de France. A gigantic photograph is on display as one enters the city, and I read and listen to odes written by poets that almost deify him. There is a lesser celebration of Édouard Glissant (1928–2011) in the airport, with huge banners with his photographs and selections from his essays. Both of these men had articulated transformative visions of the Caribbean. But one notices with a jolt during a tour of the city that the policing of the country is still manned by white French policemen. Subsequent questioning reveals that not many Martinicans are able to ever get into that same police force. Clear markers of colonialism remain sometimes invisible but nevertheless present in the state apparatuses, even though there is a visible large black population living their lives in this French overseas territory.

An earlier 1990s visit to Guadeloupe for an African literature conference, without having acquired a visa from France, meant that upon arrival, since I was not then carrying a U.S. passport, I was not allowed entry, though from another Caribbean country. My children who had accompanied me and were U.S. citizens passed through the immigration controls with ease, and I remained on the other side while my Trinidad and Tobago passport was scrutinized. I was reluctantly let in after I called my children back from their smooth entry. Returning in 2012 now with a U.S. passport provided smooth entry in a beautifully redone airport. But the city of Pointe-à-Pitre downtown seemed abandoned and uncared for compared to Fort de France, and I understand why there were demonstrations in 2009, as colonial neglect is palpable and visible. Still, there is a not-so-quiet pride in black identity in Guadeloupe.

* * *

Getting to Cuba from Miami with a U.S. passport seemed a smooth-enough exercise in 2011, but this ought not to camouflage the years of embargoes, blockades, and whittling away at legislation that argues instead for full isolation and block entry for other than cultural exchanges. Ten years or so ago, I arrived during the Elián González drama via ship as an interport lecturer from the Bahamas to Brazil on the University of Pittsburgh's "Semester at Sea." As the ship docked in Havana in the early morning, we were recipients of a spirited welcome of rumba music, dancing, and singing. After the excitement of arrival, what I saw then was a city with beautiful but sometimes unpainted buildings and people suffering under the weight of the U.S. embargo. That time my Trinidad passport provided smooth entry. Moving beyond the initial excitement of what it means to be in Cuba, the special dated charm of Havana and its old American vehicles and billboards and mementos, to the revolution provided additional tangible markers. People were spirited in their defense of their right to their children, Elián becoming emblematic then of resistance to U.S. (especially Miami Cubans') assumptions. Elián González, who had been found on an inner tube following his mother's failed attempt to make it to Miami with him, represented that sensibility, with posters showing him imprisoned in the United States symbolically behind the bars of the gate of his Miami residence. A young man we encountered on the street, though, explained that he had been arrested and served jail time because he tried to leave for the United States by boat but ended up circling the coast, as he was not sure of the navigational path.

But in 2011, this time with a group visiting for an academic project, after a two-hour wait at the airport in Miami, in forty-five minutes the plane landed through a turbulent and cloudy afternoon with applause by the returning Cubans, at an airport at which numerous people waited Caribbean style to welcome family, friends, and visitors. Since U.S. currency is not official, changing money to Canadian dollars in the United States and then to pesos provided money to spend initially. Huge billboards announcing the revolution's continuance and celebrating its major figures still dotted the landscape.

As we arrived at the hotel across from the *malecon,* I heard steel-band music as we waited with a group to be checked into the hotel, and instantly I felt at home as I walked to see who or what was playing. Poolside at the hotel, a steel band that bore Trinidad flags on its instruments was named the Trinidad and Tobago Steelband of Cuba. I told the guys in the band that I am from Trinidad, and smiles erupted as they began a new tune with even more passion for what they recognized as an informed audience.

In Santa Clara, a derailed train is a monument to Che Guevara's tactical ingenuity, and his statue towers in this little town that loves the fact that he lived among them and that they helped the revolution to its victory. Roads are well managed throughout Cuba, and the Escombray Mountains reveal themselves with numerous possibilities for disappearance. Travel through numerous small towns and cities identify management by the Committees for the Revolution and signs announcing their presence. I learned from the tour guide what "Guantanamera," that popular song of our childhood, means and, surprisingly, that it describes people from Guantánamo Bay. I wonder if Americans who now manage this U.S. off-shore prison understand this emotional connection and debasement of Cuban history and why a prison camp there is an affront.

Later in the trip after a week or so in Cuba, I panicked as I had underestimated how much money I would need and began to see myself running short of Cuban currency. My Caribbean wisdom prevailed, though, as a Visa debit card from a Trinidadian bank that I had traveled with, just in case, worked after I inserted it into the ATM machine that did not bear any of the familiar markings of PLUS systems and other U.S. networks. Suddenly, money in local currency came out of the machine, as I imagined. I was relieved and thankful for this Caribbean connection.

Out in the streets, I could observe, ironically in socialist Cuba, that women wear fancy patterned French stockings to work even as nurses. Caribbean sensuality is visibly present in people's bodies and postures. Children in a school across from the hotel were oriented each morning with lessons for living as their parents watched the morning assembly outside of the school grounds before heading off to their day's activities. The Caribbean spatial connections work better here, and for me there was a sense of continuous recognition as I saw streets lined with flamboyant trees and compared Cuba to the other Caribbean locations I have seen. The United States in local lexicon is referred to euphemistically as "the place." People seem to live their lives in an even way, with work, celebrations, the normal shopping for vegetables, fruits; music is everywhere. Cubans at home dance with exuberance, knowing the meringue and rumba moves as instinctively as Brazilians samba in Rio or Salvador. The Celia Cruz voice is replicated in several other women such as the popular Malia. The old and the new continuously collide. Miami narratives about Cuba are outdated. Buildings are being reconstituted in Old Havana; a *santera* sits next to the Catholic cathedral and can tell you a few things for a small fee as she pauses from her engrossed reading of a book. A *palador* provides hot midday meals at low cost.

* * *

An understanding of space presents the interplay of movement, escape, and return that allows agency. *Space* is also the reconstitution of the modern Caribbean subject around and outside of the nation, the region, and movement. In this space, the production of desire moves outside of an encapsulated frame of smallness. At the same time, the Caribbean becomes simultaneously a source for raw materials or natural gas, a market for U.S. products, an easy destination for tourism.

"Boat People": New Middle Passages

It is ironic that Haitians trying to leave the Caribbean for the United States were identified as "boat people" and Cubans were not and that this was enshrined in policy via different legislations for each group—"Wet Foot/Dry Foot"! Students are still surprised that this is real official language. In a way, all who made the transatlantic journey were technically "boat people." An interesting and representative image remains of an innovative Cuban who turned one of those older cars into a floating device and actually got part of the way to South Florida. Several swimmers have tried to undertake this journey, only to give up somewhere along the way as the tides and sea life are often too deadly. In some cases, these are innovative traveling experiments or acts of desperation. Still, they follow the routes of sea travel that native peoples engaged in for years before Columbus, connecting the Americas.

In Miami there was discovered a native landmark that may have been the base of a trading post at the place where the Miami River meets Biscayne Bay. Humming Bird, the Miami Carib queen from Trinidad, holds vigil there every Tuesday evening, and one can still visit this site, as hotels and huge buildings tower and are built almost just up to this landmark discovered during the excavation for new buildings. Some bones and artifacts and other materials were found there, and some turn up from time to time and are housed nearby. A visible and independent Caribbean island geography has no viable meaning for economic and sociocultural interaction outside of a *remapped, recovered, reconfigured* Caribbean with all its connections. Antillean art, Walcott reminds, is the restoration of our shattered pieces.

* * *

Puerto Rican writer Mayra Santos-Febres in a book of poems titled *Boat People* (2005) describes the loss of hopes and dreams of those now residing at the bottom of the Caribbean Sea, the end of desires of those who, seeking new lives, risk everything sometimes, including those very lives. Its last poem describes lost lives at sea, adrift in the Atlantic, in these new middle passages. The logic of boat people carries with it a host of historical narratives of discovery and loss, successful navigation and return, which accompany archipelagization. An artist from the Dominican Republic, Julio Valdez, has a series on the Caribbean/Atlantic that similarly captures this contradictory movement in his *Mar Abierto* series, beauty yet pain, fragility and "spatial uncertainty" (www.juliovaldez.com).

The writing of migration has been a substantial component of this process of defining and redefining Caribbean identity, of re-membering or "gathering the pieces." Moving from a discourse in which identity was located in the first-level diaspora's dispersal—largely India or Africa—Caribbean writers began to signal a second-level Caribbean and American diaspora. Kamau Brathwaite's *Middle Passages* (1993) is an example of this, as contrasted with his earlier work *The Arrivants* (1967), a trilogy that deals in three movements with the nature of migration, the nature of an African return, and the nature of islands. The more recent pluralizing of the Middle Passage to "Passages" captures the redefinition of a Caribbean diaspora identity in migration.

In contemplating Caribbean space in the context of its relation to the United States, one recognizes then that the macro, meta, or giant transatlantic Middle Passage (deliberately with a capital *M*) has also spawned a series of micro middle passages via the crossings of a series of people from one location to the next. There has always been an intra-Caribbean migration with indigenous peoples traveling across the seas and between islands and to Miami, as the still-existing Miami Circle documents. And various Caribbean people in the enslavement period were moved for work purposes with plantation owners to and from the Caribbean and North and South Americas.

In the postemancipation period, a variety of trans-Caribbean movements have mimicked those of indigenous peoples, with people moving to various other locations for family reconnections, better economic opportunities, new starts, adventures, work, entertainment, and so on. So intraregional communication is not new but has become instead the purview of those on cruise ships or others able to own the means of their own journeys—a range of vessel types—and able to travel through the Caribbean this way. At the other end of the spectrum, drug traffickers now also assume an unlimited space for their own movement of products, challenging Caribbean sovereignty. Ivelaw Griffith's *Drugs and Security in the Caribbean: Sovereignty under Siege* (1997) describes how coast guards of various islands struggle to keep up with the more advanced technologies of drug dealers. In one story, drug dealers use submarines or have faster vessels than some island governments.

An assumption of space for these business interests clearly exceeds the smaller business activities of the ships one sees at Caribbean ports loading produce to take from one island to the other. Interisland ferries, for example, allow passage and trade in small goods between Caribbean islands. From Trinidad to Tobago, a ferry crosses in front of the city and makes the journey around and over the top of the island to reach Tobago. And this is repeated, with more or less comfort, in various island connections across the Caribbean—from St. Lucia to Martinique and Guadeloupe, from Antigua to Anguilla and Montserrat. Various small business operators or Caribbean "Informal Commercial Importers" travel across the Caribbean, buying and taking goods from place to place.

But micro middle passages, or difficult journeys from one location to the next, remain a consistent pattern, depending on difficulties in some countries. Patterns of migration push and pull and cause each group to reformulate its locational identity. As each zone operates, there is an emergent and new diasporic countergeography. These cross-geographies are contradictory but fluid: South to North, across the South (Haitians and Dominicans to Puerto Rico, Martinique and the Bahamas and Jamaica, the United States), South to farther South (Guyanese to Brazil and so forth), and global (Caribbean people in general to wherever they choose and continental Africans to the Caribbean, Brazil, the United States) in a series of movements for economic, political, and other reasons to a variety of locations in Europe, the United States, the Caribbean, and other African nation-states.

A growing body of sociological and legal literature has developed on migration as a field of study and provides the data that intersect with the more experiential articulations (Jardine). Within the larger discourse of Caribbean migration, one can identify its various levels: temporary for short visits abroad, which includes seasonal work (H-2 workers) and even extended tourism (which sometimes includes work); migration for study, which may vary from one to eight years if one assumes terminal degrees; and the more permanent economic or family-reunification migration, which creates diaspora communities in host countries. Caribbean migrations can also be delineated as intra-Caribbean migration (island to island), the movement to the Americas (especially Panama, Costa Rica, Venezuela), north to the United States and Canada, and across the Atlantic to European centers, following each colonial relation to its metropole. Each of these migrations has created a locational nodal point that cumulatively creates the Caribbean diaspora. The reception in the host countries has not been uniformly positive, as the encounters have been often with racism (Jim Crow laws in the United States and racist riots in England, racial exclusions in Europe). The state regulates via various immigration acts (the Immigration and Nationality McCarran-Walter Act of 1952, and subsequent versions up to the present in the United States, and the Commonwealth Immigration Act of 1962 in England and its various amendments and revisions are examples).

Aerial Space: Caribbean Global Positioning

If the unity is submarine, it is also aerial. Space, we learn now, is infinite; even as we claim our own space, it is also someone else's. From my small iPhone, I am able, during a period of mind traveling, to access Google Earth and to actually find the neighborhood of my childhood; the streets of my family and friends appear, and I can actually zone in on some familiar houses. But what does this mean in terms of surveillance? Varieties of satellites have been positioned for military communication but have thereby created the technologies that allow us to see ourselves relationally and in minute detail. I can see my family house in Trinidad, neighbors, friends, new stores, and highways if I extend outward a bit. I can also see my house in Miami and the neighbor's parked car. The point to be made is that aerial space transcends narrow nation-state boundaries and assumes a different mode of engaging the world for good or ill.

Dated preoccupations with "ship" and "Atlantic" metaphors reduce the range of imaginative possibilities to a particular post–Middle Passage time frame. Imperialism, we have already indicated, assumes an aerial movement way beyond ocean-space or earthbound geography: the control of airwaves, the production of desire, the acquisition of technological items, the development of U.S. tastes (McDonald's and Kentucky Fried Chicken's popularity in the Caribbean), the assumption of the use of Caribbean labor inside or outside of U.S. borders.

Flight metaphors of proto-Pan-Africanism observed in the genre of stories of flying-back Africans give way to more advanced reading of Caribbean migration. Reading beyond the mythology of return, inherent in what is clearly an open myth of flying Africans, is the possibility of a transcendence of local space and the assumption of another geography. So as the Internet and other cable media provide both access and simultaneous control, the production of desire as well as the possibility of resistance are also available.

A journey to the island of Mauritius in the Indian Ocean reveals almost a mirrored replica of the Caribbean in terms of archipelagization, landscape, geography, cultural practices like food preparation and diet, housing patterns, clothing, and the actual physicality of the people. The same mixtures that one sees between Indians and Africans reappear there. Creole festivals and cultural mixes are cultivated in Seychelles and Reunion, which have similar colonial histories and relationships to the land and sea. A much larger global positioning, then, allows us to understand some of these geographies relationally. But they also allow us to see how coloniality re-created island botany and zoology. A walking tour through the botanical gardens in Mauritius produced similar results to what one experiences in the Caribbean. Experiments with plants and trees as with people repeat themselves.

* * *

One gets to San Andrés through Panama, I am told, but I could have also gone via Colombia. Arriving in the little island of San Andrés reveals a Caribbean people who see themselves as being colonized by Colombia. There is a mixture of a Jamaican variety of English spoken here along with Spanish, which is seen as a colonial tongue over the local patois. A visit to one of the oldest churches puts us in close contact with the fact that there is an independence movement here with its own flag. One witnesses a people, though, who seem to be cut off from the rest of the Caribbean, unaccounted for in any of the major discourses, caught somewhere in a Latin American discourse that also does not recognize them. Seeing Caribbean space means also seeing missing islands, but reading between islands as navigating space.

Diaspora and Middle Passages

In cultural studies, migration and diaspora discourses have become ways of linking issues of hybrid identities and shifting locations. But anticipating these by decades, the themes of migration and the meaning of identity in diaspora have been among the most dominant in Caribbean literature in each of its generations of writers. The concept of diaspora enters as history advances (largely post-1970) and connotes the idea of dispersal but also the creation of large and definable resident communities in host countries that have a common origin in a different location (Lemelle and Kelley; Edwards; Boyce Davies, introduction). Whereas the first generation of Caribbean writers, largely the children of colonial families who were raised in the Caribbean and then returned to England for study, can be identified, they were not a large-enough community to constitute a diaspora (Ramchand).

Thus, diaspora has been applied at the first level to the Africans who were "dispersed" or commercially deported from the continent and brought to the Americas for purposes of plantation slavery and thereafter created African communities in the "New World." The same would apply to East Indian migrant workers who were brought to the Caribbean postemancipation and similarly created residential diasporic Indian communities. These first-level diasporas, because of their enforced nature, carried themes of exile and the dream of return, which in the African diaspora case created Pan-African movements like that of Sylvester Williams's 1900 Pan-African Congress, which gave the movement its name. Diasporas are created, then, by induced, forced, economic, and voluntary movements of people from one location to another and the subsequent reconstitution of communities in those new locations (Boyce Davies, introduction).

Research on the "Caribbean diaspora" reports a persistent and steady migration throughout the Caribbean. Thus, Jardine, using the migration data, concludes that "whereas workers from Barbados were encouraged to migrate to Guyanese plantations under the aegis of the British colonial state and Grenadians formed a continuing stream of inter-island migration to the Trinidadian oil as many as 100,000 West Indians had migrated (mostly from Jamaica and Barbados) to become workers in the Panama Canal zone, and many of these had settled in Panama as a distinct black enclave in an Hispanophone Caribbean world" (270). Following the first major flow via the Middle Passage and enslavement, there would be a series of secondary movements across the Americas for economic and familial reasons. Lara Putnam's recent *Radical Moves: Caribbean Migrants and the Politics of Race in the Jazz Age* (2013) introduces the places and people who come to form "circum-Caribbean migratory sphere." What she defines then as the "circum-Caribbean migratory sphere" are the migratory destinations in and around the Caribbean, island to island, island to continental locations, and the residential locations that began to be created.

A representative illustration of this secondary flow comes from Stokely Carmichael's description of his family. Carmichael, who would later become Kwame Toure and a major voice in the Black Power movement, was born in Trinidad and migrated to the United States as a child. This is how he describes his family's migratory pattern, which becomes one version of similar migration stories that typify the Caribbean experience, within the context of a diaspora discourse:

> Like most African families of the diaspora, . . . we are simply the survivors of the dispersal. . . . Although I was born in Trinidad . . . [m]y mother's mother was born in Montserrat to an Irish planter and his wife, an African woman, said to have been his former slave. But my mother was born in the U.S. Canal Zone in Panama, from whence as a child she returned to the care of maternal relations in the "Emerald Isle," as Montserrat is known, while her parents and older siblings left for New York. (14)

One of the largest tertiary migratory flows would be to the larger continental United States following the construction of the Panama Canal. Here there would be a large influx of former workers in the Canal Zone to places like New York and the beginning development of a residential Caribbean diaspora community in Harlem and later on in Brooklyn. The question of where is home would therefore engage all African diaspora writers, given the nature of the rupture that was created via the Middle Passage and its forced migration through enslavement and subsequent migrations that create new diasporas and extend the quest for belonging. Beginning with World War I, though, and continuing in the wake of World War II, Caribbean people began to see migration to the colonial center as a real-life option.

One hastens to add that each migrating generation has engaged a feature of the meaning of home and of their existence in the destination locations. The creation of new identities in nation-state contexts pre– and post–political independence and the desire for return or its actual experience are also central concerns. What is different perhaps in Caribbean migration is that the idea of home has shifted from the original distant homeland (Africa or India) to the Caribbean nation-state homeland. Clearly a product of the independence movements of the 1960s that deliberately had to create new national identities, and the development of Pan-Caribbean organizations, home is more immediate, accessible via new communication links, and the distant historical homeland remains at the level of mythology, desire, aesthetic and cultural returns, and occasionally the actual pilgrimage. Diaspora citizenship has created the logic of identity in location: return if possible, but not as an absolute (Boyce Davies and M'bow).

Middle Passage Aesthetics

The Middle Passage has been a major topic or trope for many thinkers—creative artists and intellectuals (writers, filmmakers, historians, political scientists, artists, musicians) across the African diaspora, thus creating a kind of Middle Passage aesthetic, as we have indicated at the start. For some, like Michelle Wright, in her ongoing thinking on this topic, it is also an epistemology, or a knowledge-producing system. Although there have been other pain-filled journeys across the Atlantic, the Middle Passage has become representative for the level of degradation, dehumanization, and exploitation it entailed. Difficult journeys from Africa to the Americas via confined slave ships generate a great deal of emotional meaning. Thus, the iconic slave-ship image of Africans chained together in ship holds repeats itself in many ways in art, in craft, even in jewelry, and for some in media as a kind of subordinated memory, as it recurred with surprise in the treatment of black bodies in post-Katrina New Orleans.

Although poet and historian Kamau Brathwaite sees migration as part of the human condition, but particularly African migration as part of the whole narrative of human advancement through time, he is well aware of the current economic conditions under late capitalism that become triggers in this period. So early African migrations for climatic reasons met other harsher realities of slave trades (Arab and European) and colonialism and neocolonialism. The contemporary destruction of historic sites in Mali, for example, has a recognizable history, as does the Sudan-Nubia struggles. Displacement creates further displacements, as the quest for more favorable locations and experience becomes almost linked to identity.

In attempting to account for a Caribbean aesthetic, through the work of artist LeRoy Clarke, ethnomusicologist J. D. Elder indicates three visible elements: life force, the mask of the female face, and the blankness and nothingness of the open space that can also be the sublime oceanic phenomenon of "the Middle Passage." For me what became salient in contemplating that same artist's work was what seemed to be appearing in every work, "the aesthetic of the shadow." I have defined this as the ability to deeply embed and emboss African diaspora memory textually in art as in other forms of creative expression. For LeRoy Clarke, the African diaspora memory of the Slave Ship and the apparatuses of slavery "whips, scales, chains, ports" that produced the modern Caribbean archipelagoes challenges official history and its pretense of amnesia. The poet and artist is dedicated to an art that is tasked with excavating ourselves from the tendency toward amnesia or forgetting; to bring back to life, then, to remember, as in bringing back the members together, becomes an urgent task. Thus, his "Archipelago" memorializes the difficult birth of the Caribbean.

Sylvia Wynter has been very definite in identifying a Caribbean "cultural matrix" that she says "sprung out of a people's response to that dehumanization which would convert them into merchandise" ("One Love" 65). In spite of it all, the cultural history of the Caribbean is one that attempts to "humanize the landscape by peopling it with gods and spirits, with demons and duppies, with all the rich panoply of man's imagination" ("Jonkonnu in Jamaica" 35). One finds, therefore, certain tropes in Caribbean history that are almost harvested responses, which are then gathered and rearticulated or updated in each generation. The Middle Passage is one of these.

* * *

My uncle Eddie, who had migrated to England when I was a child, lived in the last leg of his life in the George Padmore housing complex, built for retired Afro-Caribbean people. I was comforted that it was named after Padmore, thinking that somehow that made sense and put him for a moment in some aspect of Caribbean political space. Learning too that there was a hospital wing in Hackney named after Mary Seacole and where I visited him once was also reassuring. Uncle Eddie had worked for years in a post office in Birmingham. He was the person I boasted to my friends: "My uncle lives in England." He would send me books and five-pound notes to buy nice things and once had been the source of a blonde-haired European doll mailed from England that was not really played with but sat dressed in the house on some piece of furniture. I realized after the fact that life for him in England could not have been as romantic as I made it out as a child. On one of Claudia Jones's petitions among her papers, I saw his familiar signature. What was left when I visited him in Hackney was a spare apartment with basic facilities, including a pull cord in the bathroom if one was ill, surrounded by books and magazines and a few bare pieces of furniture. It is here he spent his final days. When I saw him last, I asked if he would not prefer for me to arrange for him to return to the Caribbean so he could be with my mother. His response was that he wanted instead to be by the sea anywhere. My daughters, who had also grown to love him instantly upon meeting him, and I deposited his ashes at sunset one day about a year after, under a tree in Maracas Bay, Trinidad. He had owned land in Maracas, St. Joseph, not far away, given, I learned from my mother, by the government for his service "during the war" in family lore, but which he abandoned as he traveled to England in that mad rush of his generation of men to leave in the 1950s. Somebody else is occupying that land now, and the family is unable to pinpoint its exact contours, as he never shared those details.

My uncle George was even more complicated. I was able to get his death certificate in a town called Hastings, which I walked around afterward to discover it was the same site as the Battle of Hastings I learned about in my history classes in the Caribbean. White seabirds walked along the beach adjacent to what was now a marine museum, and facing it are new waterfront condos. Uncle George had been a marine engineer, but little else is left of him except that he went away before I was born. He also wrote me cryptic letters and sent money whenever I asked ostensibly for money for books, or to play mas.' I learned from my mother that he was a bit of a lady's man who spent his money on women as quickly as he earned it. In family photos, he is a tall, gangly man who had been an athlete, a high jumper, I am told, in his youth. I wonder if he had any children! In the London Underground and as I walk the city's streets sometimes, I reflect that I may be next to cousins and not know it.

"Inglan is a bitch," says Linton Kwesi Johnson.

"London is burning," a rhyme of my childhood resurfaces.

"Back-Ah-Yard Cabirian" restaurant, 1974. Courtesy of Armet Francis.

Brixton Station, 1974. Courtesy of Armet Francis.

Afro-Caribbean museum in Panama, honoring Panama Canal workers from the Caribbean. Courtesy of the Carl Juste/Iris Photo Collective.

Buildings with flags—Havana, Cuba. Courtesy of the Carl Juste/Iris Photo Collective.

Shashemane billboard showing Bob Marley, 2010. Photograph by the author.

Artist painting wall in Rastafari compound, Shashemane, Ethiopia, 2010. Photograph by the author.

6

WOMEN, LABOR, AND THE TRANSNATIONAL
From Work to Work

"WOMEN HAVE TIME"

Women have time
To breast feed,
Raise children
Clean house
Wash, iron,
Fold clothes
Carry water,
Gather wood.
Plant, weed, harvest,
Bake bread,
Make sauce,
Brew beer,
And more:
Do their hair,
Kohl their eyes,
Add makeup,
Dress and undress.
Women have time
For a day at the office
And then to shop
For breakfast, lunch and dinner
That they prepare.

Women have time.
Men, have no time.
      (Reesom Haile, 2001)

I begin with this poem deliberately as it offers an extended cataloging of a selection of assumed daily work obligations for women but in fact offers a succinct commentary on larger ideas about the exploitation of women's labor. It also demonstrates both a creative and an extensive manipulation of space and time. There is a second poem introduced later about agency or the ability to act affirmatively in leaving exploitative situations. These two combined produce some of the bases of women's migration.

The well-known trade routes, triangular trade, middle-passage economies that we discussed earlier, still have residual effects, that is, the economics of slavery and colonialism that accompanied the rise of European modernity, created the conditions for contemporary American economic globalization. These serve as the larger backdrop for Caribbean women's labor in migration. The sexual division of labor in feminist political economy assumes the control of women's time and work as normal. Additionally, a segmented pattern of labor based on gender and class creates assumptions about the value and availability of certain women's work. In particular, the labor of women of color is assigned lower value, while it is multiply extracted and linked, therefore precisely, to that long history of imperialist exploitation that began in enslavement to plantation economies. Claudia Jones refers to this as the superexploitation of black women. In the Caribbean-U.S. domestic context as it relates to labor exploitation and citizenship rights, lives caught in the "commuter nation" or the "translocal nation," as the Puerto Rican experience is described, are exploited by business, governmental, and medical research interests. A certain continuity between Puerto Rico and the United States shadows the same relationship internally in the continued difficult location of African Americans in working-class (or unemployed) contexts. Similar points can be made about Mexico and the use of Mexican labor within the United States, and particularly along its borders in the legendary *maquiladoras* or in Florida, where Mexican labor is still used for difficult jobs like roofing in the hottest sun or the picking of fruits and vegetables in Homestead or Lake Placid. Other Caribbean countries face either an incorporation into an American zone of economic domination or the wrath of the United States, as Cuba has for fifty years for daring to choose another path.

One has to see the large-scale Caribbean migration to the United States from the 1960s onward as a visible identification of that recognition of the operations of U.S. imperialism, in much the same way that the migration to the United Kingdom, in the immediate preindependence period (1940s–1960s), was a formal manifestation of access to the seat of the colonial empire. And Caribbean women's migration into the U.S. labor pool as well as Caribbean women's labor exploitation in home domestic and factory work contexts become other instances of a particular linkage of gender, race, and labor mobility.

So, as there continues to be a range of exploitable locations that island political and business interests use for economic gain, parallel migrating subjects operate with certitude in and against all borders but always mindful about where the possibilities for managing one's economic life successfully exist. Agency exists precisely in the deliberate contestation of larger U.S. assumptions of space.

Caribbean Women as Migrating Subjects

"LEAVING"

"Who shall kindle the fire now
and pick the coffee at harvest time
feed the chickens
water the cows and goats
and boil green herbs
to bathe away
the baby's fever?"
"not I"—she said
"surely, not I"
standing half-in/half-out
the door
The years falling naked
from her face!
　　(Weir, 1996)

There are two common meanings of the word *subject*: (1) being subject to someone else by control and dependence and (2) having one's own identity by a consciousness of self-knowledge. Being a migrating person and a subject presupposes both of these in a way, and the play between these two options or positions for women becomes a reality in what seem to be sometimes independent decisions. It is a shocking thing to realize that what seems like one's own personal decision is actually part of a pattern or a "flow," as the sociologists like to call it. After the fact, then, one feels sometimes cheated of a set of home relationships as one also feels the thrill and excitement of new locations.

The research on the migration to the United States of the 1960s and 1970s identifies that much of it was female and work-driven migration. Indeed, some of the major writers on this assert that most of the younger women in their samples were not concerned with what kind of job they would find in the United States, or what it would pay, but just with getting one. It was a consensus of opinion among working-class Caribbeans in that time period that any job in the United States would have to be better in terms of working conditions and wages than what they had at home. They knew too that their labor would be more exploited than American-born workers because of their immigrant status (especially if illegal), but they saw this situation as temporary, with an ability to perhaps earn money that could improve lives of family at home as they managed their own lives. Economic advancement and access to specialized education that can lead to upward mobility at home were identified as the primary indicators for many who migrated. In some studies, women also indicated that they were able to gain greater "independence," had more money of their own, could purchase consumer goods, or could invest in the advancement of their own or their children's or a relative's education. It is not unusual for a nurse in Trinidad to leave her service or complete her service, as one friend, Jackie, and one cousin of mine, Cathy, have done, and then travel to the United States or United Kingdom to work as trained nurses. If they started a nursing career at home at eighteen or nineteen years of age, having put in thirty years of service, then at forty-nine or fifty, they could start a new career life in the United States or United Kingdom and, with their solid experience of nursing under difficult "Third World" conditions, move rapidly through the ranks of respectability and reliability in the field. Interestingly, this kind of move also provides enough money and energy, even though sometimes generated from difficult twelve-hour shifts, to allow them to go directly out to a store and buy an expensive outfit to attend a wedding that weekend, or perhaps to fly home to Carnival or some relative's funeral at another time, or perhaps save to send a child to university, or to execute repairs on a house back home.

Studying the individual life experiences of a number of women is a useful approach to contemplating issues of globalization and women's work. Additionally, one has to differentiate between islands as between race and ethnic identification but also between time periods. Some of the research in this area has served to denaturalize migration and to link it deliberately to particular economic linkages between countries, particularly linked to foreign investment and military interventions. Thus, what is revealed is also the shift in the nature of work done on the various islands. Each island and its home economy and therefore its relationship to the global economy allow different readings of the experiences of migration and work in the United States.

Still, a buoyant local economy does not deter migration, as there is always family reconnection or curiosity or the desire to live elsewhere, or an escape from a series of negative patterns of local interaction. A series of fine distinctions must be made in the home context in terms of the various types of workers now made desirable under global capitalism. And interestingly now with the contemporary downturn in the U.S. economy, following the George W. Bush presidency, many see returning home or not leaving permanently as more desirable than being caught in U.S. unemployment patterns and the various hustles to make a living, often without the benefits of healthy social lives, family connections, and other recognizable benefits.

Some answers to the open question "Why do Caribbean women leave?" reside, then, in an analysis that looks at the sexual division of labor. A number of scholars have pursued this discussion and offer helpful analyses on the migration circuits, various studies on globalization and capital mobility, and work on domestic labor in a global context. Still in home contexts, studies done on the Caribbean provide the historical backdrop to the study of Caribbean women's labor.

The sexual division of labor, while an old process, was exacerbated in the Caribbean through the colonial agencies that had actual policy in place to keep women from access to employment outside of the service sphere and male dominance in the workplace. Additionally, from the end of the nineteenth century and into the mid–twentieth century, there was a general "housewifization" process. And it is only in the period bracketing postflag independence that one sees a new increase in women in the workforce. Still, the majority of women tended to be employed in service work, like serving the hotel industry, agricultural work, government service, factory work, dressmaking and other craft professions, teaching, nursing, and clerical work. While today one can see black women like Eutrice Carrington, with degrees in Economics, at the top echelons of financial institutions, in the immediate post-colonial period the requirements for certain positions included some class and color expectations in order to get access to employment in certain areas like banking and the airline industry.

In my view, the issue of women desiring a means of escaping unsatisfying relationships, wanting the adventure of travel as they simultaneously wanted control of the fruits of their own labor, and to improve their own lives and that of their children, as well, has been less articulated than the economic reasons for migration. Additionally, it becomes clear that as a number of women enter the workforce, a variety of them searched elsewhere for more advanced economic remuneration. The pull to the United States via more liberal immigration legislation and also some of the gains of the post–civil rights period that began to open some doors provided additional opportunities for migration.

Women who were not able to earn a decent wage, had aspirations for more developed futures, were leaving unsatisfying relationships, or wanted to educate their children abroad unhooked themselves from constraining conditions that stagnated their desires. Migration and the shifting working relationships in the United States provided an avenue largely for working-class and lower-middle-class women. The various rationales behind these moves have been already identified in a great deal of the research on this pool of largely female Caribbean women who migrated in the '60s.

Recent ethnographic work done on some of these women in the New York area concludes that racial discrimination as it manifests itself in inadequate housing and city services, high crime rates, and inferior public schools remains. What one sees in subsequent generations, though, is that while there are many success stories, more often than not, by the second generation, the combination of low wages and poor working conditions and children who use American and not Caribbean standards of performance for black children creates a disappointing result in some families. Thus, among children of the same cohort, some are successful and go to university; others, on the other extreme, do not make it at all and become occupants in the prison industrial complex. A study done in 2001 by a Caribbean Research Group in Miami found that the same issues that plague African Americans also plague Caribbeans by the second generation—police brutality, the unequal judicial system, housing discrimination, and inequities in education and salary scales. And despite the success of a Nicki Minaj, or some of the male hip-hop artists of Caribbean American descent, many parents reveal disappointment if their children express desires to become hip-hop artists rather than go on to higher education. They know that the chances of attaining that kind of success or media recognition remain elusive for most.

$$\ast \quad \ast \quad \ast$$

From my experience of witnessing my mother's cohort, the aging group of women of that 1960s generation seemed to have succeeded in getting a second generation successfully located. Some were able to return home and live out the last years of their lives in familiar surroundings. But the second generation, women in my group, tended to be centered on educational and professional advancement, now with children born in the United States, and having a more complex set of choices. Some are beginning to have grand-children whom they want to help raise. The rising crime rate and what some see as inferior medical services in some Caribbean countries have discour-aged many who work in the United States now from what they saw as an assumed return to live well on pensions and U.S. Social Security benefits. The increased cost of purchasing a house as well in some Caribbean coun-tries has left several thinking that it would be too difficult to invest now in a home property. Some have opted for building investment real estate such as a six-flat rental property rather than having the dream home return. Many have decided to make Caribbean space wherever they are.

On the other side, since the economic dramas following the post–September 11, 2001, terrorist actions in the United States have led to a redefinition and tightening of immigration into the United States, there is a parallel reluctance for people at home, already comfortably located, to migrate to an unknown and potentially difficult future. The combining of databases such as the link between Social Security numbers and immigration files has functioned al-most as a net in which some are sometimes caught in more recent and hostile legislation like the PATRIOT Act on the U.S. side. A friend of mine who is a university professor revealed that her brother was detained upon his return from the Caribbean after attending a relative's funeral. When he got to the United States, he was held under detention at the Miami Chrome facility, although he had lived in the United States for many years and had served in the U.S. Army. The combined appropriately named ICE (Immigration and Customs Enforcement) listings showed him as having committed a felony at one point years before. She in turn had to spend a great deal of her own resources to ensure that he had adequate legal representation to eventually successfully get him out of that particular situation after a six-month period of detention, pending deportation.

In pursuing my own ongoing understanding of these related migration issues, I repeatedly conducted informal conversations with a number of women, some of them friends of family members. My earlier work *Black Women, Writing, and Identity: Migrations of the Subject* (1994) had discovered that migration stories were readily available in even casual conversations of friends and acquaintances. Indeed, this is source material, I suspect, from which several novels have been built. What I found out is condensed into some sample narratives below. I noticed two generations appearing in a pattern: the generation that migrated in the 1960s and the younger generation (a smaller group) of women migrating in the 1980s and 1990s. As usual, many of the women felt that their lives had nothing to contribute and so rejected formal interviews in favor of conversations in which I was able to raise the major questions prominent in this study: The reasons for migration? The nature of the process? The relationship to families back home? And the plans for the future and the possibility of return? Written in an earlier period, these narratives have not been altered, although there have been age-related developments in some cases.

Migration Narratives

MARVA

In preparation for a forthcoming marriage in 1996, Marva, a twenty-eight-year-old mother of a four-year-old daughter, came to the United States to do domestic work and earn some dollars in order to organize the event, shop, and get enough money for a down payment on her home in the Caribbean. Marva, who is close to six feet tall, did some light modeling in her home country in the Caribbean, doing enough to have some photographs in the local newspaper. She has a high school certificate, has some dressmaking skills, and has been employed seasonally. Visiting the United States first for about three months and spending that time with her sister, who has lived in the United States since the late 1970s, she actually went, at the insistence of her sister, to some modeling agencies in New York, hoping for a big break. Strikingly beautiful, but not exactly what they were looking for at that time, perhaps older than the age at which models are recruited, she settled on some light domestic work, largely because she did not have legal papers to do anything else. She worked for about six months for a family as a nanny, taking care of an infant and doing light live-in housework as well for an upper-middle-class professional/corporate couple. At the end of the time, when she was scheduled to return home, she told the family the truth, that she was getting married and wanted to return home. To her surprise, the woman she worked for excitedly helped her with shopping for her wedding, gave her presents, reluctantly let her go, but indicated that if she wanted to return, they were so satisfied with her work, they would rehire her. Her fiancé came to the United States, and together they both shopped for the wedding reception, returned home together, and had a lavish event. About a year into the marriage, Marva realized that she was very unhappy in that situation, was used to having her own income and freedom, and decided to try to return to the United States to work again, this time planning that she would try to stay a few years and then decide what to do about her marriage, thinking also that time would take care of the uncertainty. Fortunately, she had kept a pleasant relationship with the family, who now had two other children, and the wife was trying to return to work but would do so only if she could find someone truly reliable. She trusted Marva, who had helped mind the first baby. Marva found this to be great fortune; they paid her transportation and arranged her immigration papers.

Four years later, today, Marva, now thirty-three years old, is still in the United States and has settled into being a domestic worker for the time being, with Sundays off and a half-day on Thursday. I saw her once at her work-place. I had gone with her sister who lives in the same state and works as an executive secretary to take an item to her. She was dressed in a way meant to camouflage all of her physical attractiveness (sweats, scarves, hair pulled back). On another occasion, in her sister's (my friend's) home, in preparation for a night out, she was stunningly beautiful by contrast, and I wondered what it meant to that family to have a woman of that physical attractiveness in a home working as their domestic. Her seven-year-old daughter from a premarital relationship is going to school in the Caribbean and lives with her maternal family, and Marva spends a lot of money sending things home in the customary "barrel." Her plan is still to work long enough to set up her home in the way she wants, not to bring her daughter to the United States until she is ready for university, but to keep her well in school in the Caribbean and make a life for them. Her daughter still lives with the extended family, and as a result her money goes to assist in the smooth maintenance of the entire family. Her marriage is for the time being on autopilot, with both of them clearly free to do whatever they want to in terms of other relationships. She shops and returns to the Caribbean whenever she can and plans to live at home finally once she has raised enough money and perhaps gotten some educational credentials.

ESTHER

Esther, from Montserrat, came to the United States through Canada in 1982. She traveled to Canada on vacation with the full intention of trying to get into the United States. After spending a few weeks in Canada just before the local Caribana, in a prearranged situation, she traveled to the United States, crossing the border one night, lying flat on the back floor of a car under the legs of two or three men who were occupying the backseat, all of whom had legal papers to be in the United States. She describes the experience as scary but relatively easy, as the border guard asked few questions that night. Instead of going the route of domestic work, which she hated, Esther, who had hairdressing skills in the Caribbean, worked in a beauty shop and developed a clientele of her own. Because she was very enterprising and talented as a hairdresser, within a few years she got a male friend to invest in her own hairdressing shop, which she still owns and is a thriving business in Brooklyn. Throughout all of this, Esther never secured her residence visa but has been able to travel in and out of the United States for family and social reasons, using various forms of disguise (age, gender) and the passports of friends. She has been technically eligible for the various amnesties, and when I asked her why she has not bothered to regularize her papers, she surprisingly expressed fear that if she does, it will alert ICE to her illegal status and send her home. During this period, she has been able to bring her daughter to the United States and send her to middle school and then high school. The biggest problem she has faced is that because she worked long hours, her daughter remained unsupervised and gradually became part of the urban youth culture, became sexually active, and did not make her way through school as her mother intended. Instead, she has left home, lived with boyfriends, and now has a young child.

Esther, now a very attractive fifty-one-year-old, meanwhile, continues to thrive; runs her business; helps out people looking for work when it is possible; travels to the various U.S. Caribbean Carnivals, boat rides, and Atlantic City trips; lives well; and has a healthy social life. Fliers and posters for various local Caribbean events are available in her shop, which is one of a number of popular spots for Caribbean peoples in Brooklyn. She was planning a Mother's Day concert with one of the popular calypso singers when I last talked to her and was thinking of getting some other educational certification, as she did not want "to do hair for her entire life."

MONICA

I met Monica, from Colombia, in her brother's frame shop in North Miami. The first time I met her, she had then a little daughter who was about eight or nine years old and very much the darling of a caring family. The family migrated to the United States gradually one by one, and Monica came here around sixteen with her brother to visit family and never returned home. The mother lives with them in the same apartment and manages many of the day-to-day domestic operations of the household. Monica indicates that even though she could have, she did not finish high school in the United States because of language barriers and ended up getting a job in a local dry-cleaning shop, where she still works, not far from her brother's shop. Dark haired and attractive, she lives in the apartment the family has acquired, and her brother is very generous with all the extended family and helps her from time to time to get school essentials for her daughter. Her daughter's father is not really in the picture, as she indicates that he had done a little jail time and was not dependable. Now in her midthirties, she does not project much into the future but lavishes attention on her daughter and participates in family beach outings and social events. Every time I see her, she is friendly and is always fashionably dressed.

VELMA

Velma is a forty-five-year-old police officer who recently built a house in Grenada. When I met Velma, she was about to move into the house, talked with pride about having gone through the process of acquiring the land and beginning construction of the house, and was waiting for it to be completed. Located in a fairly residential area now, the three-bedroom house was sparingly furnished. I stayed with Velma for about three days last year, and conversations were conducted during that time. Because of her police service, Velma had amassed about six months' leave, which she decided to use to go to New York to work to furnish her house. She thought about working as a security guard because of her police training but decided that a live-in domestic job would provide accommodation and food and thus maximize what she could save. Through her sister in Brooklyn, she found a job in New Jersey and was assigned to take care of an aging white woman who had little connection with her family. She indicates that the woman was very rebellious, did not want to bathe, was particular about what she ate, and also had a wound on her leg from a fall that she was not tending to. Velma indicates that under her care, the wound healed. She detailed, with pride, the steps she took to make the woman's life better: that she insisted that she bathe and that she made her eat balanced meals. Taking it on as any other project she would see well to the end, as a trained police officer, she felt great pride on cleaning up this old woman's life and indicates that she actually felt great pity for her. She indicates as well that upon the end of the six-month stay, she felt great sadness and guilt at leaving. Rather than prolong the departure, she decided simply not to go back after a long weekend and called the agency on Sunday night to say that she needed to be replaced as she had an illness in her family that necessitated that she return home. She felt that since this was in part true, she was justified, because her twelve-year-old daughter's father with whom she had an on-again, off-again relationship had been in an accident; though he lived at home with his mother, she wanted to be there for him if he needed her. Back home when we talked a year later, she was awaiting the furniture that she had shipped, she had a nice collection of household appliances, and she and her daughter were comfortable. She sends her daughter routinely to the United States to spend time with her cousins in New York during the summer months. She is well respected, likes her job in the Caribbean, has returned to her police service work, and is studying for a promotion to a higher rank. Only close friends and family know how she spent her leave time.

NANCY

The Richardson extended family lived for years in a decrepit shack in an area not far from one of the branches of the University of the West Indies. The mother and one daughter and her children inhabited the front and main house; another daughter erected a smaller house on the same property behind the main house. The other houses in that neighborhood are well kept in an otherwise clearly upwardly mobile neighborhood. It would not be unfair to say that their style of living must have been an eyesore to the other neighbors. Once the grandmother died, the two daughters and her now grown daughters and their children who shared the space realized that the land had been left to them. One daughter, now in her early sixties, decided to go to the United States and work for as long as she could and amass some money along with what she already had accumulated at home. From the United States, she made plans to begin the erecting of a massive two-story house, with about four bedrooms on each level. The initial money that she had was enough to erect the frame and to enclose one or two rooms in the bottom floor. Subsequent trips (about three in number) to the United States and short periods of employment there facilitated additional work on the house: to enclose the rest of the house and to include windows on the top floor. Her plan when we talked was subsequently to return to the United States for work again and to complete the house, but she did not have any anxiety about this and felt when the opportunity arose (God willing), she would travel. If not, something else would work out. When I talked to her subsequently, she indicated that she is older (early seventies) now and has done as much as she could, but as it exists now, she does not plan to return to the United States to work. She felt that her children have gotten a good start and that it is up to them to do the rest. She is active in her church, has distinguished herself as one who prays with dynamism, visits with the sick, and is otherwise an active member of her community. One of her daughters recently came to New York to live with the New York branch of the family and to get work. Not long after that, her visiting male friend and father of her two children followed her to the United States and proposed to her in a very romantic way, and they got married in Brooklyn. Interestingly, she is seeking hairdressing work in the United States, as this is her training and for years she had maintained a small beauty shop at the front of her family home and was able to make a fairly good living that way. Life in the United States, without the official papers, is one of hustle. She plans to send as much home as she can but feels that the house was her mother's project, and while she may help, she has to establish something for herself now. The house is almost completed, as various of her children contribute when they can, in particular one of her sons who drives a taxi in the Caribbean and lives on the first floor with his wife and two sons, in a partially enclosed area. The other sister of the family still lives in the same house toward the back of the property and has not done much to alter its condition, nor does she express any desire to migrate.

MARY

Mary came to the United States first in 1965, at age fifty-four, and spent three months with her son, leaving her daughter, who was taking her final exams, in the care of her cousin, who was also a schoolteacher and ran a day care. She had spent most of her adult life as a primary schoolteacher, beginning, in her words, at age fourteen as a "pupil teacher" in the government schools. A pregnancy cut short her ability to stay in this service, and after that she took her teaching skills and worked in the private-school circuit, developing some still-thriving schools in neighborhoods wherever she lived. Her first visit to the United States was completely a social visit. Not satisfied with the arrangements for her daughter, she returned home from the United States, though she could have stayed longer, and her friends told her she was crazy not to have done so. Instead, she decided to see her daughter through high school. Struggling with the end of a difficult marriage, she endured for another year or so while she made plans to go to the United States, this time permanently. She left home in 1967 with her daughter, settled her in university, and then headed off to Brooklyn to join the larger Caribbean community there and find work. She got a certificate as a nurse's aid and started training as an LPN. Her days were spent working as a nurse's aid to geriatric white women, providing in-home care and sporadically training for her LPN certificate. Her employment history was checkered, as she often went home in the winter months, not wanting to deal with the cold, and spent time with her older sister, who needed companionship and later care. Eventually, after fifteen years of inconsistent work in the United States, now sixty-nine, she returned home for good and declared herself retired. She lived on inheritance and some other pension money but had not put in enough Social Security time to earn a check if she did not live in the United States. She traveled annually to the United States to retain her green card, and after a while did not bother anymore and let the grace period at which one can stay expire.

Eighty-five now and an ailing diabetic, confined to a wheelchair, she lives on a pension and remittances from her children abroad. Her health is not good, and sometimes she laments not living anymore in the United States, saying that the services would be better. Two local women are employed to take care of her, mornings and evenings, and their services are paid for by her daughter abroad. Her return home was enjoyable nevertheless. She joined a senior citizens' organization that provided social interaction such as dinners and parties. The transition to the eighties has meant deaths of many of the group; infirmity, advanced aging, and nursing-home living have cut down on the activity and travel to the United States. Many of that group had provided care services for elders abroad and are often dissatisfied with the service they get at home.

PHILOMENA

Philomena lived for years with a man much older than she and in the interim had six daughters with him. She traveled to the United States in 1966, also in her midfifties, settled in Brooklyn, and easily found work as a live-in servant to a quite famous differently abled woman who painted with her feet and frequently appeared in local news programs for her work. She spent at least ten years of hard domestic service and all her free time either working extra jobs on her days off or shopping for furnishings for her home, which she took down in crates or mailed from time to time—everything from toilet bowls and matching sinks to furniture, lighting fixtures, and appliances—planning to finally have the type of ideal home in the Caribbean. In the meantime, she went home and made sure that she got married to her children's father, the owner of a substantial piece of land, since other women were attempting to move in on an otherwise healthy man living in a house by himself. Philomena spent the next five years or so sending all her money home to improve the house with the plan to return home after all her children were settled and happy in the United States. She oversaw her last unmarried daughter's college education, graduation, marriages, and first babies and returned to Brooklyn occasionally to shop.

She returned home finally in 1992 and happily settled into her life at home in a nicely organized and decorated home. However, in 1996, at age seventy-five, she returned to Brooklyn and while at her daughter's house had a stroke that left her solidly brain damaged and living only on life-support systems. In the end, the family made a determination that she could not survive anymore and allowed the doctors to disconnect the support systems, and she died shortly after. She was buried in her rural village in the Caribbean. Her aging husband died a few years later. The home she struggled for remains empty except for occasional visits by relatives from the United States who want to spend time at home and a family friend who lives in makeshift quarters adjacent to the house.

GEMMA

Gemma went to a school in the Caribbean, where she passed a few of the subjects required to graduate to higher education and so embarked on a career in nursing. She enjoyed dressing in crisp nursing uniforms and walking down the streets to the respect of her neighbors and community. After a few years, she became pregnant and had a son without the benefit of marriage to a recalcitrant partner who later on married someone else. A few years later, she had a daughter and continued to live in her family home and work as a nurse while her mother helped with the children. After twenty or so years of working, she migrated to the United States through a scheme that was recruiting nurses for work. Attaining employment in Pennsylvania, she continued to work, but to her surprise and now over the age of forty-five, she became pregnant with another child. She saw herself now as having to work until that child made it through high school and into college. A very successful nurse, she maintains a very demanding work schedule and indicates that she cannot see herself living back home again. Her mother has since passed, and her neighborhood is now crime ridden and not the same as when she grew up. Her youngest child, born in the United States, is fully enmeshed in American structures, which keep her in the United States. Her oldest son, who migrated with her, did two postings in the U.S. Army and actually was one of the first group of soldiers who entered Baghdad at the start of the war.

SUZETTE

Suzette came from St. Vincent as a fortyish woman and lived for a while in Brooklyn. She had three children at the time and wanted to get into a different economic situation in the United States. She was able to secure employment from an agency with a male couple who had a house on Fire Island. Since the couple was fairly well off and traveled a lot, all they wanted from Suzette was for her to maintain the house in good condition and take care of their dog when they were not in the United States. This couple, according to her, live a very high-end life, with a lot of entertaining. Suzette has worked for them now for about fifteen years, and in the process they have helped her to travel back home and bring her children to go to school in the United States. Her children have gone on to do really well and are in university now. Suzette feels that she has lived the best possible and no-stress life, as the gay couple for whom she works are very liberal in their support of her, and she in exchange has maintained a very positive and open relationship with them, though she whispered when she mentioned to me their sexuality. She indicates, though, that she has ended up being the companion for the dog in a large house with televisions all over the place and a great deal of freedom to do what she wants and drive back and forth to Brooklyn, as she had the day I interviewed her, to get her hair braided. This is where I met her as she told her story. She does not see herself as ever returning to the Caribbean, as this is her life now, and she has maintained a small apartment in Brooklyn where her sister lives, and for her children Brooklyn is home.

DOMINIQUE

Dominique was living well in Haiti but with a husband in government, an official under the Aristide regime. When Aristide was deposed and sent into exile, her husband thought it better if he sent his wife to live in the United States, as she had U.S. residency and had gone to school and had sisters in the United States. He stayed at home to rebuild a life and a home that was destroyed by gangs of marauders after the demise of Aristide. Now they commute, still in a loving relationship. Their three children, now very Americanized, live and go to school in South Florida, but because of the proximity to Haiti and the fact that she has good credentials to work and earn a good living, the family is able to travel frequently to be together. Following the earthquake devastation of 2010, he is even more committed to the rebuilding process, but for her, there are no immediate plans to return home until things are more stabilized.

JASMINE

Jasmine, a young high school student in a good college in the Caribbean, came up on annual visits to visit her mother's siblings in Brooklyn and determined to stay rather than go back and complete the advanced level of her exams. She easily got into Brooklyn College, overstaying her visa, and it seems no questions were asked as she made her way through an accounting degree and graduated. But without proper papers to remain in the United

States, she never fully realized her potential, living with friends in small apartments and doing extra babysitting duties for family. After a few years, she went back home, having reached the end of her possibilities. But feeling limited by what is available in the Caribbean, she left for Canada, again with a plan somehow to get back into the United States. She is still in Canada, but many will not be surprised when she turns up in Brooklyn again, where she has lived for the past ten years of her life.

Finding Meaning in Migration Stories

At the center of each narrative is the need for economic and personal well-being and a definable better life. Home, in some cases, is the physical building itself, but it is also the accoutrements of a good home or education for one's children. Migration then is linked to the globalization of the economy and the absence of certain opportunities for women of working-class origin, if they do not follow the route of mobility through education or the more successful realization of familial goals. Maintaining family connections is the other central feature in each case . . . the need to see family advance and the (grand)children cared for in a much better way. Third, the return home, imagined or fulfilled, is a feature that is ever present. It can move from dream to reality, even if the reality is often not borne out in a positive way. In some cases, age and infirmity precluded full enjoyment toward the end of long lives; in others, the economic gains were minimal in a relative way—cheap furniture and U.S. fittings in houses.

Recent scholarship identifies that migration is circuitous—that it is never one-sided and that a series of movements back and forth perhaps more closely identifies this migratory pattern. David Harvey links contemporary globalization to capitalist labor flows consistently in *Spaces of Hope* (2000). For Harvey, in terms of "contemporary globalization," four recent shifts are identifiable: (1) financial deregulation, which began in the United States in the early 1970s and moved from a hierarchical system controlled by the United States to a more decentralized system of international finance with power blocs; (2) the waves of profound technological change and product innovation; (3) the media and communication systems and the ultimate "dematerialization of space" that had its origins in the military apparatus now controlled by the financial institutions and multinational corporations; and (4) the cost and time of moving commodities and people. These were accompanied by (a) geographical dispersal and fragmentation of production systems that transcend national boundaries and produce commodities globally; (b) doubling of the world wage labor force, bringing women largely into the market with a parallel exploitation; (c) a global population on the move; (d) hyperurbanization; and (e) a deterritorialization of the world on the backs of the nation-states but operating at the supranational level along with parallel environmental and social problems.

So Caribbean migration that relocates people in different locales than the ones they were born in has to be read in complicated, nonnativist ways. One of the questions that one gets at times, surprisingly from some African Americans who should know better, is, why did you all come here? It is a loaded and conservative-in-intent rhetorical question that baffles, as the gains and losses of migration are so varied. Some of the answers are offered here. One of my friends indicates that her mother packed up the family and moved away from their home and their father to Toronto when she was about nine or ten and that she and her siblings had little say in the decision. A major feature of her professional life has been to reacquire a home in the Caribbean island of her birth, which she has recently. But she still feels an impossibility to recapture those years, though she has been professionally successful in North America. Versions of this narrative are common.

The women represented here all have as primary reasons for migration the search for a "better life," as the sociologists have described it, linked to family advancement, often in comparison not with U.S. African Americans but as measured against the success of their cohorts back home. At times, people who remained in the Caribbean are clearly just as or sometimes more successful.

The proximity of the United States to the Caribbean means that there is a much quicker passage between the two locations, as opposed to the distance between the Caribbean and Europe, where preparations for return home, even now, are much more planned. Still, economic well-being of self and family and educational and professional advancement, leading to a measure of comfort and happiness, are primary motivating factors in the drive to self-empowerment.

The "superexploitation" of the black woman as outlined by Claudia Jones is again worth being recalled here in the context of this chapter's concerns. Jones had early asserted that the Black woman as mother occupies a particular position in terms of defense of the black family and that this then is what renders her as pivotal to struggles, as it explains her possibilities for militancy. Jones, who had included women's domestic labor as central to her analysis, approached women not with romanticized views of motherhood as some sort of essential identity but with an analysis of the role of superexploitation in black women's lives. Her larger point is that the U.S. boast that American women possess the greatest equality in the world cannot hold up when one identifies the actual location of black women in American society. So, Jones, in the 1940s and '50s, made a point that still can be argued through a number of surveys of women's rights internationally today and if one looks at census statistics that still locate women's labor and women of color's labor as below what is assumed as normative in society for economic security and transcendence of social limitations. Women of color, including African Americans, earn 62 percent and Hispanic women still earn 53 percent of every dollar a white non-Hispanic man makes, 83 percent of every dollar a white woman makes, and 85 percent of that made by black men, according to the 2009 Labor Department statistics.

So whereas the generation that included women who had identified "the Bronx (Brooklyn) slave market" (E. Baker and Cooke), in which middle-class white women could select a maid for a day to do a week's work, Claudia Jones in studying this phenomenon had concluded in 1948 that Black women were generally confined to the lowest-paying jobs. In 2009 the situation has not radically improved as far as remuneration and types of employment were concerned. And in some readings, it has deteriorated, as a 2011 Pew report, "Wealth Gaps Rise to Record Highs between Whites, Blacks, and Hispanics," indicates that it is now twenty-to-one (Rakesh Kochhar, Richard Fry, and Paul Taylor, "Pew Research Center's Social & Demographic Trends," July 26, 2011). Clearly, we are in the middle of an escalated economic disparity beyond any reasonable standards of equity, which has an impact on subsequent migrations.

Since black women are often heads of households, then the poverty of black communities is ensured if the black women stay underpaid and superexploited, Claudia Jones's analysis of Department of Labor Department statistics revealed. The majority of Black women workers tended to be employed in the 1940s and '50s primarily in private families as domestics and as cooks, as waitresses, and in a range of other service industries, as well as in agricultural and clerical work. Professional black women remained the minority. Importantly, as well, she identified domestic work as the kind of "catchall, fallback" profession for black women and, in the postwar period, the job made to seem most desirous for black women. Again, she correctly identified media representations of black women as one of the sources for maintaining this identification of black women in service roles. Today it may not be so much domestic work in homes as the assumption of service work of various sorts. Essentially, then, migration of Caribbean women for reasons of work, allowing some mobility and personal satisfaction within a larger context, suffers from that tension between the larger construct of transnational labor-market flows.

So, although one may finally have a "leaving" strategy, as the earlier cited poem indicated, is there ever an "elsewhere" that is completely untouched by all of these machinations at the political and economic levels? True, the United States is used as a work space and the Caribbean is linked to fun and relaxation, and a healthy social life, within the escape-route paradigm. The contestation of U.S. boundaries, legislation, policies, and rules of conduct is fundamental and natural. Many indicate that the policies are ridiculous, given U.S. people's mobility throughout the Caribbean, and Caribbean people therefore assume the same right to unhindered mobility. Migration is therefore linked to access to resources that are, in regional terms, plentiful and unbalanced in the United States. There is an assumption of mobility that spells a certain resistance to fixity in intimate relationships and economic and social life.

Contradictory Narratives of Caribbean Working Girls: Rihanna and Nicki Minaj

When Rihanna was battered by Chris Brown, her bruised and bloody swollen face remained so etched in my consciousness that a professional friend of mine decided to write an open letter, seeing it as one of the negative end results of a type of unthinking Caribbean participation in dominant culture. But Rihanna's descriptions to Diane Sawyer (ABC News, *20/20*, November 6, 2009) of her mother's abuse at home at the hands of her father seemed to suggest a continuity across borders and a patterning that foregrounded some issues of the circularity of violence against women that remain understated but centrally part of the abuse cycle. Rihanna's subsequent participation in being presented as a more adult sexual Caribbean woman, willingly involved in sadomasochism, also embraced another stereotype, loaded with all sorts of meanings of island female accessibility, as young Caribbean women enter the African American public sphere. She says in an interview in *Rolling Stone* (April 14, 2011, 80) that in some ways, her masochism is linked to having witnessed abuse in her household. Her public return to and the termination of a relationship with Chris Brown reveals recognizable features of the abuse cycle. Still, these are young women whose lives are still unfolding, and so their stories are yet to be fully realized, and here conclusions remain provisional.

A more completing aspect of the story, though, was the report that her grandmother Clara Braithwaite, whom she affectionately called Gran Gran

Dolly, died in Brooklyn on July 1, 2012. News reports (*Barbados Nation* and *Huffington Post,* July 1, 2012) of the singer's visits to her grandmother's bedside prior to her passing and Rihanna's subsequent tweets about her loss recapture an aspect of the missing U.S. family-migration context. After her abuse episode, one of the open questions was, where was her family in this? The father seemed predatory; the mother seemed absent. Still, that Chris Brown and his mother also tweeted and sent love at her grandmother's passing indicates that they too knew Gran Gran Dolly. I wondered what kind of conversation she had with her granddaughter when she was in pain. The Caribbean family story and even the photographs of Clara Braithwaite appear familiar.

Nicki Minaj's lyrics to "Fly" put a bit more meaning behind what has turned a pair of Caribbean island girls into huge public personas but who nonetheless carry the Caribbean migration impetus:

> I came to win, to fight, to conquer, to thrive
> I came to win, to survive, to prosper, to rise
> To fly
> To fly

Here we get an awareness in lyrics generated out of personal pain of the ways that representations often try to limit the full understanding of one's history and current conditions, that is, "Paint their own pictures then they crop me in." But, above all, we see a determination to triumph: "I am not a word, I am not a line / I am not a girl that can ever be defined / I am not fly, I am levitation / I represent an entire generation." Similar to Rihanna, Nicki Minaj's (Onika Maraj) personal narrative is one that also describes violent abuse of her mother by her drug-abusing father who attempted at one point to burn down the family house and at another dragged the mother two blocks down a street (Halperin). One has to read these determinations of young women to prosper as an attempt to get beyond the pain, while still caught at times in the larger constructions, created before them, and into which they as black women walk. It is for this reason that her comments to a Liberian performer on *American Idol* were criticized as too generalizing or making faulty equivalences between war-torn Liberia and oil-rich Trinidad and Tobago. "I'm so proud that this place gives people like you and people like me, who came from absolutely nothing, a place that we didn't think we'd make it out alive from, it gives us the chance" (Nicki Minaj to Zoanette, *Mail Online,* February 28, 2013). Although the *Daily Mail* makes the link more about underprivileged status than place of origin, many people from the Caribbean were not amused at the comparison, as a number of blogs indicated.

Still, a more assertive version of the Caribbean American identity in migration is also at play here. Whereas Caribbean American male performers have always been acknowledged, Caribbean girls, born in the Caribbean and working in the entertainment industry in the United States, seem to present a new generational levitation that presumes space even as it struggles through difficulty. Although the impetus for migration remains and can be lined up in a trajectory with the struggles of the first generation of Caribbean migrants of the 1920s or the subsequent 1960s migration, there is a determination in the most visible of this contemporary generation to assume transcendence as they attempt to move in an era of economic difficulty against constraints of race, gender, class, and foreign birth and place. The determination to "fly" resonates with the logic of Caribbean space.

7

CONNECTING STORIES
My Grandmother's Violin

As a little girl, I always remembered my grandmother Edith Gordon Boyce playing a violin. She also taught everyone in the family to play the piano. A love of music always permeated a home in which it was not unusual for aunts and uncles to sit at a piano and play jazzy tunes. In his teen years, my brother was a member of a Barataria group that would entertain at events. In my mother's words, he was a bit of a piano virtuoso at a young age, playing at five for Edric Connor, a musician who would subsequently migrate to England. When I was eight years old, my grandmother died, so I never got the full benefit of the transfer of this musical legacy. But I still remember my grandmother playing the violin as clearly as I remember her bathing me in the backyard and rubbing my skin hard with her fingers as she spoke to me in a French patois. My aunt played the organ and piano in the A.M.E. church in Barataria. And in her old age, all that was left in her memory was the ability to direct a choir, which she did to the amusement of those around her.

My grandfather died before I was born, so I never met him, but I have a memory of a photograph of him, a tall, brown-skinned man in a military uniform, on the wall of our family home in Barataria. His birth certificate surfaced among my mother's papers, as born in Arnos Vale Estate, St. Vincent. There is a Barbados connection somewhere, which I was told as a child, but of course did not listen seriously enough then to remember and perhaps told myself that Boyce was a plantation owner's name in any case. Still, there were only two or three families with that last name in Trinidad in my childhood, with a family suggestion that they were all related in some distant way.

There were also always family stories of a great-grandfather who was a wealthy Tobago entrepreneur, but they always seemed like just that, family fiction. My uncle Eddie related to me several versions of these stories, including an ownership of horses by the Gordon brothers. None of this had any tangible meaning until a relative came through to visit me a few years ago as she made a brief tour through the United States. As though on a mission one evening, she shared with me some photographs of this family ancestor, Baker Gordon, and some material that she thought I should have that a historian had collected and passed on to her. Earnestine Cordner, my cousin who shared this detail, died the year after we had this conversation, which seems remarkable now. But in many ways, it reveals how tenuous family stories in the diaspora can be if connecting stories remain like broken threads in a tapestry. Still, there are so many loose pieces yet to be connected, abandoned memories that seem unconnected until a bit more detail is provided. I finally understood the family history, which explained why my grandmother played a violin.

Notes on Sinai Josiah Baker (Gordon) (1855–1926), Musician and Businessman, from Tobago Newspapers

The News, November 14, 1885, p. 2

S. J. Gordon, formerly of Plymouth, has now opened his tailoring establishment in Main Street, Scarborough, in the premises recently vacated by *Daylight* newspaper (12 Nov. 1885).

Mirror, November 30, 1909, p. 4.

S. J. Gordon started a new soda water factory opposite the Blue Store and Mr. J. E. Roberts' store in Scarborough. He imported Herman Lachapelle's improved machinery, and his "aerated drinks are of excellent quality." He can supply all of Tobago at a very cheap rate.

Mirror, May 1, 1913, p. 4

Scarborough Brotherhood [an organization that was started in the Methodist church in 1909 and continued well into the 1920s, open to people of all religions, held debates and discussions, and promoted lectures on agriculture, pest control, health, and so on] held a farewell for Rev G. Godson, who was leaving for Barbados. . . . Archie John, S. J. Gordon and George Wheeler played the violins. . . .

Mirror, November 27, 1916, p. 12

S. J. Gordon read a paper on Duty to the Scarborough Brother-hood on Tuesday evening last.

Labour Leader, February 6, 1926, p. 13

Sinai Josiah Gordon died 23 Jan. 1926, aged almost 71 years; therefore his dates are 1855–1926. Wife already dead in 1918. Children are Mrs. A. Cordner, Harold Gordon (Trinidad constabulary), Mrs. E. Quinlan, Mrs. E. **Boyce**, Mrs. Pierre, Miss McKay and Miss Olive Gordon of Tobago. His brother is Frederick Gordon, Gordon Stables, Port of Spain.

From "Notes on Sinai Josiah Gordon, Tailor, Entrepreneur, Musician," provided by Susan Craig-James based on research for her book *The Changing Society of Tobago, 1838–1938. A Fractured Whole,* vol. 1, *1838–1900.* Vol. 2, *1900–1938.* Trinidad and Tobago: Cornerstone, 2008. (Notes dated December 4, 2002.)

Reversing the Pattern (My Mother in Her Words)

My name is Mary Boyce Joseph, a senior citizen of the United States of America. I was born in Trinidad in the Caribbean islands of parents of various origins. My mother was born in Tobago, the sister island of Trinidad, and my father was born in the island of St. Vincent. His father came from Barbados and had been a slave. My mother's father, Baker Gordon, owned a great deal of property which was rudely and crudely taken away from him in the island of Tobago. He was too black to own such a property and besides that he was also the first generation after slavery for his father had been an African who was a slave there. My mother's father's name was Gordon so her name was Edith Gordon before marriage to my father then she became Edith Boyce. My mother's mother was from Africa from the Ashanti and her name was "Nana"—Nana Pilgrim of Tobago. She had five sisters and four brothers and was related to the Pilgrims, the Armstrongs, Elders, Quinlans, Pierres and Cordners. I have one sister, Olive Boyce Elder Thomas, and three brothers, George Boyce and Edward Boyce (England) and Albert Boyce, who lived in England and the U.S. and returned to Trinidad.

*I have two children, Joseph Anthony Boyce and Carole Boyce Davies.
Joseph has three boys (Anthony [Tony], Jevaughn and Joseph [Joey]
Boyce Jr.). Carole's husband is Dr. John Davies and she has two daugh-
ters (Jonelle and Dalia).*

*I was born in Port of Spain, Trinidad and Tobago. I am a resident
of the United States of America now about twenty years now and am a
practical nurse. I recently became an ordained minister in the Ethiopian
Orthodox Church but I have been for years in Trinidad a member of the
African Methodist Episcopal Church. I also was initiated into the ancient
order of Mechanics to the 12th degree but am no more an active member
in this order.*

*I have been a teacher, social worker, practical nurse and minister
of the gospel but am now a retired person. I went to the public schools in
Port of Spain. My daddy could not afford to send us to the high schools
or colleges so when I reached the highest grades and being the most intelligent in my class I was moved to the school leaving class and began to be
trained as a teacher and was put in the pupil teacher's class to study. There
you had to take examinations for teaching which I passed. Sometimes I
had to deputize for teachers who were out sick and so I began to learn
practically how to teach a child in all its aspects. I was trained to teach
preschool and kindergarten up to grades 1 to 3. But moving from one class
to the next, I taught children of all ages at the government school. This
experience was very good for me as even now, children mean very much
to me. The Bible says "suffer little children to come unto me and forbid
them not for of such is the Kingdom of heaven." I am quoting Jesus Christ
talking to his disciples. These years of training I have never forgotten
for I kept teaching kids, privileged and underprivileged children. I just
wanted to see them learn. Wherever I lived, I opened a school for small
children and the last of them in Laventille grew into a large pre-school
and kindergarten. I also opened youth groups wherever I lived.*

*My father worked for a number of years in the Fire Brigade in Port
of Spain and after resigning received a small pension so we moved from*

Woodbrook, Port of Spain, to Barataria, San Juan, and bought a house on the Eastern Main Road. At one point, my father went to Venezuela on the promise of work that would bring a lot of money but when he got there was told that there was no work so he had to find a way to get back to his family and returned after a year of travelling around the country to tell us many stories of his travels. On arriving back to Trinidad he got a job in Brighton working as a company officer for 10 years in La Brea. I lived there with my mother and father and continued my teacher training there and passed my first teachers examination there. I joined the choir in the Anglican Church and my father would walk me to church there on Sundays. He liked that as I was quite attractive and the boys were beginning to buzz around me. My father warned me to be careful and take time in choosing and of course the boys thought he was too strict and over-protective. I was inexperienced about young men but ended up learning the hard way in the years to come.

This young man came to my father's house after telling me he was in love with me many times. I told him he had to get my father's permission to see me. So after visiting my father's house several times, he approached my father one night telling him of his undying love for me and that he wanted to marry me. My father listened intently and then called me to ask me if this was true. I told him yes and we became engaged. His name was George Osborne. We began spending a lot of time together in those romantic Caribbean evenings of stolen kisses; I discovered I was pregnant with his child. His mother though was against him marrying saying that she was not ready for her son to marry and he had to listen. I was tormented by this throughout my pregnancy and nearly lost my mind. This was a turning point in my life anyway and I had my baby with my family's support and gave myself to the Lord as I believe he saved me and brought me through.

Because of this experience, I had to stop teaching after passing two examinations and had to move on to something else. I learned to sew and did so well that I became a seamstress and was able to maintain work *and secure enough money to take care of my child. I opened a small sewing shop in Port of Spain, sewing for some of the stores around. I taught many people to sew, to earn their daily bread and be an asset to their families. Many people still sing their praises about learning to sew from me, one of them my god daughter of Indian descent who became quite adept at it and was able as many to make their own clothes and those of their children.*

My little girl has come a long way. She came about ten years after her brother by choice as I wanted another child. Her father and I were engaged to be married but at the same time I learned that he had got another girl pregnant in the south. My daughter was a lovely little baby and when she was born, he came back and tried to patch up differences, vowed to be faithful; but I did not accept him at that time. He soon went to Grenada where his family was from planning to go to England. The next I heard was that he had died in a fire. Well I worked very hard to take care of my two kids. I opened private nursery schools and my daughter learned to walk and talk amidst children. I tutored her myself and she progressed quickly. She just kept learning and learning and reading was her special subject.

In retrospect on my life and living, I have taught my two kids the love of God and the appreciation of the good things of life. I have learned life the hard way. It was no bed of roses for me. I did learn to stand on my own two feet believe it or not. It was a very great struggle up the hill of life for me and I did all I could as a black mother to educate my children and train them up in the way they should go, and that is to seek God first and help themselves to become somebody and go somewhere in this great wide world.

My mother was always busy in her spare moments writing her own book as she termed it, handwritten pages on typing paper, sometimes typed, and put together in a folder. After she died, I found her journal, which she called a personal diary and in which she had started writing reflections on her life as an eighty-year-old. As such it contains a bit of early family history and centers on selected moments in her experience, particularly disappointments in love and having and raising children and finally developing a faith in God as the ultimate protection. The difference in historical period is important. I comment on a period in my mother's life when she was in her prime as a sexual being. At eighty and with writing as an ordering experience, what appears is a much more subdued, reflective person, conscious that she was writing a document she wanted her grandchildren to read. I decided to reverse the paradigm in order to provide context, with my great-grandfather's history first as reported in Tobago newspapers, my mother's reflections, and my deliberate construction of a more playful mother I remembered.

My Mother's Wings

Growing up with what I saw as an already sexually liberated mother in a time before the sexual revolution of the 1960s and '70s is something that I now cherish. For the first nine or ten years of my life, I was blissfully nurtured, loved, cared for in an extended family situation in Trinidad, but one in which my mother was always my center. Then, as I entered adolescence, I began to get a sense that there also existed a bourgeois social standard, though many others around lived lives that resisted compliance and expressed themselves more naturally and organically.

Not surprisingly, it was in church and school contexts that my state of blissful innocence in relation to the official patriarchal norms was disrupted. On one occasion, when I proudly declared my family name in a church youth meeting, one of the elder women of my mother's generation looked at me with disdain and told me that I had "fudged" my last name. Not understanding precisely the implications of such a statement but clear that it was not positive, I went home to ask my mother what that meant and to report it to her and my family. What followed was the inevitable family anger and verbal recriminations against that woman who, it seems, had her own even more problematic narrative. But more important, what occurred was the extended family's rearticulation of my right to my name, accompanied with a relevant family history of dignity and accomplishment. I have learned subsequently from colleagues who work on African philosophical and social history that far from being social pathologies, Caribbean family practices often reveal African gender systems and kinship structures that survived the Middle Passage.

Still, the tendency to transfer the pain that we carry onto others similarly located has to be seen as colonially derived with vestiges of enslavement. Indeed, this woman I refer to had also had a daughter, by other than officially sanctioned means. That a child could be her malicious target with words like the ones she uttered, when her own family life was similar, is an amazing expression of the self-hate and alienation that Frantz Fanon identified as an end product of colonization.

In the Caribbean of my childhood, it was not uncommon to witness the trauma suffered by girls, who I (and they) thought were from respectable nuclear families, having to bring their birth certificates to school in order to take the common entrance exam for high school. The pain they experienced on discovering that their parents did not have the same last names and were not married and that the prejudicial word *illegitimate* appeared on their birth certificates was palpable in that period. Still, for many of us, though, in our working-class worlds, the nuclear models were not something we yearned for. My friends, relatives, and neighbors were perfectly happy with the extended family lives we lived, full of uncles, aunts, cousins, noise, and excitement. Fathers resident in their homes were distant or often unavailable, even oppressive, and later we discovered had sometimes completely intact other nuclear families in other locations. One illustration suffices: A friend, a light-brown-skinned member of our group of classmates, came to class one morning crying, with her face and ears a bright red. She reported, between sobs, that her father had dealt her a stinging blow across her head and ears as she was about to leave for class. We would learn later on that his approach to fathering included a great deal of bullying and physical abuse from which his children are still recovering. Another friend had a taxi-driver father whose car was a source of a great deal of spare change that she would salt away by offering to clean his car whenever we had to go somewhere or she had to amass resources to buy an item. In other words, consistent beneficence was not ensured to the few of us who had fathers at home.

So bits and pieces of family narrative provided the information that clarified my early life. I gathered that my mother, who had been on the upward path in the ranks of a schoolteacher career, successfully passing the various exams, became pregnant with my brother at about the age of nineteen. Of course, this proof of her sexuality followed her in the Caribbean of my mother's youth. In those days (the 1930s), unlike today, when many young women may actively choose to have a baby, family narratives of both protectiveness and shame persisted in the Caribbean in such a context. In our family's case, on the one hand, there was pride, as my brother was the first grandson in the family, but still, on the other hand, my mother obviously experienced some economic difficulty in raising my brother without a father present, with stories of an inability to provide things like a bicycle, for example, when he wanted one. For my brother, this situation embedded his compliance with a range of family prescriptions about service, but as a male, it also made him the recipient of a family pride and control of resources, ensuring his place as the "big brother" in the family hierarchy and thereby the ability to manage and dispense a range of economic resources.

Toward the end of my mother's life, my brother was her other primary caretaker, and he demonstrated a level of deep devotion for her that I had not seen in him before. I realized that perhaps it mirrored the closeness they shared during the first ten years of his life, before I was born, when he was my mother's constant companion. I saw him tenderly lift her from her wheelchair to the front seat of his car to take her to church. I saw her have to trust him completely and hold him around his neck like a child. There is a photograph of my brother at about six or seven, with a winning smile, wearing an outfit, complete with cap in a kind of plaid material that our mother had lovingly made for him, that captured for me this relationship of mutual nurturing and pride.

I came along, as my mother told me often, out of her desire to have another child, and happily a girl, some ten years after my brother was born. There were opportunities offered her by her older sister to abort, which she refused. I have no evidence that she loved my father, whom, it seems, was dispensed with, because of his recalcitrance, soon after my birth, and he made his way to England in that wave of migration in the 1950s. Her comments about him were always indifferent or dismissive. Still, my presence was the legacy of whatever that encounter was, and though reaping a great deal of spoiling as one of the positive benefits of being the youngest child in the extended family, I lived my life determined to make my mother proud. Suffice it to say that I became my mother's eyeball, as they say in the Caribbean, sometimes referred to by friends and neighbors as "Mary's little lamb," as I was seen to follow her everywhere. I was the little girl she sewed pretty dresses for and took to meetings and outings of all sorts.

Growing up in that period, with a mother who, I thought, was one of the most attractive women around, I felt only love and admiration. My mother, full of personal style, could wear dark-red lipstick (with an elegance I have tried to emulate); made herself beautiful fifties-style black flared satin skirts, screen printed with coconut trees in gold or silver; wore blouses with folded-up sleeves and wedge-heeled sandals, her hair pressed and curled as other women in that period. My classmates in elementary school often told me that my mother was better looking than me: smooth, dark, flawless skin; a winning smile; and a height and confidence to match.

I thought I was the luckiest girl in the world to have several godfathers. I did have an official godfather who was a chemist and whom I loved dearly and was proud of as he drove one of the biggest American cars around at the time and always stopped his car to chat with me and give me sometimes spending money with which I could show off and buy all my friends candy or ice cream. His questioning presence always made sure that I was doing well in school, explaining at times some Latin phrases that I asked about. But some of these other godfathers, I realized with a shock much later, were without a doubt some of my mother's boyfriends. I remember going to a house with my mother to visit one of them, and while I played for hours riotously with the children around, my mother had somehow disappeared. But I was safe, as I knew she was somewhere inside the house. Another of my mother's friends helped me to land quickly my first job after high school and before I went to the United States to university a year later. When he learned about my success in the exams, he directed me right away to the appropriate place and person to get employment in government service.

I forgot to say that my mother got married when I was about ten and seemed happy enough, though I could tell she had exchanged a certain freedom for marital responsibility but was never fully satisfied. But she did not abandon at least one of these prior friendships. Mr. P., let's call him, who had directed me to my first job, remained a staple, it seems, throughout her married life. He himself was married to someone else who stayed at home mostly, and they had two or three well-cared-for daughters. In his nice car, he would meet my mother every day after work and bring her home, would even sometimes pick her up at home in the presence of my stepfather and take her wherever she wanted to go. That my stepfather did not have a car and would wait for a bus or taxi did not comport with my mother's sense of elegance, and she refused to see herself in those limited terms. Indeed, the observation of several around was that she had married only to make herself respectable, and not for any deep love, as was clear even to me. One Carnival day, my mother, in the company of her husband, ran into my brother's father—who was obviously her first love. Sparks flew between them, and I witnessed him, this tall, lanky man, pull my mother to him, and lingeringly tell her sweet things in her ear, which made her blush, and plant a juicy kiss on her lips before they reluctantly separated and he walked away. I believe my stepfather looked the other way, pretending he was looking at the passing Carnival bands. My little-girl eyes wondered at the revelation of this sexuality that my mother maintained outside my own framework, and about the fact that this formidable woman could be reduced to such vulnerability.

Yes, a free and liberated sexual identity surrounded my mother. There are many other stories like that I can recall but, of course, will not tell all here. All the way up to and through her seventies, she always maintained "gentlemen callers" or introduced me to some new beau. Her greatest sadness was when, at age eighty-three, she had a diabetic-related leg amputation that greatly altered her sense of self, though not her spunk. It is reported that she told the doctor, "If you want to take my legs, then you have to give me some wings!" At first she found the humor in it. For example, postsurgery, when she had to stay in a nursing home to recuperate, I flew in from the London study abroad I was directing to see her. She laughingly told me two stories. One evening, when she was wearing her wig and had spruced herself up, a little girl who perhaps was a daughter of one of the nurses and who frequented the nursing home, and with whom she had chatted before, asked her, "Where is the old lady who was here before?" On another occasion, she told me that old women in nursing homes had to be careful because old men, confused or suffering from dementia, would often try to find their way into their beds, perhaps confusing others with their wives. She indicated that she found the possibility of a wandering senile man absolutely nightmarish and undesirable.

I wrote this initially in the Caribbean a year after losing my mother when I visited her grave frequently. It was the day before Mother's Day. In Trinidad on the radio, people called in with greetings; women called in with flirtatious comments for the deejays; there was much talk of honoring mothers, and I wrote this as I thought fondly of my mother . . . always sexy, always beautiful. Several anecdotes still make me smile. Once, toward the end of her life, spending some time with her, I returned to her house, accompanied by an old professor of mine, whom I had gone to visit and whom she knew well. He was in her age group, perhaps a little older, and they had done social work together in the 1950s during my childhood. I thought it would cheer her up to see him. Her nurse reported to me later that as I approached, she told my mother, "Look, Carole is bringing an old man for you." Whatever she had said had generated a loud laugh from the nurse, which I had heard (prompting my question later). It seems my mother had responded: "She must be bringing him for herself. I don't want any old man." Now by this time, she was mostly confined to a wheelchair, but still with her characteristic sauciness.

It reminded me of those days when the formidable female friends of my mother and aunt would come by the family home to spend a few hours. Often the children around were chased away. But if you lingered, as I did at times, you could not help but overhear their stories, accompanied with raucous laughter, about sexual escapades with men. In one of those scandalously reported narratives, one man, it seemed, in those pre-Viagra days, was unable to perform with a friend of my mother who was an amply endowed and much-desired-by-many light-skinned woman, who interestingly also had a husband well older than she was. They laughed hysterically at his comments at the moment of sexual failure, as it seemed the man had lamented loudly about his inability in comical words. "Tell us! What did he say again?" "She wants it! She wants it!" was the reply. Scandalous laughter!

Another story she shared with me was about a cousin in her age group who had left her husband for a famous dancer. When the dancer died suddenly after a performance in New York, the story goes that the now dead man, who was very powerfully involved in African spirituality, was still returning to the house where he visited her, running up her stairs in his characteristic style, but, even more than that, still having sex with her whenever she was in bed. Of course, this was one of those occasions for "suspension of disbelief." I was told conspiratorially by my mother that her cousin was able to secure peace from this sexually active dead man through consulting a Shouter Baptist relative in Brooklyn, who performed the required ritual to send the dancer to his rest or at least stopped this disembodied sexual activity. Later, I wondered jokingly, as I was telling this story to a friend, whether after the man's spirit had been laid to rest, she had missed her sexual escapades with the deceased. One of the Caribbean remedies for this, I gathered from my mother, was "wearing black panties." In our discussion, though, we concluded that such continued activity would have sapped her energy over time and would have led to her death.

Yet the cousin Vi story still fascinates me. It remains an unconnected portion of a longer narrative. Teacher Violet as she was called, a Spiritual Baptist in Belmont, Trinidad, whose expertise was sought, we are told, by Roman Catholic priests, migrated to Brooklyn also in the 1960s. From a spiritual angle, this migration can be seen as a process of almost accompanying her clientele, for cousin Vi never entered the world of work, as the other women around her did. That there began to be visible Baptists in places like Brooklyn, with sisters traveling from places like the Bronx for Sunday services or to take part in rituals, can be credited to people like her for sure. The links between spirituality, sexuality, and power for women are strong ones that for women like mother were never contradictory.

Photograph of grandmother's father, businessman and musician Baker Gordon, in Tobago. Courtesy Susan Craig, Tobago history. Family photograph.

Photograph of grandmother Edith Gordon Boyce taken in Barataria (circa 1956).

Portrait of Boyce extended family (*standing, left to right*): Albert, Mary, Edward, Olive, and George. Grandmother Edith Gordon Boyce is seated, and brother Joseph Boyce as a boy is standing to her left.

Passport photograph of brother as he leaves for study in the United States. Found in mother's wallet after passing.

Passport photograph of author as she leaves for study in the United States. Found in mother's wallet after passing.

Photograph of author and unknown childhood friend taken on the same day as grandmother photograph in Barataria (circa 1956).

VOICE LESSON

Cimarron.

Cimarron.

Remember to roll the r's

(Think of the sound of galloping mustangs on a Nevada plain)

Cimarron

(or the pound of buffalo hooves)

Cimarron

(or your grandma's mules broken loose last year)

Maroon.

Maroon.

Breathe in deep.

Say it like a warrior hurling her spear through the air.

Maroon. (Now think of bloodhounds, armed men at your heels)

Maroon (or Nanny's boiling cauldron set to catch them)

Maroon (or women wearing the teeth of white soldiers around their
     ankles.)

Maroon. Maroon.

Pronounce the "a" soft like the "a" in "alone."

That's right,

Marooned

(Imagine dangling from an orange tree blindfolded—stockings from
     someone's clothesline noosed around your neck)

Marooned (or the one dollar to your name, the eviction notice taped to
     the door)

Marooned (think of a cold, soundproof room.)

Maroon. Maroon.

Say it slow like a rich, full thing to the mouth.

Maroon. (Remember yourself six years old, talking sassy in your
     mother's dark lipstick)

Maroon (or Zora's lips mouthing "just watch me," her felt hat tilted to
     the side of her head)

Maroon (or all those women's mouths in Ebenezer choir, *Free at Last,*
     singing for the fire locked up in their bones.)

Maroon. Maroon.

Here's your chance now, follow the instinct of your tongue and say it
     your way, Maroon.

Put on that hat you wear when you're all stirred up and need to have a
     word or two.

Maroon
Hurl your spear if you like,
Or change the accent on the "a" perhaps something wide, free like the
     "a" in gallop Maroon Maroon
(Hear the call of an old abeng?)
Maroon Say it Say it rich Say it full
(The twitch near your ear is only the remembrance of thunder.)
Maroon
Breathe in deep
Maroon
(This dust kicked up on the plain is sweet as nutmeg!)
Maroon
Say it!
Maroon
(Listen to the feet of summer rain behind you)
Say it strong
Say it now
Break loose speckled horse,
and take yourself back.

Marcia Douglas, now a recognized writer, wrote this poem for a class booklet during her days as a graduate student at Binghamton University.

8

"CHANGING LOCATIONS"
Literary Pathways of Caribbean Migration

Capturing the dynamics of migration via song, poem, play, film, or novel has been consistently a theme in the Caribbean experience and is perhaps one of its central aesthetic features. Just as movement is a central component of the blues aesthetic in the African American cultural field, I propose that we similarly read the assumption of space in the Caribbean as similarly potent. One can see this movement perhaps most visibly in the written literature with the same directional points identified earlier. Although there are several literary movements, I propose to focus on two visible largely Anglophone locations, two pathways among a variety of possible entry points to this discussion.

Caribbean American Challenges

It is perhaps useful to begin with Claude McKay, of Jamaican origin, as the signature writer of the Caribbean encounter with the United States and the beginning of Caribbean diaspora formation, primarily because McKay was a leading contributor to the Harlem Renaissance of the 1920s. In his poem "Harlem Shadows" (1922), he describes the Caribbean working experience in the following terms: "The Shadows Wane / The Dawn comes to New York / And I go darkly-rebel to my work." There is an echo in the "darkly-rebel" phrasing that reappears in his poem "America," in which he confronts, as Malcolm X would later, the contradictory meaning of America for a black person who also experiences U.S. racism, at the structural and personal level.

However, before McKay, as a meticulously researched recent work by Jeffrey Perry (2009) tells us, there were Caribbean activist intellectuals in the United States in the early twentieth century who put tremendous time and energy into the common struggle of delivering the African American community, broadly defined, from one of the most oppressive racist systems in the world, South Africa being the other. Hubert Harrison was a leading figure in ushering in the Harlem Renaissance. It was Harrison, we learn, who actually coined the term and provided the philosophical and argumentative basis for the "New Negro Movement": "a race conscious, internationalist, mass-based movement for 'political equality, social justice, civic opportunity, and economic power' . . . urging defense of self, family and 'race' in the face of lynching and white supremacy" (243).

The available research on Harrison's Afro-Caribbean background indicates birth in St. Croix, the U.S. Virgin Islands, childhood there, and migration to New York in 1900 at the age of seventeen. His development as a major orator, organizer, and agitator for black rights combines with his entry into the Socialist Party, and he is reported to have influenced Marcus Garvey. His formation of the Liberty Congress in 1918 rounds out an amazing life that is necessary information for understanding Caribbean migration to the United States and the nature of the challenges that Caribbeans faced as well as their defiance of an oppressive state.

The early generation of Caribbean migrants to the United States and the coterie of activists that they formed and above all their instantaneous identifications with black struggles are important to understanding Caribbean space conceptually. Thus, Claude McKay can be taken as a representative member of a generation that experienced the conflicting emotions of notions of migration, as he would move from Jamaica to the United States as a student but would develop some major identifications with Harlem and the African American experience (W. James and McKay). His famous poem "If We Must Die" (1919) captures the unquestioning identification of this group with U.S. African Americans as they battled racism. Several other sonnets in his 1922 *Harlem Shadows* capture as well the sense of duality that African Americans like W. E. B. Du Bois had articulated in his "double-consciousness" formation but also the sense of resistance to a state-level terror that was unleashed on Third World and native peoples as they experienced its power.

But McKay, who began to see Harlem as home, as the titles of his books *Home to Harlem* (1928) and his autobiography, *A Long Way from Home* (1937), suggest, would also write wonderful nostalgic poems throughout *Harlem*

Shadows about the Caribbean. For example, "The Tropics in New York" is triggered by seeing familiar Caribbean fruits—bananas, mangoes, tangerines, grapefruits—in a different location: "My eyes grew dim and I could no more gaze / A wave of longing through my body swept / And hungry for the old, familiar ways / I turned aside and bowed my head and wept." It is worth noting that his theme of "shadows" also carried the logic of twilight. Still, it also becomes clear that "home" is a repeated trope for McKay, used titularly and thematically in several of his works. But this is a home that varies, it seems, from the Caribbean homeland to his new Harlem "home."

According to Joyce Moore Turner, "The development of Harlem provided the opportunity for African Caribbeans to join with African Americans to help forge a cohesive organizing arm" (53–54). She explains the activism in Harlem in several ways: Harlem was on the way to becoming a global city, and many of these Caribbean people were meeting each other for the first time and were able to compare notes on colonialism; they had moved out of the insularity of the single island or colony; they were encountering black people from all over the world; they were affronted by the hard-core Jim Crow racism of the United States. They therefore threw in their lot with U.S. African Americans in order to struggle against this oppression; they saw this condition, in Du Bois's terms, as "a local phase of a world problem"; and they therefore struggled at the same time against racist colonialism and built links with their home countries.

Caribbean women in each period also appear as writers and activist intellectuals whose work is worth noting, as they often engaged in the same considerations as their male counterparts, covering subjects ranging from the political to the personal. Some recurring themes are noticeable: considerations of the economic conditions of black peoples following enslavement and colonialism and contemporary economic globalizations, which have rendered many of them in situations of financial lack. Added to the particular racial location and economic disparity, the location of gendered subjects who were resolved in migrating for work adds another piece to the economic mosaic.

In the U.S. context, the major women writers who capture this experience beginning in the 1950s, Paule Marshall and Rosa Guy, do a credible articulation of the human dimensions of these movements. Rosa Guy, from Diego Martin, Trinidad, who died at age eighty-nine, would have lived through all these varied twentieth- and early-twenty-first-century movements. She is identified as having written fifteen books, most of them young adult fiction that dealt with issues of Caribbean migration to the United States but also race and ethnic relations in an urban New York context and definitely sexuality (Fox). But Guy is also identified as one of the founders of the Harlem Writers Guild in 1950 and, like her close friend Claudia Jones, had studied acting in the Harlem-based American Negro Theater group in the 1940s.

More attention has perhaps been accorded to Paule Marshall, whose *Brown Girl, Brownstones* (1959) became the signature text of its generation. Another generation of Caribbeans, this time in the 1950s, living in New York, took on the desire to make these cities home. Marshall depicts her central character as a Caribbean woman migrant in New York whose quest for a brownstone is driven by her ambition and determination to develop a secure home base in the United States. The daughter, though born in the United States, by contrast heads toward the Caribbean. The father remains outside of the economic drives of the family, is finally crushed by the American machine, but in the end chooses a creative and religious path, still with some conflicted outcomes.

Marshall's more recent memoir *Triangular Road* (2009) describes autobiographically the movements of her parents, a father who goes from Barbados to Cuba as a contract worker but ends up back in the same cane fields he was escaping, decides to stow away and arrives in New York to factory work, and, still dissatisfied, later joins the Father Divine socioreligious movement. Her mother, who migrated to Brooklyn to join a sibling, ended up being a depressed residential domestic worker and later a day worker and dissatisfied wife. Ironically today, the Barbadian community's foresight is recognized in their purchasing of those brownstones, which now are worth millions. Subsequent works such as *Daughters* (1991) and *Fisher King* (2001) and earlier works like *Reena, and Other Stories* (1983) and *The Chosen Place, the Timeless People* (1969) each engage these issues of reconnection, diaspora, movement, and the construction of new lives.

There are few writers who navigate the various points of the African diaspora with the confidence of Paule Marshall. In early bibliographies, she was listed as a Caribbean writer, but also as African American. Unabashedly now Caribbean American, Paule Marshall is also identifiably an African diaspora writer, operating outside of rigid nation-state belonging. In other words, she was an African diaspora writer before the category was created. Her *Praisesong for the Widow* (1983) was set in the African diaspora of the U.S. South and the Caribbean, specifically in Grenada, and reaches its climactic moments in Carriacou using the Big Drum Ceremony as its African foundation. Along the way, though, she has her characters remember Igbo Landing, where the Africans in local mythology walked back to Africa, relive the Middle Passage, and make family reconnections, always reengaging the mythologies of the African diaspora conceptually. Marshall clearly was ahead of many of her contemporaries in recognizing this important feature of our experience, not quite continental African, but fully African descendants in the "New World." So when she goes to Brazil and meets the old women of the *Irmandade da boa morte*, it was, as in my experience, like meeting family elders, meeting old women who had held on tenaciously to their history in the African diaspora, as a cultural life-sustaining device. She is able to provide her character Merle in *The Chosen Place, the Timeless People* with the ability to travel to Africa from the Caribbean without returning to the United States, bypassing Europe, showing thereby the use of an alternative geography. Marshall reminds us of those triangular roads that our ancestors took and that we continue to take as we complete some of their journeys and initiate new ones for ourselves.

In the generation of the 1960s and '70s, Jamaica Kincaid captures the high point of that migration to the United States. Her *Lucy* (1990) reveals an observer of American bourgeois culture who can write critically, almost anthropologically, about the white family for which she works, as the writer herself moves from au pair girl to writer and becomes in some ways representative of the generation of women who would strike out from the Caribbean, as her character does at the end of the novel *Annie John* (1985), determined to make a life abroad for themselves. Her more recent *See Now Then* (2013) captures the internal falling away of that idealistic incorporation into an American success narrative, which seems to trace some aspects of her own experience, as she often does.

So, even as she writes subsequently about gardening in Vermont, in *My Garden Book* (1999), the author realizes that her garden "resembled a map of the Caribbean and the sea that surrounds it. . . . I only marveled at the way the garden is for me an exercise in memory, a way of remembering my own immediate past, a way of getting to a past that is my own (the Caribbean Sea) and the past that is related to me, the conquest of Mexico and its surroundings" (7–8). Here, as she details and critiques some aspects of American culture, the past intervenes, as she compares her present house with the house she grew up in and the assorted punishments associated with that era of Caribbean parenting (44). But the house in Vermont in *See Now Then,* is almost twilight zone–like in its hidden tortures, as difficult to read as being forced to be a participant in a couple's argument.

Articulating some of the other aspects of the Caribbean migration experience of the Spanish-speaking communities, though written in English, Angie Cruz in *Let It Rain Coffee* (2005) situates her work both in the

Dominican Republic and in New York. The same can be said for Cristina Garcia, in *Dreaming in Cuban* (1992), which narrates the back-and-forth movement between generations and locations and the conflicted engagement with the American challenge to the Cuban experiment with socialism. Perhaps a more troubling capturing is Loida Maritza Perez's novel *Geographies of Home* (2000), which begins with an experience of racism at Cornell University, but instead of moving outward has her protagonist return to Brooklyn and to a troubled family that ends up victimizing her. Another version of the migration as a student into the United States is Elizabeth Nunez's *Beyond the Limbo Silence* (2003), which is semiautobiographical in nature and identifies the writer as a student participant-observer in the U.S. racial systems in the 1960s and 1970s. Marcia Douglas in *Notes from a Writer's Book of Cures and Spells* (2005) imaginatively expresses movements between Jamaica and the United States and in one case creates a character who becomes a captured experiment in a university lab in upstate New York. Staying at home in the Caribbean, though with a consciousness of this migration, Earl Lovelace has a wonderfully nuanced, at times humorous, story titled "Joebell and America" that narrates a Caribbean gambler's failed attempt to get into the United States, though he makes it to Venezuela and Puerto Rico along the way.

The most phenomenal contemporary writing of the discourse of migration, though, comes through the contributions of Edwidge Danticat. Her *Brother, I'm Dying* (2007), a family narrative, and therefore autobiographical in nature, can be taken as that detailed narration of the discourses of migration to which I referred at the start. The memoir narrates the lives of two brothers—one Edwidge's biological father who migrates, definitely "in search of a better life" but ends up sick, dying from the debilitating life of overwork in Brooklyn, New York, as a gypsy cab driver, the other detained in Chrome Detention Center as he attempts to leave Haiti legally.

Ironically, both brothers end up being buried together in exile in Queens, New York, the one who decided to stay at home determined to make life on the island and the one who migrates as well. The entire oeuvre of Danticat has focused on the discourse of migration, from *Breath, Eyes, Memory* (1994) to *Brother, I'm Dying* (2007).

The elements of migration that are identifiable in *Brother, I'm Dying* are those that create the Haitian diaspora, which provides the extreme of the larger Caribbean migration narrative: (1) difficult, troubled island nation-state life with its unrelenting poverty and dysfunctional state apparatuses; (2) migration of parents leaving the children behind with a relative pending reunification; (3) other children born in the destination location while the children at home learn to live without their parents and bond with the extended family members; (4) reunification of the nuclear family in the host country; (5) the consistent presence of the economic and social problems of the extended family at home; (6) the concomitant obligation to send remittances; (7) the difficult and increasingly violently poor conditions of the home country; (8) the deaths of members of the extended family, some of whom one will never see again; (9) the final destruction of the church and residence of the uncle and the humiliating escape; (10) the attempt to get to the United States legally when faced with deteriorating conditions, which is changed to an illegality that renders one (11) incarcerated in Chrome Detention Center in Miami, pending (12) deportation and in this case (13) his final death while being interrogated to determine (14) the refugee status that is never acquired.

Importantly, then, this young girl or woman becomes witness on both sides—the nation and migration—to the navigation of issues that spiral out of this process of migration. Born in Haiti, and migrating as a child herself to New York, she remains emotionally if not physically lodged in both aspects of her extended family dynamics. Indeed, the drama of the interplay of these two locations is central to the narrative, as are the contemporary histories of Haiti and the United States, operationalized through U.S. power relations. In her first novel, *Breath, Eyes, Memory,* then, the concern is with women, raped and destroyed by the nation, living abroad now, still carrying that pain from generation to generation. In the second, the sense communicated is that the violence wreaked by some state actors like *tonton macoutes* also migrated and thereby could maintain a shadowy presence in our communities. *The Dew Breaker*'s (2005) central metaphor, the scar that runs through the family, the nation, remains so far unable to be repaired.

In the final analysis, the interplay between migration and nation in the Danticat oeuvre offers a perpetual encounter with history, a past of pain and a history of oppression that identify themselves in Caribbean history in different ways, perhaps more visibly in Haiti. Her subsequent works, such as *After the Dance: A Walk through Carnival in Jacmel, Haiti* (2002) and *Behind the Mountains* (2004), similarly return home through actual journeys with the parallel documentations of those experiences.

Reversing the Installed End of Colonialism

Thomas Glave has a wonderfully imaginative story of a desire for another ending in "He Who Would Have Become 'Joshua,' 1791." Here he creates an idyllic narrative of a sensitive and creative African young man who rejects many of his society's cultural mandates for being in the world and in the end actually attained flight but never crosses the Atlantic and so also never becomes enslaved. Glave here preempts the automatic logic of enslavement and instead allows his character a sensuous relationship with the river and with another man that in the end protects them both from harm and actually envelops them without any sense of personal destruction.

The various enslavements and colonialisms in the end culminate in a large migration to the Caribbean and then outward to the colonial centers such as England, only to face an uneasy welcome there. This secondary migration, which has created a Caribbean diaspora and a similar set of identifiable nation-state diasporas, was notable in England with the arrival of the Windrush (1948), though there were small pockets of Caribbeans living in England before that. The identification of Afro-Caribbeans as a category in the last British census perhaps makes a particular community identification even more possible. Still, the tension between the needs of a constructed nation-state diaspora and a larger Caribbean diaspora remains an issue yet to be worked out, even as the African Union in 2005 claimed the African diaspora as its sixth region.

For Stuart Hall, theorist of diaspora, in describing "dislocation and disjuncture" as the formative conditions of his identity as a Caribbean diasporan subject, there is also a clear decision to stay and participate as a resisting subject and world citizen as he supports the second generation as it establishes itself. Writers of the Anglophone Caribbean colonial period documented well the rejection they experienced from their colonial "motherland" as the dynamic of this failed relationship, meticulously cataloged in texts like George Lamming's *The Emigrants* (1954), Samuel Selvon's *The Lonely Londoners* (1956), and Beryl Gilroy's *Frangipani House* (1982), the latter written, as she indicates, in the earlier time period but published in the 1980s, when black women's writing was able to find its audience.

For the writers of the first generation of Caribbean experience who migrated to the colonial centers of Europe or the United States, the engagement is with what it means to migrate as a colonial subject. The writing in this group is classic now, an entire body of literature based on migration. In these works, the reality of racism in the colonial center and the logic of rejection but also of re-creation of identity in a new place mark the narratives, but also the relationship of home to exile, which remains a major theme of these works. A similar version of things produced the *Négritude* movement of the 1930s with writers like Leon Damas, writing in his classic "Sell Out" about his disgust with the pretensions of French culture and its colonial extensions that produce fake individuals.

The creation of institutions that would support this writing has been fundamental in providing a context in which this work would appear. Thus, the role of journalists like Una Marson in developing the BBC's *Caribbean Voices* (Jarrett-Macauley) and Claudia Jones the *West Indian Gazette and Afro-Asian Caribbean News* (1958–64) (Boyce Davies, *Left of Karl Marx*) would give writers of the 1950s and '60s access and audience.

And in the 1980s and beyond, Caryl Philips with texts like *The Final Passage* (1985) and *The Atlantic Sound* (2000) captures a variety of movements, pulling in the various migrations undertaken in the African diaspora. The onward migration to Britain, the United States, Canada, or elsewhere becomes the material for the shifting discourses of nations and migrations and a parallel sense of "unbelonging" in either location. Migrating to London, as indicated above, produced a series of displacements, generationally articulated as a struggle for a Caribbean identity in diaspora. Beryl Gilroy, who died in 2000 and served as one of the first black teachers and headmistresses in England, has written about some of these initial encounters with racism in her autobiography, *Black Teacher* (1976), and, in her view, the female counterpart of E. R. autobiographical narrative that would become the 1967 film *To Sir with Love,* which starred Sidney Poitier.

Goulbourne and Chamberlain have suggested that familial contexts, both in the Caribbean and in the United Kingdom, favored the maintaining of transnational family links, and this was facilitated through a variety of common relations, such as "shared heritage" and common assumptions of possible futures. Still, one can perhaps now identify three generations: the first came with the Windrush (1948) and through the 1950s, the second was the post-1960s generation influenced by civil rights and Black Power discourses and not willing to accept racism, and the third generation was the Afro-Caribbean children who grew up and assumed the rights of the state. *Leave to Stay* (1996) with its subtitle, *Stories of Exile and Belonging,* edited by Joan Riley and Briar Wood, Riley having previously written *The Unbelonging* (1993), captures a genealogy of nation and migration movement in her introduction, which identifies that whereas her grandmother lived in the "same house all her life," in the Caribbean, as, say, Paule Marshall's grandmother character "Da-Duh" had, her mother's generation "had larger ambitions and more potential to realize these in the labour shortage of the post-war boom years" (1). Thus, by the time it gets to her:

> Migration played a large part in my formative years located as they were in the period of mass emigration from the Caribbean and similar regions. For me the concept became synonymous with economic advancement. . . . Despite

this, the experience of being migrant was not an easy one. It was isolation, being cut off from even the most basic aspects of cultural norms. Everything that had been immutable and changeable in our lives was suddenly called into question. It meant painful rethinking of values that had previously appeared universal as they came up against those values of equal strength in both England and the USA. (1–2)

For children of the succeeding younger generation, born in the host country, the determination to access the benefits of the state becomes as consciously identified as it is loaded with all the contemporary urban conflicts that one finds in youth culture in the United States. A variety of reports in London are beginning to identify some major urban problems brought on by glaring social inequities and treatment by policing officials and inequities in the educational systems alike. Much of this culminated in the riots in Tottenham and Hackney in 2011.

The (Im)Possibility of Return

Writing from Canada, though, Dionne Brand's *A Map to the Door of No Return: Notes to Belonging* (2001) suggests a kind of impossibility of any full return anywhere. Located at the intersections of the two diaspora—African and Caribbean—the metaphor of the actual "door of no return" at the exit of the slave castles to the New World and the imaginative door that exists once one leaves and enters "readiasporization" presents a major contradiction: "How to describe this mix of utter, hopeless pain and elation leaning against this door?" (41). Dionne Brand, in a series of self-reflective narratives, offers a contemplation on the meaning of migration, loss, and recovery, moving skillfully between island and metropolitan center, rural and urban, the sea and land, Africa and the diaspora. It is never a happy ending, for always it seems all of the levels of migration generate loss in an unhappy tension with (im)possible recovery. The Caribbean identity that she recuperates is one that has to be ready for continuous self-invention. "The place where all names were forgotten and all beginnings recast. In some desolate sense it was the creation place of Blacks in the New World Diaspora at the same time that it signified the end of traceable beginnings" (5).

One gets a similar sense in the creation of the pain of history in Marlene Nourbese Philip's *Zong* (2008), a work that returns to the past to recapture the Africans lost at sea, deliberately thrown overboard in the famous 1783 case by that name. It is a difficult work in which the writer seeks to recover the madness of that journey and, along the way, the sense that the islands, including

Tobago, always figure. The movement is, then, as suggested here, between the "long journey/long memory" and the more contemporary home and journey experience that the writers themselves carry forward in a range of imaginative experiences. Significantly trained as a lawyer, though, and as an established writer, it is as though she takes on the Zong case, again this time imaginatively representing the voices and silences of the victims of this massacre.

Thinking further about migration and the formation of the diasporic subject also allows us to examine how location produces identity. Thus, the same can be said for writers like Nourbese and her classic *She Tries Her Tongue: Her Silence Softly Breaks* (1989) and Dionne Brand's *In Another Place, Not Here* (1997).

Austin Clarke of Barbados, also living in Canada, provides a wealth of experience in the writing of home from migration. Memory, then, becomes significant to the articulation of a voice, as does actual experience. His autobiographical book *Pig Tails 'n Breadfruit: A Culinary Memoir* (2000), on good food, as he calls it, reminds one of the nostalgic Claude McKay poetic uses of food as a means of reconnection in ways more practical than achievable in his fictional writings. One sees a similar sensual use of Caribbean food in Opal Palmer Adisa's *Caribbean Passion* (2004).

Kamau Brathwaite had signaled a move to a second-level Caribbean and American diaspora identification in *Middle Passages* (1993), as we have shown earlier, the pluralizing of which captures the redefinition of a Caribbean diaspora identity in migration. Moving from a discourse in which identity was located in the first-level diaspora's dispersal—largely India or Africa—Caribbean writers assume a series of "unfinished migrations."

The contradictions in identification on either side of the migration movement indicate simultaneously a dual allegiance to family in both locations so that it is impossible, as Danticat's work reveals, to choose one group over the other but to embrace both aspects of these identities. Perhaps in a world in which being "posted" is not always possible, as she reveals most recently in the essays collected in *Create Dangerously: The Immigrant Artist at Work* (2011), the writer as immigrant navigates the writing of experience deliberately, adjusting to each as appropriate with the recognition that living at home may become completely untenable. Even if one had made a choice, as her uncle did, to remain home, circumstances in an unstable nation may rapidly change that sense of fixity. Dionne Brand offers a final thought in this continuing migration/nation/identity discourse, claiming that one is left with a series of continuing definitions, especially at the level of the imagination and through language.

"HAITI, I CAN SEE YOUR HALO!"

Living on Fault Lines

> In a scattered series of disparate islands the process
> [of the Caribbean quest for national identity] consists
> of a series of uncoordinated periods of drift, punctuated
> by spurts, leaps and catastrophes. But the inherent
> movement is clear and strong.
>
> —C. L. R. James, appendix, "From Toussaint L'Ouverture
> to Fidel Castro," in *The Black Jacobins*

Modifying the words of her song "Halo" for the "Hope for Haiti" telethon, popular singer Beyoncé, in a formation that seemed to exceed her own self-awareness, mouthed the words, "You're everything I need and more / it's written all over your face! / Haiti I can see your Halo." Indeed, the catastrophic experiences and the entire *Hope for Haiti Now: A Global Benefit for Earthquake Relief* (MTV Networks, January 22, 2010) fund-raising telethon, as did other efforts, served an amazing function of putting back on the table for consideration the important iconic history of Haiti as the first place where black resistance to enslavement became manifest as black freedom. I use the logic of the halo not in the way it appears in Christian iconography, but in the way the halo of what Haiti means radiates as a series of spatial principles across the African diaspora.

The contradictory history of Haiti that produced today's American hemisphere's poorest country runs up against a history of glory and transcendence. Thus, in many ways, Haiti becomes an important and extreme representation of the black condition: on the one hand, a past of dignity and legendary greatness; on the other, the starkness created by the initial history of dispossession, subsequent economic difficulty, brought on sometimes by horrendous leadership, often in collusion with external actors, environment, climate, location, but through it all, an amazing resistance of its people matched by an outstanding creativity.

The "halo" that Haiti throws out, then, is a series of conflicting representations, but above all a definition of an unrelenting humanity for African people: from what it takes to survive in the harshest conditions to how one begins again after everything falls apart. In other words, we see in each encounter with Haiti what it means to be human in the world, minus all the trappings of material possessions. Examining these conflicting representations and what they mean in the larger African diaspora, first of all, there is the gravitational pull of the history of Haiti that consistently radiates outward as representative of a series of configurations of African diaspora identities from enslavement to resistance, culture to literary and artistic transcendence.

Quickly looking up the scientific meaning of *halo*, one gets an energy field with gravitational pull, such as around a planet, a series of readable energies that radiate visibly and invisibly outward. Not only does a halo structure have a fairly small mass, even compared to a small moon, but the mass is evenly distributed radially. One instantly thinks, then, of one reading of the Caribbean as small island spaces that nevertheless radiate outward. Newer readings of space as infinitely expanding are also applicable.

An amazing series of articles and visual representations circulated on the Internet and other media in the wake of this 2010 earthquake and its aftermath of displacement of epic proportions. Interpretations of the meaning of Haiti proliferated: from the Caribbean, Latin America, and Black America (these are our brothers and sisters); North America and Europe (aid and recovery and an attempt to control the discourse); Africa (these are our people or I never knew they existed); Asia (how can we help—we feel your pain); a Euro-descended Brazilian diplomat (it is *macumba* [voudou] that has caused it); from Pat Robertson, an American evangelist (they made a pact with the devil to get liberated from slavery and so are paying back for this freedom now).

Caribbean responses, intellectual and political, have been consistently informed of the relevance of the historical meanings of Haiti, as was historian Hilary Beckles, principal of the University of the West Indies, Cave Hill, in his essay "The Hate and the Quake" (available on numerous websites). In this essay, Beckles, who had already discussed this point in an elaborate way in larger lecture and academic paper formats, was able to seize the occasion to rapidly distill some of the important historical research on Haiti and gesture to some kind of Caribbean-based initiative that seemed to be eroding under the U.S. takeover of the airspace and its plans for reconstruction.

It is important to indicate that Beckles was leader of a Caribbean delegation to the 2001 U.N. Conference on Race in Durban, South Africa, which had requested as part of a reparations package to the African peoples of the world that the French government repay the 150 million francs (then estimated by financial actuaries as US$21 billion) that had been levied against Haiti in exchange for its independence. This, it was argued, could be used to rebuild Haiti and end the ongoing suffering. A subsequent Summit of the Americas in Trinidad in 2008 had as central themes Haiti and Cuba being regularized not for goodwill or political expediency but to indicate that the Caribbean and Latin America and indeed the world could not afford, at this point in history, to have two isolated countries barred from full participation in the economics of the Caribbean, the Americas, and the larger international operations.

Caribbean responses such as this one have been geared to challenging the "popular perception that somehow the Haitian nation-building project, launched on January 1, 1804, has failed on account of mismanagement, ineptitude, and corruption." Instead, "Buried beneath the rubble of imperial propaganda, out of both Western Europe and the United States, is the evidence which shows that Haiti's independence was defeated by an aggressive North-Atlantic alliance that could not imagine their world inhabited by a free regime of Africans as representatives of the newly emerging democracy." Thus, while the American nation had been founded earlier but chose to retain slavery of African peoples as a fundamental flaw in the construction of a new world nation, Haiti, which also fought for and won its freedom, "proceeded to place in its 1805 Independence Constitution that any person of African descent who arrived on its shores would be declared free, and a citizen of the republic. For the first time since slavery had commenced, Blacks were the subjects of mass freedom and citizenship in a nation."

Thus, most significant to the systematic destruction of Haiti, Beckles argues, is the fact that Haiti, not being recognized by the French or the Americans, was isolated, as is Cuba still in 2013. Additionally, Haiti, called then the pearl of the Antilles, was desired by all of the other imperial powers who could not stand the idea that there was a free black nation in their midst while they were enslaving and colonizing everybody else. European powers jointly executed a stranglehold on Haiti, culminating in the 1825 French request for reparations "in return for national recognition."

Of course, it does not end there, as the Americans continued where the French ended and invaded and occupied the country more than once, in the early twentieth century, at one point for more than fifteen years (1915–34) and since then have maintained a relationship of control. Zora Neale Hurston in *Tell My Horse* (1938), who visited Haiti toward the end of the occupation, has some documentation of sentiments of Haitians in response to the American occupation. But she also describes a class/race scenario that continues as almost two Haitis: "Haiti of the wealthy and educated mulattoes and the Haiti of the blacks" (73). The combination of support for a horrible dictatorship by the Duvalier family and the subsequent interferences in the economy contributed to years of degradation. The most recent removal of Aristide by Colin Powell and Condoleezza Rice for the Bush II administration in 2004 provided the final gutting of the basic democratic state infrastructure and prepared the way for this most recent cataclysmic event. According to many Miami-based Haitians, this 2004 coup, which removed Aristide, took out the last vestige of Haitian control of its state, leaving it vulnerable to nongovernmental organizations, business interests, and nominal generic and ineffective leadership. Thus, at the earthquake of January 12, 2010, the collapse of the palace, the center of governance, and then President Preval's impotence, its people trapped and in pain became a final symbol of the destroyed promise of revolutionary Haiti.

The conclusion, according to Beckles again, is that "Haiti did not fail. It was destroyed by two of the most powerful nations on earth [France and the United States], both of which continue to have a primary interest in its current condition." Thus, the appearance of Americans and French as rescuers has to be put into this larger historical context. In more recent times, then, we see that the neocolonial business and foreign interests have always wanted access to Caribbean state power, in a way that they have achieved it in other places in the Caribbean. A version of "life and debt" continues, and the local and foreign bourgeoisie continue to buy up and kill local industry and replace it with imports, creating another consumer nation.

Haiti's halo appears also in the history of black enslavement and the resistance to it, the ongoing desires and struggles for black freedom, and the ongoing attempts to curtail it in myriad ways. We live a protracted struggle as we move individually and collectively against these twin extremes that work against black freedom. We see as well a not-so-pleasant aspect of that halo in failed, incompetent, uncaring, or "predatory leadership" in other parts of the Black World.

Haiti and the rest of the Caribbean and the entire Black World are therefore inextricably linked symbolically and through history. C. L. R. James, in *The Black Jacobins* (1938), perhaps the first history of Haiti from a Caribbean intellectual, writes that the idea of modernity for New World black and Caribbean people begins here: the first place where *Négritude* stood up. "West Indians first became aware of themselves as a people in the Haitian Revolution" (391). It is also important to remember that once Haiti was liberated, any formerly enslaved person arriving in Haiti was free once she or he reached its shores. Put in context, then, is the often levied terror threat floated by those against full independence for Martinique and Guadeloupe or Puerto Rico that if they got independence, they would end up impoverished like Haiti.

With this history articulated, casual fears of this nature have deep-seated historical intent to work against a unified Caribbean nation. So, just as the quest for human rights stirred the Haitian Revolution, the success or failure of Haiti has continued implications for Caribbean, African, and African diaspora human rights internationally.

On January 16, 2010, when then Senegalese president Abdoulaye Wade told a meeting of his advisers that Haitians are the sons and daughters of Africa, because the country was founded by slaves, including some believed to have come from Senegal, and offered free land to Haitians wishing to "return to their origins" following that week's devastating earthquake, which had destroyed the capital and buried thousands of people beneath rubble, it actualized one of the African diaspora entitlements identified in an essay, "Toward African Diaspora Citizenship" (Boyce Davies and M'bow). The argument advanced there was that the claims to be realized beyond the emotive, cultural, and spiritual connections included refugee rights, retirement rights, and travel, trade, and educational exchanges. Thus, following the passage of the African diaspora as the sixth region of the African Union (2005), what was left to be realized was a series of activations of this principle. The Wade declaration became the activation of but one of these. In a way, then, the African response to the Haitian tragedy corrected the paralysis following Hurricane Katrina in New Orleans and was the beginning of the reversal of some of the losses black communities have suffered. Wade had insisted that if a region was handed over, it should be in a fertile area—not in the country's parched deserts (Associated Press newswire, January 16, 2010).

Living on Fault Lines

An awareness that we are all "living on fault lines" allows us another way of understanding Caribbean space. Caribbean land- and seascapes not only are beautiful but can also include the violence of the environment. First is the violence of the abuse that has taken place throughout history on these same beautiful landscapes. The beauty camouflages at times that history of violence. Massive earthquakes and devastating hurricanes are not unusual phenomena. Following the destruction by the 2010 earthquake in Haiti, there was renewed clarity that we all live on several intersecting fault lines—economic, social, political, geographic. In this reading, and as it pertains to the Caribbean, all of these levels of violence also act tectonically, moving into place and then moving again, creating thereby the crises that seem to recur in our day-to-day existences.

As he confronted the intensity of the Caribbean landscape, Rochester, a representative Englishman, felt overwhelmed by everything: "Everything is too much, I felt as I rode wearily after her. Too much blue; too much purple, too much green. The flowers too red, the mountains too high, the hills too near" (Rhys 41). But such is the reality of the Caribbean.

The representative work of Caribbean artists is often marked by the dramatic palette of color, which dazzles in its intensity in the landscape as it does in the work of the artists who are not afraid to fully represent Caribbean realities. But what if that same beautiful landscape hides centuries of pain? What if this beautiful landscape exists on a fault line that can erupt with deadly result? This is also the reality of the Caribbean that generates often another submerged, inner text that produces the "catastrophe" that James identifies above.

Thus, human actors also make catastrophe. Jamaica Kincaid captured it in a different way in her *Small Place* when she described small and beautiful island locations that hide in their beauty centuries of evil and destruction, islands that exist on fault lines—geological, economic, and historical. Indeed, we all live as human beings with an illusion of safety and dominance until forces larger than us make us aware that we exist at the mercy of nature and can in one second be removed to an elsewhere with tragic consequences. It is that beautiful/ugliness of Paule Marshall's capturing of Barbadian speech that we have to keep always in our consciousness as we confront the meaning of a Haiti.

The intersection of the reality of beauty with the reality of violence in various forms provides the drama that resides in the work of the Caribbean artist. Thus, one often gets at times a clash, at others a dramatic contrast or a startling intersection, maybe a layering of the beauty of the landscape with that shadow text that startles in interesting ways, maybe a landscape that is totally harsh and no longer friendly.

Perhaps it is the artist who is able to render this most evocatively, as we see in the LeRoy Clarke piece titled "Haiti" from his *Douens* series. Attempting to capture the black condition, trapped, he says, in that place between becoming and destruction, his "Haiti" painting is stark black and white, did not have legs, he says, because he was working in a room that did not give him enough height to complete the painting (conversation, Cascade, February 22, 2010). We see an uncanny prophetic warning sometimes in the images of the artistic class, able to capture ahead of time and with poignancy some of these difficulties, a certain amputation of the dreams of transcendence in the wake of postflag independence. Following the 2010 earthquake, Clarke was able to complete the painting, which was, it seems, being created with some kind of inner sense of time and space. This has resulted in an entire series called *Eye Hayti,* which includes seventy-five black-and-white paintings, two of which are included here.

The way that James framed it, "From the start there had been a gap *[read: fault line],* constantly growing, between the rudimentary conditions of the life of the slave and the language he used. There was therefore in West Indian society an inherent antagonism between the consciousness of the black masses and the reality of their lives, inherent in that it was constantly produced and reproduced not by agitators but by the very conditions of the society itself" (*Black Jacobins* 407). It is significant that James here used language in a sense signaling one aspect of the discursive violence of which we speak. James interestingly makes the point here that Césaire's *Cahier* had united elements in modern thought, bringing together the African sphere of existence with the modern, that is, "No longer from external stimulus but from their own self-generated and independent being and motion will African and Africans move toward an integrated humanity" (402). Still, the delay in the full participation of women in the wake of this movement toward an "integrated humanity" has already been recognized in a variety of now at least three generations of Caribbean feminist scholarship.

Sylvia Wynter, as a Caribbean woman thinker, very early in her intellectual trajectory, began to analyze the gaps in our understanding of relevant questions of humanity. She asserts: "For it is with the discovery of the New World and its vast exploitable lands that the process which has been termed, 'The reduction of Man to Labour and of Nature to Land under the impulsion of the market economy'" (35) was able to be executed. There is, then, a direct relation between the Industrial Revolution seen as one of the key elements of modernity and the exploitation of the land-labor-capital relations in the New World. Thus, "In this aspect of the relation, the African slave represented an opposing process to that of the European, who achieved great technical progress based on the primary accumulation of capital which came from the dehumanization of Man and Nature. In general, he remained a transient, a frequent absentee, his society without roots in the new soil. The African presence, on the other hand, 'rehumanized Nature,' and helped to save his own humanity against the constant onslaught of the plantation system by the creation of a folklore and folk culture" (36).

Still, Wynter sees the Caribbean subject as caught in a "dual role, ambivalent between two contradictory processes." Thus, via culture Caribbean people have been able to make sense of this landscape, this environment, this new place, in which they had to "root" themselves and in several cases, as in the Maroon communities, creating replicas or new versions of social relations that existed in Africa.

Wynter had earlier suggested that so far, it was Fanon who had best grappled with the "complexity of our problem" that "we the New-World blacks, the first total colonials of capitalism, have internalized the 'standards and needs' of the external audience" (74). Here too was already the question of education, again following Fanon, that in her view was the "chief agent of indoctrination by which the colonized black internalizes the standards of the colonizer other" (75). So when Fanon says, "Black self-alienation is not an individual question; besides ontogeny and sociogeny," she says it makes perfect sense, as she had been experiencing the contradiction, the tendency to see everything African negatively and through the eyes of the colonizer. We are also mindful that Fanon had already addressed this question of colonial violence in *The Wretched of the Earth,* in this case violence not only as physical but also as epistemic, economic, social, and cultural.

A phenomenal contemporary challenge to the violence of landscape, political actors, and social and cultural forms of violence, though, comes also through the creative expression of Edwidge Danticat. Hers is a multilayered and textured representation that captured ahead of this particular 2010 trauma the experiences of difficult lives, a pain and disappointment that permeate a consciousness of being in a world that seems to reject one's humanity at every turn. Thus, the massacre of 1937 at the border between Haiti and the Dominican Republic is brought back for reconsideration in *The Farming of Bones* (1999). She sees in the logic of zombification an experience that parallels Clarke's *douendom* and finds common reference in other sleepers (the sleepers were then actually zombies) who need only salt on the tongue to wake them up (Florida International University, Eric Williams Memorial Lecture, Miami, 2004). A consciousness of living next to death, of innumerable funerals capturing the incremental deaths of the oppressed and impoverished Haitians that she writes about in *Brother, I'm Dying* (2007), is writ large in this recent tragedy, as bodies of Haitians were strewn everywhere, buried in mass graves, yards, or unaccounted for and carted off with the rubble. The violence of human actors that destroy her uncle's church and send him into hiding and then in search of refugee status meets the violence of the American state, determined to keep as many Haitians away, and detention in Chrome and his death. Had this not been a memoir, the actions seem as fanciful as if they came from a writer of the imagination of Edwidge, but alas, this is a documented event.

In the final analysis, in the Danticat oeuvre, there is a perpetual encounter with history, a past of pain and a history of oppression that also identifies the extremes in Caribbean history in different ways. In engaging the Haitian landscape, Edwidge Danticat presents layered diasporas: the larger African diaspora emanating from the trans-Atlantic enslavement, the other "middle passages" via the Caribbean Sea that create the Caribbean and Haitian diaspora, the intra-island migrations, and inter-island movements within the island of Hispaniola, but also a black women's diaspora. Violence acts on and causes subsequent actions of violence in those consigned to difficult lives on a Caribbean fault line.

Short essays like "We Are Ugly but We Are Here" capture economically and creatively the challenging history of Haiti, from the beginning rape of the native queen Anacaona to her contemporary daughters who migrate, sometimes because of a constructed hopelessness, and continue to battle via the sea their subsequent middle passages. A sense of hope permeates all, though, in this phrase that women tell each other in recognition of difficult conditions. "We are ugly but we are here." Ugliness captures the Fanonian wretchedness of the way that we are presented to the world but still a resolve to survive and transcend:

> "My grandmother believed that if a life is lost, then another one springs up replanted somewhere else, the next life even stronger than the last. She believed that no one really dies as long as someone remembers someone who will acknowledge that this person had in spite of everything been here. We are part of an endless circle, the daughters of Anacaona. We have stumbled, but have not fallen. We are ill-favored, but we still endure. Every once in a while, we must scream this as far as the wind can carry our voices: We are ugly, but we are here! And here to stay."

Similarly iconic, "Children of the Sea" presents a creative narration of two Haitian lovers, one migrating because he was pushed out by the threat of violence to an uncertain future. Along the way he witnesses a willed death reminiscent of enslaved Africans crossing the Middle Passage and foresees his impending death at sea. The other lover remains at home dealing with loss and his absence, trying still to continue a difficult life and always beginning again.

Each group claims its humanity by distancing itself from the one occupying the most wretched identity. This paradigm is indeed what had the promise of being challenged in the more recent global identification with Haiti. What we get in situations of intense pain, as the Haitian experience shows us, is how to stay human in the face of degradation, pain, large environmental struggles, and cataclysmic changes.

Sylvia Wynter in "Unsettling the Coloniality of Being/Power/Truth/Freedom: Towards the Human, after Man, Its Overrepresentation—an Argument" asserts that our current struggle is to "secure the well-being and therefore the full cognitive and behavioral autonomy of the human species itself; ourselves" (260), in the face of the Western bourgeois conception of the human that represents itself as though it were the human itself. That is, for her, struggles of race, class, gender, sexual orientation, and ethnicity, and struggles for the environment, global warming, severe climate change, and the sharply unequal distribution of the earth resources, "with Haiti being constantly produced and reproduced as the most impoverished nation of the Americas," are part of a systematic pattern to claim our humanity in the face of Western bourgeois ethnic class "man," which claims humanity as it leaves us constantly having to reassert ours.

Césaire's "Poésie et connaissance" ("Poetry and Cognition"), which James cites, needs to be recalled in this period, particularly since his lecture was delivered in Haiti in 1944. He had asserted then, "Poetic knowledge is born in the great silence of scientific knowledge." So, let us consider Trinidadian calypsonian David Rudder's classic "Haiti, I'm Sorry" (1988), which fulfills this argument of Césaire, as it captures the history but also the current condition in the ways that artists are able to do. It offers an apology for misunderstandings that resonate more than twenty years later in the 2010 earthquake. Here is what the third verse says:

When there is anguish in Port au Prince
Don't you know it's still Africa crying
We are outing fires in far away places
When our neighbors are burning
The middle passage is gone
So how come
Overcrowded boats still haunt our lives
I refuse to believe that we good people
Will forever turn our hearts
And our eyes . . . away

CHORUS
Haiti I'm sorry
We've misunderstood you
One day we will turn our heads
And look inside you
Haiti I'm sorry
Haiti I'm sorry
One day we'll turn our heads
Restore your glory.

Of course, there have been many other poetic versions that identify the iconic nature of the understanding of Haiti in the larger Caribbean or African diaspora context, from Brazilian chants, for example, accompanying groups such as Olodum and Ile Aiye, to a range of more formal poetic representations. Indeed, the chant "Remember San Domingo" (Boyce Davies, "Politics of African Identification") is identified as one of the early versions of the current calypso form when enslaved Africans in other parts of the Americas used the meaning of the Haitian Revolution to negotiate for their own liberation, as this had inspired a range of other liberation movements across the Americas. Thus, Wyclef Jean's "We are Africans Living in Haiti" (at the "Hope for Haiti" telethon) was echoed in the Senegalese president's offer of a homeland for Haitians in Senegal, as in Hugo Chavez's "Haiti does not owe us anything. We owe Haiti!" gesturing to Haiti's role in the Bolivarian revolution that liberated the first Latin American states.

As we confront the meaning of a Haiti, it is the artist, the creative spirit, who pulls from that well of inspiration and creates images that linger who is able to render these most evocatively. From Haitian artists Philippe Dodard to Gregory Vorbe, in canvases marked by intense blues and reds that serve as background, sometimes monstrous figures, other times historical or iconic, come alive to confront the viewer with a presence that haunts. They are a series of conflicting representations, for sure, but above all a definition of an unrelenting humanity: from what it takes to survive in the harshest conditions to how one begins again after everything falls apart—what it means to be human in the world, minus all the trappings of material possessions.

The iconic pilgrim of Gregory Vorbe's "Pilgrim of the Future" shows us what we do not want to see but must, the human condition and its ability to survive and still be there. But it is a representation that the artist presents as a signature for where we are today. A man/woman figure, with all his/her possessions on his/her back makes his/her way out of the fire, it seems, stick in hand with a gas mask covering his/her face, deliberately contemplating the next move through to a future that is yet to unfold but seems very dark on the horizon—a landscape now obscured by darkness. On the body of the figure are all the emblems from the African past. Recognizable patterns from Malian *bogolon* fabric recur as part of a skirt. And charms around the neck, perhaps indigenous, seem to provide the spiritual ammunition. A warrior figure in the end, arrows in a quiver, and a readiness to respond to danger give us a self-defensive if necessary but inquiring and contemplative posture. Leaves mimicking military camouflage also adorn the body, and a lone companion dog also contemplates the horizon. But it is a figure that is still standing, still here after the destruction, as is the indigenous native figure who remains still present in "I'm Still Here" or "We Are Ugly, but We Are Here." In other words, there is a determination to survive and be witness to the future even as those in charge of it prove they cannot lead, or have no answers to grave human problems.

The long cry of humanity is what embodies LeRoy Clarke's *Eye Hayti* series. There was for him a conjunction of events that allowed the creation of the series—the tsunami in Indonesia, the impact of the Darfur crisis, the world's capitalist economic collapse, culminating in the Haitian earthquake. Thus, in the work, he attempts to capture the scars let loose on the body of humanity, seeing Haiti as representing the cry of anguish, an enduring cry that echoes again the earthquake of 2010. So whereas an initial work was titled "Cry!" we see a series of anguished cries from various locations. The environment or landscape also cries in this imaginative rendition. Clarke returns to the idea that each work is like a chapter in his ongoing "languaging," as he terms it. This is a process that includes destroying existing motifs, removing rubbish, sifting through various elements in order to put oneself, as Wilson Harris does, in the spherical bombardment of space. Thus, the work becomes a reauthorizing of space, his way of looking at this through the various screams. His initial single "Haiti" piece then, a thirteen-foot piece now, attains symbolic release in this now seventy-five-piece *Eye Hayti* series, giving birth, as it were, to numerous versions or aspects of the experience that is Haiti, but is really also the world in pain. The mythopoetics of Haiti that Clarke creates in *Eye Hayti* move backward and forward through Caribbean historical time, but also across the breadth of spaces we inhabit, extending to a way of engaging the world (conversation in "Legacy House" Cascade, Trinidad, February 17, 2013). In this way, the halo that Haiti produces, with which this chapter began, also has global resonances artistically.

LeRoy Clarke painting (from series *Eye Hayti . . . Cries . . . Everywhere*), "Forged in de Iron of My Word" (2011).

Using a veranda as a seamstress workspace, in Haiti. Courtesy of Noelle Theard.

Bar and restaurant, Haiti. Courtesy of Noelle Theard.

Street scene in Haitian village showing opposition of big house and small house. Courtesy of Jean Willy Gerdes.

LeRoy Clarke painting (from series *Eye Hayti . . . Cries . . . Everywhere*), "Eye Thunder Say
. . . Say!" (2011).

10

CARIBBEAN GPS
Compasses of Racialization

Caribbean Global Positioning Subject

There is always a moment of quiet pause when I encounter Caribbeans who casually declare that there was or is no racism in the Caribbean. Some indicate that the United States is where they first encountered racism. Others, in even more extreme articulations, say that Caribbean people do not experience racism in the United States in the same way as do African Americans. From the African American side at times comes an argument that Caribbeans are treated differently than are African Americans. Yet all research reveals that racism is an international phenomenon that appears differently nuanced according to historical and cultural locations; it is also a structural socioeconomic organizing system that creates a hierarchy in which race determines how individuals and communities are able to access resources and power; how they are located in systems from education to criminal justice, athletics to the entertainment industry.

I try to think back to my home Caribbean experience, of course, with the hindsight that comes from contemporary awareness, and recall that there were schools, Carnival bands, certain types of jobs, and residential patterns for white people, many of whom were expatriates, but some of whom were also Trinidadian by birth and belonging. I also remember stories told by the senior friends of our family about visiting Englishmen, during the colonial days, who were incompetent but who were placed as supervisors over more adept local workers and of white children who casually disclosed the working-class-level jobs their fathers held in England before coming to the

Caribbean to managerial posts. Not long ago, a friend drove me around Point Fortin in southern Trinidad and casually showed me the residential patterns of different working categories in the oil industry in days past. White workers were accorded more privileged accommodations. And returning home as an adult, and attending a performance of a friend in the Trinidad Country Club in Maraval, in the 1990s, it was evident that there was still a largely white membership and that workers tended to be of African descent. Put into racial context is the barring of an African American couple in the 1970s who attempted to use the relationship with the Trinidad Hilton Hotel where they were staying to play tennis at the club. Although there had been a long history of this being a space that privileged whiteness, the obviousness of this affront became one of the generating incidents for the Black Power movement in Trinidad, as it clarified the international nature of white supremacy and its manifestations in the Caribbean. Indeed, there were locations that remained so far removed that they remained invisible to black people in their day-to-day interactions. So in the normalized combination of internationally practiced racism combined with colonialism, but also with a legacy of slavery, race was used as an organizing system for societies across the Americas. Benefits still accrue and are carried over into contemporary times to those who were beneficiaries of resources acquired in earlier periods.

As in the United States, examples of everyday racism become normalized. In the Caribbean, these often manifested as intragroup color differences and access to certain kinds of employment. Teachers, in my experience, tended to privilege the children who were lighter and with certain Euro-derived hair textures. Some cousins ensured that they had children with men who were of some Euro-descended or other ethnic racial origin and as a result changed in one generation the physical appearance of all the succeeding children.

The point is that the obvious racial terrorism of the U.S. South or the hardcore Jim Crow racial segregation and sharecropping systems that African Americans experienced up and through the civil rights era are taken as the marker of what racism is by Caribbeans in the United States. But activists like Marcus Garvey indicated that as he traveled through the black world at the beginning of the last century, everywhere he went the condition of black people was subordinated by racialized economic structures. This, after all, was why international political movements emanated from various locations. And it is why the Universal Negro Improvement Association was formed. This was also why Caribbean activists saw their struggles as linked to African Americans. A young black man from the Caribbean, Stokely Carmichael, first mouthed, in the United States, the phrase *Black Power,* and Caribbean students were active in Black Power activism in the United States and in the Caribbean. And even in the contemporary period, there have been examples of Caribbean people caught brutally in the web of racial subordination. An understanding that racism is a structural phenomenon that uses epidermal racial characteristics to create a hierarchy of subordination and domination into which everything is ordered from leisure to the judicial system is a necessary safeguard. Even if one is living in a Caribbean self-governing country, this system is in place at invisible levels—economic and political.

I have already identified myself as coming of age in the United States in the 1970s, in a context in which Caribbean identity saw itself as linked to a larger Black Power struggle in the United States. Indeed, the Caribbean developed its own Black Power movements that markedly changed access for Black people. But I was a child of independence and the practical politics of a prime minister who was also a historian who had written *Capitalism and Slavery*. In the United States, I attended the historically black Howard University, which for many Caribbeans was a fulfillment of a deep historical desire, given the iconic meaning of this university across the African diaspora.

* * *

The Caribbean offers an important understanding of how a history of diasporic dispersals can shape the historical and contemporary consciousness of a people. This begins with the coming together of the experiences of suffering and exile that grew out of slavery and colonialism and therefore provided a consciousness of a resistance to enslavement. The Caribbean diasporic imaginary then includes the first iconic revolution against slavery, the Haitian Revolution (1804), which in the end was a movement with trans-Caribbean actors and the Pan-Africanist movement (which, held in 1900, was organized by Trinidadian Sylvester Williams), whose aim was the bringing together of Black world political thinkers and actors from the Americas and Africa in a common opposition to Western domination of Africa and its peoples worldwide.

Pan-Africanism then served as the ideological anchor for much of the twentieth century, with Hubert Harrison (1883–1918) from St. Croix who provided an oratorical and organizational example in the United States or Dr. Harold Moody (1847–1922) from Jamaica among those who would influence some of the thinking and strategies of the Garvey movement, which itself successfully mobilized Black racial unity within working-class communities in the Caribbean, the United States, Latin America, the Pacific, and Europe beginning in 1914. In the wake of that movement, but from the late 1920s on through the 1950s, iconic diasporan Caribbean political actors like George Padmore, Amy Ashwood Garvey, and C. L. R. James created Pan-Africanist institutions like the International Friends of Abyssinia and the International Service Bureau. In the 1960s, Kwame Toure and Walter Rodney did student and grassroots organizing at the popular social-movement level.

Although many Caribbeans, Africans, and African Americans now teach, work, or attend major universities as though it was automatic, or out of their own self-generated successes, it is important to recall Walter Rodney's assertion: "Black people are here in these institutions as part of the development of black struggle, but only as a concession designed to incorporate us within the structure" (112–13).

As it relates to the Caribbean activists, Joyce Moore Turner provides an informed analysis in her *Caribbean Crusaders and the Harlem Renaissance* (2005). The daughter of Richard Moore, the author of *The Name "Negro": Its Origin and Evil Use* (1960), she provides interesting detail and background to this period that illustrates the activist work of four friends—Hubert Harrison, Otto Huiswoud, Cyril Briggs, and Richard Moore—identifying how they came to their positions as young men and indicating that they were four of a much larger and more diverse population.

My recent work on Claudia Jones, from Trinidad, a black radical intellectual who was solidly working class in orientation and joined the Communist Party USA (CPUSA) at age eighteen and indicates that her family, as were others in the 1930s, were victims of overt racism, confirms Moore Turner's analyses. Claudia Jones engaged directly in intellectual and activist work that has located her solidly within both the Caribbean and African American history as well as an international African diasporic radical intellectual tradition. Importantly, Jones indicates that her activism was precipitated by Jim Crow racism and the Scottsboro Boys trials and defense, 1931–37.

Reading Racism in Theory and the Academy

Talking to a Puerto Rican colleague who works on race a few years ago, I lamented to him that entering these discourses on race is like entering a field of mud. You never know when your feet will sink into the oozy mess, but you know that you have to get to the other side, only to discover that the field is bigger than you thought and the other side recedes into the distance the more you walk. I was actually imagining a walk across Port Meadow in

Oxford to a pub on the other side, as I had just returned from teaching in a summer program there.

He responded laughingly that for him, it would be more like entering a field loaded not with mud but various types of fecal matter, though of course he did not use such polite language. I have to admit that I had also thought of the latter, again recalling Port Meadow, but thought it would not be such a nice thing to say to someone who works on race. And so I chose the more polite mud metaphor. So, here I am sharing it with you and having you enter the field with me but letting you choose your matter—definitely not a promising prospect for those who want to keep their shoes clean! One of my daughters, then a little girl, said, when I told her the story, maybe hip-length boots, as the ones seen in those fly-fishing commercials, would be best. But choose the filth metaphor of your choice, for messy it is.

The messiness of race actually helps me understand why when we encounter the most rabid forms of racism, it feels precisely like being confronted with something nasty, something foul and evil, why the discourses are so cloudy, the theoretics so arbitrarily located, so unfinished, inadequate, the emotions so raw. We are all implicated even as we try to be color-blind, or try to see past race to the already premature "postrace" or "postblackness" that some attempted to introduce into U.S. racial discourse. But that too quickly became a form of racism-engineered denial, as even President Obama had to admit that he never bought into postrace as a construct: "I never bought into the notion that by electing me, somehow we were entering into a postracial period" (*New York Times,* May 4, 2012).

The agency then comes only in the confrontation, the challenge, and the possibility of transformation, or what Khalil Gibran Muhammad calls "historical literacy" (conversation with Bill Moyers, 2012). Confronting racism then begins appropriately with a healthy realization of this dirtiness, this smelliness, this foulness, an unpleasant history that many would want to forget.

One other contextual narrative is important. Once at a very elegant dinner, a dark-skinned Caribbean woman responded openly to her fellow table mates after a nationally ranked African American lawyer had recounted some of the history of struggles against racism as part of his speech. She indicated publicly that she could not relate to his talk, as in the Caribbean there was no racism. Several at our table remained politely silent. A few table guests, including other Caribbeans, not wanting to let such a blanket statement sit unchallenged, tried vainly in hushed tones to clarify for the woman the way that racism manifests in the Caribbean and that she would have been a victim of it without knowing and that many of the gains that people assume as rights now were indeed part of that struggle with which she was disidentifying.

Several variations of this story exist and are recounted from time to time in a normalized way by Caribbean people. But I have heard of stories of African Americans also telling Caribbeans that they are not black. Definitions about what constitutes blackness or who is able to claim blackness persist, as do the confusions about racism. Sometimes there is an attempt to suggest that the children of Caribbean and Africans have ended up being the beneficiaries of educational systems meant for African Americans who should have traditional, third-generation, claims.

The problem is that the U.S. standard of virulent racism is often taken as the norm, so if one does not have in one's history an Emmett Till or the legal sanctioning, say, of a *Plessey v. Ferguson* or children being spat upon as they tried to integrate schools in the South or the horrendous images from documentaries like *Eyes on the Prize* or movies like *To Kill a Mocking Bird* or *Mississippi Burning,* then for some racism did and does not exist. A more developed historical literacy is required, as there are several practices that use race as the lever for social hierarchies throughout the Americas of which the Caribbean is a part that qualify. One can often be a victim of racism in the Caribbean and not realize it, as it may be conjoined with class subordination, as it often is in Latin America and the Caribbean. Whitening—at the aesthetic, social, economic, demographic levels—occurs in various forms across the Americas. Thus, the ways that racism gets masked in the Caribbean include being located historically in the larger world context in a series of racialized frameworks. In these contexts, the Caribbean occupies an exotic space, racialized, under a variety of colonial and global marketing practices. Mimi Sheller offers a helpful series of categories of ways that the Caribbean has been consumed from European arrival until the present time.

So confronting U.S. racism as a Caribbean subject depends on several knowledge factors from political orientation to experience. The definition that those with historical literacy work with is one less dependent on individual acts of prejudice and beyond the epidermic but more attuned to the structural or institutional organization of a society that creates a hierarchy in which all aspects of one's existence (housing, policing, educational, judicial, social, cultural, leisure, and sports) are affected and advance some groups and subordinate other groups of people based on their racial designation.

Nations and civilizations like to construct pretty narratives that mask ugliness because the national narrative comes to represent the founding aspects of the constructed national identity: cute flags, anthems, unitary histories, favorite founding fathers and leaders. And the trick is to have everybody buy into these narratives even as they attempt to subordinate the messiness of differences. For people of color, located in racially structured societies, there are daily reminders of racial location and identity so there can be no forgetting, and for those seriously confronting racism, there similarly can be no forgetting. That re-membering that Morrison identifies in *Beloved* (1987) is what can help us, as painful as it is get to the other side of this messy field, filled with the wrecks of slave ships, lynched bodies, raped women holding their dying babies, exterminations, colonialisms, children separated from their parents, bloody rebellions and uprisings, and so on that seem to keep extending without end, as much a part of the history of the New World as the Old.

I am deliberately locating racism, then, in terms of its messy past and so want to dispense with the easy notions of "reverse racism." In my view, to talk of racism in such casual terms robs it of its white supremacist overlay and somehow locates a kind of symmetry in social relations or relations of power that are not in any way symmetrical. To take racism in this way some-how also empties it of its history and denies the centuries' accumulation of scientific theories and related one-sided wealth accumulation, the erasing of knowledge systems, the trafficking in bodies, the extermination of peoples, the destruction of cultures that has been racism's legacy as it interacted with capitalist projects. The casualness of the application of "reverse racism" means that a *bloco Afro* (Carnival band), formed in Brazil because Africans were kept out of Carnival, can be accused as operating on the same terms as the former when its existence was itself in response to the exclusions of deeply entrenched structural racist operations.

Although I agree that there are different racisms, I see these as operating historically and geographically with different racial codes and in different locational contexts, all with the bottom line being a systematic organization of society on the basis of superficial biological characteristics, called race, and then the installing of a variety of oppressive practices on these subordinated groups such that every aspect of their lives is affected. The "polite racism" of the United Kingdom masks the structural inequities that keep white people of a certain class in a position of advantage from generation to generation. Racism, then, is a system of dominance, a system of oppression that interacts with, produces, and reproduces other systems of dominance so that there is a network or web of interactions that efficiently attempts to lock or contain those racialized subjects that it interpellates in these subordinated locations.

Stuart Hall's position is instructive here, as he calls for historical specificity as one delineates *racisms:* "It is only as the different racisms are historically specified—in their difference—that they can be properly understood as 'a product of historical relations' . . . [and that] there might be more to be learned from distinguishing what, in common sense, appear to be variants of the same thing: for example, the racism of the slave South from the racism of the insertion of blacks into the 'free forms' of industrialist-capitalist development in the post-bellum North; or the racism of Caribbean slave societies from that of the metropolitan societies like Britain" ("Race, Articulation, and Societies Structured in Dominance" 337). Thus, the versions of racism that Hall identifies have to do with geopolitical expressions structured in dominance and hegemony.

A variety of scholars have identified the varying theories of race, racism, and racial inequality through the years, from angles that engage social, biological, political practices. Mario Barrera in *Race and Class in the Southwest* offers a helpful overview of a variety of theories that he classifies broadly as deficiency theories, which include the "classic racist theories" that identified deficiencies in biology, social structure, and culture as the explication for racial inequities; bias theories, which are largely sociological in orientation and began the process of explaining racism in terms of social and economic structure; and structural discrimination theories, which began to look more closely at racism as a product of capitalist systems, colonialism, and so on. Barrera would find that "of the various theoretical models that have been set forth to explain the persistence of racial equality in the United States, the internal colonial model is the most comprehensive and the one that most accurately reflects empirical reality" (212). In this way, he is able to account for more than, say, African populations and to locate Chicanos, in his analysis. And this becomes important, since U.S. racism tends to identify race only in oppositional terms, leaving out a host of other, also raced and subordinated, identities.

This approach is helpful to me in my own reading, as it also has the capability of locating gender, and in particular women's oppression, as Maria Mies (1988) and others do, within the frame of oppression. Some would say that slavery normalized race or that capitalism normalized labor exploitation. The debates about race, even Stuart Hall's assertion that "race is thus, also, the modality in which class is 'lived, the medium through which class relations are experienced, the form in which it is appropriated and fought through,'" are often still inadequate, in my view, to speak to the range of representations of race as it inflects gender, sexuality, ability, class, and so on. But recent ongoing work in this area has consistently provided new paradigms needed in order to fully apprehend the workings of racism in our societies. For example, Michelle Alexander's *The New Jim Crow: Mass Incarceration in an Age of Colorblindness* (2012) provides a way of reading the parallels between the two systems that may disappear without a full understanding of the similarities in the two systems, and the derivations of the latter from the former. Thus, it may be useful, for example, to see how Latinos and Caribbeans fare in that system, how they are racialized by these means. Some racializing systems remain invisible until they reach crisis proportions. The study *Criminal Justice v. Racial Justice of Afro-Caribbeans in England* (Runnymede) reveals the overpopulation of Caribbeans in the United Kingdom. And Julia Sudbury, in *Global Lockdown: Race, Gender, and the Prison-Industrial Complex* (2005), describes an internationalizing of prison culture in which people of color remain the prime targets of the system.

In this chapter, I examine only a few of these modalities by examining the necessity of "reading" racism by Caribbean subjects. Although it is true that racial and racist codings vary from location to location, for safety only, operating in a new environment requires new and heightened protection instincts. The examples I want to work with include popular readings of race, representation of black males as raced and gendered subjects, and the issue of "blonding" as a type of whitening in the popular culture as an acting out of racial representations of desired and desirable black female subjects.

Reading Racism in Mass Media and Political Culture

The 2011 riots in Tottenham, Hackney, and Birmingham, England, provide us with an opportunity to look again at some of the early discussions on how racism works itself through mass culture. Uniformly, the British media, the police, and the political class referred to the black and white working-class youth as delinquents, badly parented, thugs from somewhere else. The positions that analyzed the provocative nature of policing, the murder of a black youth by the British police, or inner-city poverty as triggers were scarce. So a racial reading dominated all state apparatuses.

In "The Organic Crisis of British Capitalism and Race," the introductory chapter to *The Empire Strikes Back: Race and Racism in '70s Britain*, the writers assert that "racial forms of domination do not develop in a linear fashion but are subject to breaks and discontinuities, particularly in periods of crisis which produce qualitative changes in all social relations" (Centre for Contemporary Cultural Studies, University of Birmingham, 11–12). This analysis is applicable to this contemporary British urban racial situation as well. Stuart Hall has an insightful delineation of this in his "Racist Ideologies and the Media" between "overt" racism and "inferential" racism. An excellent example of the latter was the CNN initial coverage of the search for a culprit in the Boston Marathon bombing (April 15, 2013) in which John King kept insisting, in news coverage that people around the world access, that his sources indicated a "dark-skinned man." Without confirmation, a set of racial meanings and ideologies circulated and fed into dominant narratives of people of color as the enemy. These scenarios in real time allow us to see how structures of racism circulate and operate.

Racism, in its historical context and then within the locational particulars that determine how it operates in a given place and time, reemerges. For me, then, the particular racial inscriptions and reinscriptions have to be read and reread within the context of a multistranded critical analysis, at the levels of the systemic or institutional structures, at the levels of discourse and ideology, at the levels of the social, personal, and political. Necessary, as well, is an interactive mode that locates the academy, political systems, and mass culture in a constantly and mutually inflecting system. So a few months before these riots, an item was reported as "14,000 British Professors—but Only 50 Are Black" (*Guardian,* May 27, 2011) that provided the statistics for black professors in British universities as being abysmally low and unchanged in the past decade. The absence of opportunity for full participation in the society, then, can be seen as having a direct correlation with the frustration felt by inner-city youth who, if we follow the other statistics, remain disenfranchised.

Close reading, as is done in the literary field or some form of cultural critique, provides some of those skills of analysis, along with the reading of specific information from a range of other sciences. These become indispensable tools for readings of racism beyond the personal and prejudicial. I am also using the notion of "reading" racism as "reading" is used both in semiotics and in African American rhetorical practice as "signifying" or disclosing or proclaiming publicly in a confrontational manner on an adversary's general behaviors, intimate practices, and general public persona. Reading racism, then, means (1) reading its hidden and explicit codings, its various languages, behaviors, gestures, practices at the literal and symbolic levels; (2) reading the historical codes in contemporary contexts; (3) reading its public trials, confrontations, reading beyond its biological factors or assertions (brain weight and size, I.Q., physical characteristics, and social pathology) to its practices; (4) reading the range of theoretical positions; and (5) its intersections in a systems-of-dominance approach in order to reveal its hidden and explicit interactions.

Thus, contemporary U.S. "Tea Party" Republican rhetoric of "wanting our country back" is the identical language used in populist white supremacist discourses upon the arrival of black people in London in the 1960s. "We want our country back!" then becomes coded language for a return to an uncomplicated past in which black people existed only in subordinate ways or were absent. In the slavery era, it was illegal to educate a black person. In the 1950s and '60s, there had to be legal struggles in order for black elementary schoolchildren and university-age students to attend the institutions of their choice in the United States. The racist, white supremacist logics then dictated that black people should not have access to these institutions. Laws and policies enforced this and had to be challenged legally. The white population and their popular culture had maintained the notion of racial exclusion from education through hate groups like the KKK and through the popular, everyday, behaviors of women, for example, spitting at children trying to go to school. Thus, governors in Alabama and Mississippi positioned themselves sometimes in front of the doors of institutions, in order to block entry of black students; the National Guard had to be sent in; black people had to march, organize, and basically embarrass the United States internationally for their basic human rights. Reading the racist, white supremacist logics of, say, a governor standing in front of a university today would not work. Instead, a reading of white supremacist logics at the level of policy will reveal processes to dismantle affirmative action and reinscribe "family values," already racially and gender located; cutbacks in education while high-tech prisons are constructed; more frequent death penalty scenarios for a young men for whom there is "reasonable doubt," while a young white woman who was at the scene of a murder in Europe is let off on a technicality and for a minute becomes "America's sweetheart"; or domestic terrorists who carry out executions under the guise of mental disturbance. At the university level, deliberately working to dismantle or contain Africana Studies programs and departments becomes a microrepresentation of the same.

Thus, the metaphor of the governor standing and blocking the door of the university has to be read at the level of the symbolic, at the level of the overtext, as institutional gatekeeping that remains, that is, blocking access by withdrawing the resources that might make it possible for those formally excluded to enter. At the same time, the general white population is no longer jeering and spitting at the students but is repeating those behaviors in the way that they vote, which issues they support, and so on, and their saying yes to jails, to conservative leadership, to death penalties, and so on. Thus, all are located in an overarching system of racist practices at the more formal level of citizenship.

I am reasserting that there are particular constants in terms of racial oppression—that is, that a particular race occupies the position of dominance and then constructs its world as normative and then subordinates all others, on the basis of superficial biological characteristics, socially and institutionally, so that one's entire life is held hostage to these constructs, circumscribed and located in terms of a racial hierarchy that equates whiteness with privilege, oppression, dominance, and a variety of others held in relation to their intersection with this dominance. But I am also saying that at the popular level of racial practice, there has to be a variation in reading in order to come to meaning, even as one looks at the constants. Lucius Outlaw asserts that although the term *race* has not remained constant, the deployment of *race* has virtually always been in service to political agendas.

This became even clearer to me in 1995, after spending seven months in Brazil and witnessing the particular hierarchies of race in that country and the way that one has to engage in different reading practices in order to come to knowledge. Whiteness, in this context, occupies a sliding scale of power and privilege, allowing a number of people of other than Aryan appearance to enter and claim whiteness, but still holding intact the subordination of African and Native American identities. Within the logics of *blanqueamento*, or the ideology of whitening, according to do Nascimento, the aggression exists at the physical and biological level and the economic, which dictates that African-descended people must turn progressively lighter in color, in order to obtain better living conditions, employment opportunities, social relations, and respect, in short to fully exercise their very human conditions and citizenship.

What is specific here is that as a variety of people struggle to occupy a more favorable position in the hierarchy, "whiteness" as the signifier for privilege and power remains in place and is able to assert itself and maintain this dominance. So, while there is slipperiness in the in-between categories and those who get located there, an African or native identity remains abject and despised or eroticized and desired.

In September 1995, a year after the end of formal apartheid, I traveled to South Africa to work as an external examiner at the University of Durban, Westville. This historically was a university for Indian students, I was told. What became clear to me, during my brief stay, was that over time, hard-core practicing racists are able to abandon the rabid, foaming-at-the-mouth variety of racism for a calmer, gentler, more acceptable structural version. Thus, even under the leadership of Mandela and all the hope that was expressed at the abolishing of formal apartheid, the rigid racial structures were still deeply in place at the level of housing, schooling, economic systems, employment, and so on. White South Africans obviously had to be assured that their basic situation of privilege was not going to be radically changed. So what was abandoned were explicit social practices of racism in favor of the reliance on the systemic. Indeed, being in South Africa in this period was strangely reminiscent of being in the United States, where, unlike Brazil, one may have elected officials who are black and see black people represented in the media and so on, but the deep racial structure is still in place. In fact, South Africa, it became clear, was in some ways ahead of the United States in the number of elected officials, it being an African majority country, though still with the lingering structures of apartheid. Many colored South Africans benefited from the state and functioned as a buffer between the white racists and the black majority, and actually in many cases bought into the racial logics as applied to the black majority, even as they themselves recognized how they were located in relation to whiteness. Today, some colored South Africans are able to import those same race-based practices into their conduct in the United States or the United Kingdom, which share similar hierarchies. The United States would nonetheless return to the overt articulation of racial difference, ironically, once Obama became president in 2008: a congressman who shouted "You lie!" during the first State of the Union Address by a black president, a Supreme Court judge who mouthed a disagreement with an analysis publicly, a white woman governor who was captured shaking her finger in the president's face, and explicit racist commentary on right-wing news stations are only a few examples. Deep institutional racial structures persist or are even heightened as if to compensate, even as one has representative black leadership. The lessons of colonialism, neocolonialism, and postcolonialism proliferate here. And in this context, if we use the colonial model that has been part of Caribbean history, then Obama becomes contradictorily a type of neocolonial/neoliberal leader in the United States while having access to the full power and might of the United States. Still, within the logic of racism, there is a conscious decision to devalue the presidency, for the moment at least, rather than accord the normal respect for the protocols that go with the office when held by a white man.

Just as the particulars of location in these three areas (the United States, South Africa, Brazil) are on record as having the most overt forms of racism in place, present variations on the same that have to be studied and addressed in each time and context, so too the particulars of time and place in U.S. racism have to be reread and thus confronted and rearticulated. Rather, there has to be an interactive effect so that the operations of racism in policy, the academy, and mass culture are seen as creating and re-creating each other in some sort of continual motion. At the symbolic level, all the racist codes that have historically structured this society and operating both at the macro and micro texts of U.S. racism allow racial codings to remain intact.

Reinscriptions at the level of the media are loaded, particularly when media become the space of a series of popular articulations of race. In reality, mass culture, television, film, the print media, radio talk shows, magazines, and the mouths of everyday people continue to articulate very basic racist assumptions. Popular racism is then reinscribed by conservatives and liberals alike.

A number of scholars have identified the ways that racial stereotypes at the national and international levels exist in U.S. popular culture, especially the filmic, representational level. Polly McLean's "Mass Communication, Popular Culture, and Racism" has an excellent overview of the issues pertaining to racism in mass culture. Popular magazines like *People* from time to time identify the racism of the film industry in the way the academy excludes black film and black actors from recognition, or still consigns them to specific roles, still necessitating NAACP Image Awards. Additionally, mass culture and the possibilities of the Internet and various forms of social media have spawned a new generation of crude racial hatred jokes at a very base level. The proliferation of conservative radio talk shows has played a major role in the spreading of particular forms of traditional racist thinking, as has the active participation of the callers who become the everyday people who are cultivated and represented. At the same time, television talk shows, even as they demystify whiteness, present a particular pathologizing of black people and working-class whites by the very framing of the questions, as a variety of working-class people display the pathologies that then go on to deploy, reinscribe, and confirm racial and class meanings of inferiority.

Challenging Eurocentric Assumptions of Knowledge

The academy has been historically located as one of the sites of ideological reproduction. Indeed, university-based academies have always been the primary site of the assertion and reproduction of a wide range or basic racial theories. The academy has also been the site of particular creation and maintenance of racial structures, interacting with policy makers and the media. Thus, the university is never an innocent and objective bystander.

It is in this context that maintenance of a traditional curriculum ends up reproducing the larger structures and contexts of white supremacy. The classic racist theories that have shaped the way the traditional academy functioned remain in place, as the work of scholars who have done a significant amount of work on the nature and theory of race remains largely unread. The academy and the various canons have been the site of the maintenance and deployment of specific social values of a people over the years. At the level of ideology, the various interactions connect the academy with the policy makers and the popular. Struggles for "diversity" end up becoming white-washed symmetrical university multiculturalisms. Mainstream departments (English, Philosophy, History, Political Science) remain "hearts of whiteness." The academy becomes, then, another project that reproduces and reasserts racial hegemony.

The intellectual community, then, become complicit to the extent that recent advances about race, gender, and sexuality remain outside the frames of knowledge acquisition or transmission. Additionally, the disciplinary boundaries that remain intact allow reduced analyses such that Toni Morrison, in *Playing in the Dark,* makes the point that an incredible amount of negotiating has to take place to allow race to escape from the textual reading and writing of a variety of American texts.

Confronting racism as a Caribbean intellectual, then, means, for me, the ongoing interrogation of racial meaning and the hierarchies that are embedded at a variety of levels at the academy, policy, and popular culture. Thus, even Women's Studies Departments and their canons engage in a similar repetition of race-based paradigms at the epistemological and pedagogical levels. In other words, the academy becomes complicit and continues to function, as it has in the past, as the site for the production of a particular privileged reading of society.

What is interesting in this context is that the racist biological theories and the subsequent social-deficiency theories continue to drive institutional decisions in terms of hiring and teaching, and thus also affect public policy. Officials of universities still describe faculty as "minority hires." From public policy to popular culture, race-based logics operate in myriad ways.

But Black Studies?

If we periodize Black Studies as beginning as a formal institutional structure in the 1960s, then from a contemporary vantage point, we can now account for the impact of Cold War politics, which also had a lingering impact on Africana Studies departments that stayed far away from black Left scholarship and instead worked the safe integrationist issues. Not too many scholars would follow the path of a Cedric Robinson or an Angela Davis in terms of fleshing out some of the aspects of the black Left tradition. According to Sylvia Wynter, in "On How We Mistook the Map for the Territory and Re-imprisoned Ourselves in Our Unbearable Wrongness of Being . . ." (2005), once Black Studies entered the very order of knowledge it had contested, something different happened. This something different was indeed an attempt to operate by the standards of the academy, to get people tenured and promoted, to acquire the prizes of the academy such as named chairs that sometimes reproduce models of enslavement, some carrying names that are highly suspect or insulting, or both. And above all the tendency was to buy into the same epistemological frameworks—for example, the disciplines and the value of certain kinds of work, certain kinds of publications.

The delinking of activism and scholarship (the study and struggle model) that had characterized the beginning moment of Black Studies (1968) began to take place in the 1980s. This meant that for new faculty entering the institution, meeting the professional demands often led many to quiet contemplation, as they met the specter of not getting tenure and were cautioned to keep their heads low, finish a book, and stay out of the way. The lack of activism of young faculty misses at least six classes of students. The way that this relates to knowledge production is that it ruptures the organic link between theory and practice, intellectual work and activism, which had been the hallmark of prior scholars from W. E. B. Du Bois and onward and was precisely what produced the programs we have today.

April 20, 2009, marked the fortieth anniversary of the famous and now iconic image of students at Cornell University successfully leaving a takeover of Willard Straight Hall, armed in self-defense to demonstrate a lack of fear as they encountered the academic racism that accompanied the large-scale entry of black students into predominantly white institutions. April 2009 also marked the fortieth anniversary of the founding of Cornell's Africana Center as an independent unit with its own budget and reporting directly to the provost as one of the terms of its identity, and the two issues are of course connected.

It is significant to note that Cornell had a long legacy before that of black middle-class students attending for higher degrees, though not without encountering various forms of racism in housing, sports, curricular issues, and the like. A recent book, *Part and Apart: Black Students at Cornell University, 1865–1945,* by historian Carol Kammem, indicates that the title suited the topic, "because black students were part of Cornell; they participated in a number of activities. But they were also set apart by their race." *Part and Apart* also tells how black students survived by starting their own organizations, subject to a variety of explicit forms of racism, like being unable to live in campus housing. The latter point about housing is significant because Wari Hall, which was set up as a cooperative black women's housing unit precisely because of these inclusions, had a cross burned on its front lawn. This cross burning became the final straw for students experiencing various forms of institutional and personal racism and triggered the Willard Straight takeover and this now legendary history of student radicalism at Cornell.

So the 1960s were different, and 1969 was a good year. Supported by the Black Power movement at the national level and its related Black Arts Movement and integration of historically white universities and colleges, the influx of students into these institutions without the benefit of the institution's recognition of its Eurocentricity—curriculum, faculty, points of view, theoretical positions, distribution of courses, and the rest—would lead to a demand for a more representative curriculum. Fabio Rojas (2010) in *From Black Power to Black Studies: How a Radical Social Movement Became an Academic Discipline* provides good data on this movement, indicating that the forms of social protest employed by the 1960s–1970s generation actually worked in that they produced the Africana Studies departments, programs, and centers that exist today. It was gratifying to have as a colleague Audrey Smedley, who was teaching, writing, and thinking about race and ended up co-authoring the American Anthropological Association statement on race and her own work *Race in North America* (1999) and co-editing *Racism in the Academy* (2012).

Ironically, what happened in the interim was that throughout the 1980s and 1990s, faculty and students were cautioned away from those very strategies and instead were encouraged to develop the more intellectual accommodating approaches that have also worked but with a different result than was intended in the initial incarnation of these studies.

So the Cornell students' takeover of Willard Straight Hall became iconic for two reasons: students were demanding the institutionalizing of black studies as a basic offering of the university curriculum as they were challenging the institutional bases of Eurocentric ownership of knowledge and structures that marginalized their presence, and the students were presented as assertive as they made those demands. Importantly, the students were armed by the community, as there were threats against them by white supremacists from the surrounding communities, police from across New York State had arrived to "take them out" Kent State style, and white frat members had tried to break in to take back Willard Straight Hall. For many of us, it is that same iconic image and its meaning that Cornell tried to erase by its recent moves to contain and redefine Africana Studies.

A lot has changed since the 1960s in a series of forward and backward movements, as Black Studies jockeys within these institutions to maintain an academic environment where all voices are represented. There has been a long tradition of Africana Studies at the institutional level, if we are to work with some of the initial contributors of intellectual work in the field (Cooper, Du Bois, Woodson, Herskovits, Locke, and others). At the faculty level, what became concrete was a student-led assertion of a demand for knowledge, but not without an ongoing struggle for legitimacy. But thereby enters another issue. The 1980s witnessed an ongoing commodification of the field, following the entrepreneurial Gates model, so that even if this was not the Gates intent, a professoriate, often with no or little commitment or knowledge of the politics and history of Black Studies, began to populate these departments, either for convenience in getting to certain institutions or because this was a professionally rewarding, interesting area in which to work.

So at the same Cornell University in January 2010, the logic to contain Africana studies was actualized. A provost announced a unilateral move of Africana Studies into Arts and Sciences without any discussion with the faculty replayed similar white power actions in history.

Africana Studies is a field therefore contestatory by definition. Racism's institutional superstructure as applied in this context means we exist collectively in a field organized to counter a massive hegemonic Eurocentric knowledge edifice. A primary manifestation of this institutional racism is a willful institutional ignorance that often dominates. This means that administrators and colleagues from other units are often unable, too uninformed, unwilling, or ill-equipped to represent the interests of these units in ways that are to the benefit of knowledge advancement.

Claude Steele in his book *Whistling Vivaldi: How Stereotypes Affect Us and What We Can Do* (2011) laid out some interesting arguments and examples in the academic contexts in which racism at the institutional and structural level is alive and well, using as well his experience at Ohio State University as a graduate student as one of these and a more recent experience as a faculty member at major Ivy League universities as another end. In each case, a variation on academic racist practices from the explicit to the implicit occurred.

There is a phrase that the United States uses openly to talk about its subordination of the rest of the world: "It is not in U.S. interests to . . ." A similar pattern is identified in these institutions: "It is not in the institution's larger interests to . . ." The more recalcitrant or stubborn of administrators offer no retreat from hardened positions. From my experience, one fights consistently an uphill battle while the university moves on to its "more important" matters in which faculty and administrators in Black Studies or Latino Studies or Asian Studies are never or rarely included, except as decoration or ornaments, and one also confronts the quotidian microaggressions of institutional and personal racism. Often we are recipients of some advances only through informed deans and provosts, and once these leave the institution, one is again bereft of support.

The impending demise of Black Studies is held often as a kind of red flag, or an indication of a trend so that universities feel they do not have to meet minority populations' needs seriously anymore. Or if there is a problem within the program—a change in leadership, for example—a model of incorporation into some giant ethnic studies unit is floated and at times successfully activated. Reporting from the trenches as far as faculty is concerned, benefiting from reports from a variety of other institutions, within the structure of U.S. racism, pathological behavior is often supported or at least not curtailed so that dysfunctional tendencies, sometimes even insanities, are normalized. In these contexts, having standards of excellence becomes a direct challenge to the normalizing of bad behavior. Often the sympathy is with the one acting out. University structures like sexual harassment workshops can be ignored, as they are not union mandated. To the extent then that the institution can make Black Studies sites of dysfunctional behavior, places of "unrest," then they can avoid the commitment to the larger issues of equitable building, curriculum development, and student needs for education across the university. Leadership coming from some other context that has no history or knowledge of Black Studies is often sought.

One can make a similar point about reactionary leadership from anywhere, that is, not limited to geography, but it is amazingly telling when there is a disrespect for the gains of departments and units during periods of struggle and the casual dismissal of these with administrative support. Houston Baker's argument in his book *Betrayal: How Black Intellectuals Have Abandoned the Ideals of the Civil Rights Era* was partially right in addressing some of these concerns about the nature of intellectual commitment. Ron Walters in one of his last lectures, delivered at Cornell's Africana Studies anniversary conference in 2010, indicated that we have to make fine distinctions as we consider the politics of individuals. For example, earlier generations of Africans, like say Professor Chike Onwuachi at Howard, he suggests, would have been coming to the United States with Pan-African knowledge, politics, and sensibility or became, upon arrival, part of U.S. civil rights or Black Power activity. But since then, the rise of the postcolonial state has produced a variety of individuals with different and more individualist politics, ideologies, or positions, for economic advancement and with little interest in some of the historical issues of African Americans.

We can also assert that the older generation of Africana scholars, largely male, operated from either a benign or an insidious patriarchal form of sexism that had to be negotiated against consistently even as they advanced some specific nationalist imperatives to advance Black Studies. This has been well articulated by black feminist scholarship over the years, beginning with *Brave* (1982). But still, in 2011, women students at Cornell's Africana Center organized a forum, "Re-claiming Africana Studies as a Black Feminist Space," in order to find a way to talk about the nature of women's participation in Africana, given recent history in which students were verbally abused by a professor without any major intervention from the administration. A number of women students indicated that there had been a pattern and a climate from the other male professors that seemed to condone this behavior, and thus they no longer felt comfortable entering the building.

Finally, discourses of hybridity and creolization in cultural studies have created a framework that has reified a kind of Walcott-like 1970s mulatto identity. This notion of "mulatto studies" identifies a kind of grotesque framework that operates out of the logic of a "cultural void" or "anything but black" being privileged. It also refers to the ambiguous location of a kind of study that tries to represent "hybridity" in the postmodern and cultural studies sense as proposed by Homi Bhabha and others, who in their home context have not even addressed the fact that there are Indo-Africans (Siddis) horribly subordinated and marginalized by the same upper castes from which some of our definers of hybridity come.

Ironically, according to the immediate postenslavement logic, the intent was to create precisely a "hybrid" population that did not necessarily belong to Africa anymore but now tried to settle themselves accordingly in the new location without reference to a past. Indeed, building hybrid products in botany as in zoology was the passion of the science of colonizing that saw the "New World" as a laboratory of sorts. The botanical gardens across the colonial world testify to this propensity, as does the numerous naming for racial combinations across the Americas. Black Studies and the various decolonization political movements intervened to correct erasures of African presences. Caribbean Studies, as this work suggests, often marginalized in these larger frameworks, has all to do with the nature of the larger project of

Black Studies to the extent that it continues to claim that intellectual space as a founding member, as the next chapter shows, in a range of diasporic circulations.

Black-Male-ing: Popular Readings of Racial Subjectivity

The particular history of racism, sexism, and homophobia in the United States has conspired to locate black masculinity as the primary index of blackness, indeed of race, and of a heightened form of perverse masculinity. The result is that black males in the United States, unless actively resisting these inscriptions, often walk into very particular stereotypical representations. Understanding this particular racializing of black men is critical for Afro-Caribbeans living in the United States or the United Kingdom, particularly if they are raising boys. The traps that can render them within the prison industrial complex are myriad, as Angela Davis and others have shown over the years. By the second generation, the same problems that beset African Americans—educational disparities, unequal policing, low or no employment, the criminal justice system—also affect Afro-Caribbeans.

Still, the dominant construction of race privileges black male subjectivity that is constituted and reconstituted over time turns on some very particular constants that get replayed with the available items in every historical moment. The black male as subject, then, is produced and mass-produced with all the apparatuses of the media and, following Althusser a bit, via all the other ideological state apparatuses.

Fanon's *Black Skin, White Masks* identified the site of interpellation for the black man, hailing the black male subject into a very raced and debased subjectivity. The specific gendered nature of this positioning has still not been fully addressed and marks the limits of both Fanon's work in the area of gender and many succeeding positions in this area. At one level, then, a specific version of black masculinity was created and easily transferable, even if reclaimed, in hip-hop usage. To arrive at the same level of interpellation for black women, given that female identity is already located as biologically inferior, perhaps the phrase *black bitch* does the equivalent work. In other words, black women end up being excluded from both constructions of blackness and womanhood and are debased, technically erased from an affirmative identitarian position, except at the level of service, unless they actively resisted the erasure and claimed that affirmative identitarian position themselves. At the same time, this claiming of an affirmative self-defining position by black women often runs counter to the ways in which they are supposed to be located in society and thereby presents a series of other already installed conflicts. This explains, at a certain level, why the gendered reference or equivalent word *negress* remains outside the popular language, with all its loaded and sexualized meanings as they relate to service. Today, therefore, for white and black youth, the so-called *N* word occupies a gender-neutral position. What is interesting to me, for the purposes of this discussion, is that the black female identity position gets collapsed, thereby, into the racial category.

Sojourner Truth, offering a critique of prevailing constructions of womanhood and indeed manhood in 1851 at the Women's Rights Convention in Akron, Ohio, would ask that telling rhetorical question: "Ain't I a Woman?," saying in part: "I have as much muscle as any man, and can do as much work as any man. . . . I can carry as much as any man, and can eat as much too, if I can get it. I am as strong as any man."

Clearly, the man that Sojourner was talking about in this period would have had to be the Black man, as they were the ones primarily relegated to the labor-intensive chores that she identifies. But she was also locating, or calling into question, the existence of the black woman repeatedly in these very formulations, even as she challenged given definitions of gender, of white womanhood, and of masculinity. This erasure of the black woman at the conceptual level is at the heart of what I am calling *black-male-ing* in the first instance, as it is a formulation that at its heart has as the primary operatives the white man, the white woman, and the black man, with the black woman located as the excess. It is for this reason, I would assert, that countless black poets from the *Négritude* movement to the 1960s would have to sing the praises of the black woman, in a way attempting to recall her into existence.

The taking of the black male experience in the world as primary becomes a fundamental feature of this *black-male-ing*. I am using the term with all its echoes and with the knowledge in place that a whole host of negative associations have been located linguistically for black people and identified with the word *black*. But in this case, the echo with *blackmailing* is deliberate, in that a fundamental feature of racial ideology is the constructing of the black male experience as central and oppositional, necessitating that black women be blackmailed into either defending black male behaviors, subordinating themselves, erasing themselves, or occupying the service role, for the benefit of the race, which, if we read blackness as equivalent to black masculinity, means, then, for the benefit of black men. Native Americans, Asians, and Mexicans remain assigned to the margins of U.S. racial politics.

A series of social practices and thinking hold this logic in place. A study done in the early 1980s, in Washington, D.C., and on classroom practices of teachers of elementary school, identified that in terms of attention, white boys received the most attention, of the positive variety, followed by black boys, who received a large share of attention, of the negative variety, followed by white girls and black girls. Kunjufu's *Countering the Conspiracy to Destroy Black Boys* (1985) makes a related point. In other words, what was revealed then and has been borne out in the way the media and the criminal justice system have handled black men is that they pay significant, though negative, attention to young black men. The dominant representation of a black man on television until and even after Barack Obama's presidency was hand-cuffed with hands behind his back, whether it was a right-wing Republican running for president and trying to enter a Georgia television station to be part of a debate or a Harvard professor trying to enter his home. This sub-ject position of black men then plays out for capitalist society in aspects of their masculinity—brute force and physical prowess (athletics, with football players, boxers, basketball players, soldiers, and so on), sexuality (studs, a variety of players), violence (criminals, drug dealers, gang members, and so forth)—leaving white men with a variety of respectable levels of masculinity that nonetheless can mask pathologies and forms of criminality.

A few years ago, speculations on whether Colin Powell, a black military man, would become the first black president allowed a discussion that linked the lessons of neocolonial black male leadership in Africa and the Caribbean, that is, would he bomb a Caribbean country. We know now that the specific racial identity of the United States would not necessarily change, and for women, gays, and other subordinated groups, patterns of racism continue so that each one has to argue, protest, and thereby fight their way into seri-ous consideration. Thus, students in a teachers college in South Africa, and university students I taught in Brazil, were already aware of the outcome of this story before it happened via the Obama presidency and had wonderful analyses about the possibilities and their concerns. The Obama presidency allows us to read in real time outcomes of that story. Thus, under President Obama, black people end up in an ambiguous position, unable to critically challenge his omissions as they pertain to black people without seeming disloyal to the racial meaning of an iconic first black president.

Being *black-maled* in this context means being located by white society, "whitemaled" as it were, on the pole of hypermasculinity, the culture's dick as it were, while being dispossessed of full participation in the intellectual, political, economic life of the culture. Feminist work has long shown that in terms of how masculinity and femininity are coded, enacted, and performed, men are the ones, from childhood, assigned the plane of physicality, thought, rationality, and action and women assigned the plane of nurturing, emotion, hysteria, passivity, and irrationality. It is not much of a vault in argument to show how with race added, given that black people in this culture have been assigned the level of labor, exploitation, black men would come to stand in for the superphysical, while white men would claim for themselves the pinnacle of representations, as it relates to rationality, intellect, thinking, and so on. Isaac Julien and Kobena Mercer, in "True Confessions: A Discourse on Images of Black Male Sexuality," in *Brother to Brother: New Writings by Black Gay Men* (1991), would say, "Racism defined African peoples as having only bodies and no minds: Black men and women were seen as muscle-machines and thus the superexploitation of slavery could be justified" (171). Still, this predicates the erasure of the black woman and the holding of the white woman as the delicate and much-needed representation of superfemininity, with black women located in the service role, serving all, reminiscent of Hurston's "mule" metaphor.

In a way, then, black women and black society in general—black children, elderly people, and other black men—whether they support black men like O. J. Simpson or Clarence Thomas or any of the other varieties, ended up being *blackmailed* on the basis of their deep understanding of the history and complexities of race relations. To identify blackness with masculinity, and to expect it, learning to live with the cost of that blackmailing has become normalized. I mention Clarence Thomas deliberately because his was the other media spectacle, with Anita Hill's charges of sexual harassment, even though she did not make them willingly, but had confided to a colleague (then a judge) many years earlier. That Clarence Thomas called a logical critique of his behavior a high-tech lynching we know fulfilled that particular media linkage of masculinity with race that became acceptably current and allowed him to enter the Supreme Court. There his record has been one that is aiding the dismantling of many of the gains of the Civil Rights era. And the "high-tech lynching" defense became a usable defense for other black men similarly charged. Clearly, another kind of collective blackmailing of the black population occurred via Clarence Thomas. And all the key players were there—the embattled black man, the then passive and quietly self-effacing white wife, and the black woman trying to speak her truth, posed against a large, "rational" white male establishment.

For this reason, a significant act of resistance occurred when more than sixteen hundred black women and women of color signed a statement that was published in the *New York Times* on November 17, 1991, which has turned out to be prophetic:

> We know that the presence of Clarence Thomas on the Court will be continually used to divert attention from historic struggles for social justice through suggestions that the presence of a Black man on the Supreme Court constitutes an assurance that the rights of African Americans will be protected. Clarence Thomas' public record is ample evidence this will not be true. . . . We speak here because we recognize that the media are now portraying the Black community as prepared to tolerate both the dismantling of affirmative action and the evil of sexual harassment in order to have any Black man on the Supreme Court.

In effect, then, the entire "African Women in Defense of Ourselves" statement says that just as African women's interests are being betrayed, the entire community ends up being black-maled by the larger racist logics of the culture. And their statement has proven to be true, given Thomas's record of voting on the Supreme Court. Seeing a much more mature Anita Hill at the anniversary of the hearing with a new book, *Reimagining Equality: Stories of Gender, Race, and Finding Home* (2011), following her earlier *Speaking Truth to Power* (1998), and able to reassess twenty years later what had happened to her and to put sexual harassment in the context of race and gender privileges and subordinations in many ways closes one of the circles left open on this issue.

A series of racial projects has made it such that black masculinity is constructed in particular ways. Added to that, every other person in the world, once she or he arrives in the United States, gets located in the same racial paradigms, even if one is coming from another altogether different ethnic, cultural, and historical context. Audre Lorde, of Caribbean American heritage, writes in *Sister Outsider* (1984) about her son, though in an earlier time period: "I wish to raise a Black man who will not be destroyed by, nor settle for, those corruptions called power by the white fathers who mean his destruction as surely as they mean mine" (74). This desire continues to be a place of trauma for many black women who have seen their children destroyed by two forms of dangers—the dominant culture's race-based policing and prison systems and the violence of the streets in which criminality and popular drug cultures sometimes demand execution-style killings. And some who are witnesses or innocent bystanders can be hurt in the crossfire. This is a far cry from the masculinity of a Malcolm X or a Stokely Carmichael who used their masculinity in a dueling match against white power and for community leadership.

Many, of course, speculated that with a new president who wanted to re-establish some kind of link between service and community and had a wife with a thesis titled "Princeton-Educated Blacks and the Black Community" and written under her maiden name, Michelle LaVaughn Robinson, in 1985, there may have been a space created for reinvigorating black communities and in the academy Africana Studies. Michelle Robinson's thesis found a waning of identification with community in terms of service after those in her sample made it into professions of choice. But how to translate that into some tangible gains? How to move leadership so that it represents the needs of the most disenfranchised? How to fight for full black humanity and related human rights? This has clearly remained outside of any serious consideration at the highest levels and marks what I have called the (im)possibility of a black president.

But it further explains the question of neoliberal or neoimperial leadership. If we open the frame a bit and see African Americans as part of a larger international or diasporic identity, processes of Jim Crow and its extensions functioned as a type of internal colonialism. Bearing all the hallmarks of colonialism, a number of Left scholars including Malcolm X and William Patterson and others of "We Charge Genocide" (1951) had presented to the United Nations and had thereby articulated the internal colonial model to account for the continued exploited condition of black people in the United States. In this context, we have another frame with which to view the rise of certain leaders as operating as a kind of neocolonial leadership in relationship with their communities.

Being black-maled as well then here refers to being caught in the prevailing racial definitions in their cumulative effect: adopting particular sex roles, accepting a particular version of black male sexuality. For women, it means accepting erasure in a general category of blackness that excludes them, accepting location only in service categories (mother, wife, daughter, sexual partner, maid, cook, and so on), and being subjected to a kind of behavior that acts as though we never contributed to the world of ideas, and therefore the acceptance of a conceptual blindness that erases women can pass as acceptable. Thus, the decades of scholarship by black women, including the most recent accumulation of intellectual work in this new generation on the intersections of systems of dominance—race, class, gender, sexuality, and so on—remain conceptually distant from the majority of scholarly endeavors, including current revisionist theories of race.

The cost of any form of blackmailing is usually too much, or way beyond one's means, and attached to it is the logic that one could continue to pay interminably or that one is at the mercy of those holding the equivalent material product or person hostage or some information hostage that is feared to be disclosed. In this context, articulating the basis under which we are hostage to particular formulations of race and gender is a means of dismantling this attitude. My calling of the question here is another confronting of racial meanings, identifying the active position in which it appears in our communities and resisting its effects.

Blonding

Dorothea Smartt in her "Medusa" poem has an interesting sequence that ends with:

> Dye it
> Remembrances of Africa Fast-fading
> in the blond highlights
> turn us back on ourselves
> slowly making daily applications with our own hand
> my hair as it is comes
> is just not good enough.

Popular representations of the most desirable black women conceptually are analyzable in terms of current practices of "blonding." By "blonding," I am referring to the practice and preference of the entire population for extreme blondness in hair color, texture, and styling and its related implications, given all the historical meanings of this identity in terms of deficiency, desirability, and sexuality. In my view, this presents a contemporary U.S. version of *blanqueamento* (whitening or performing the meanings of whiteness), even as it has historically been a seductive play on racial exclusions. The fact that black and Asian women have entered this practice boldly seems to suggest that for women and black women to be seen in a particular way, they have to enter the given mask of an inadequate white female representation that has been the historic cultural association of blondness. In other words, white female desirability is identified with golden tresses and all the inscriptions of fun, femininity, and acceptance. If, in other words, "gentlemen prefer blondes" and if black women want a gentleman, then blond may have to be the preferred modality. Photo-shopping techniques facilitate the whitening of photographs of even white women, as a recent fiasco of Julia Roberts revealed in the British legal system's rejection of this form of whitening in advertising.

Legal scholar Cheryl Harris in an interesting essay titled "Whiteness as Property" identifies "whiteness" as property, which dominant U.S. society guards as one does an investment. White women we know came to represent the privileged site of that property, including in its gendered aspects as the white men's property. Thus, for black men, if whiteness is equivalent to acquiring a particular status, material gain, and privilege, which are its benefits, then the notion of white women as that property that accrues with its success has not shifted. In this context, then, personal choice is identical with the politics of success in North American society. Thus, black women, and the racial signifiers they carry, are also reduced to not being good enough, as are the other aspects of their blackness, unless they accept blonding as self-presentation. It is not surprising, then, that every black woman who becomes successful in the media seems to have to perform blonding even if photographically alone at some level, from Beyoncé to Lil' Kim, Mary J. Blige to Queen Latifah. Caribbean subjects who enter these U.S. racialized locations, as did Rihanna and Nicki Minaj, end up being similarly presented as blond, pink wigged, or red haired.

The way that race works in this context is in the acceptance of a certain set of ideal representations as standards of what is beautiful that, as Carolyn Cooper has shown, has to debase blackness in order to operate. A variety of beauty-queen constructions over the years, which have been contested solidly in the post–Black Power period, had tended to reify a range of European aesthetics and normalize them. A consistent vigilance to these constructions indicates several returns over time, which it seems in each generation has to be challenged, as is being done again via a return to more healthy hair for black women in various social-media "hair journey" narratives.

Confronting racism, then, in this context seems to mean perpetually uncovering the comfortable, "commonsense" logics under which racist projects are continued and normalized. For example, the avoidance of the theoretical contributions of a variety of woman of color scholars to the discussion of race, not as a unitary subject but one that inflects with gender, class, sexuality, often can find theoretical meaning only in systems of dominance theory. After pursuing a wide range of discussions on race, I still find this approach one of the most useful I have encountered and one that goes a long way toward addressing the articulated issues of class or race or gender that would want to be posed as the singular categories of analysis. Confronting racism in this context means reading race in its varied interactions on different levels, through time, and with all the various manifestations.

Confronting racism as a Caribbean subject means refusing normative understandings, especially the ways that dominant racial discourses seek to naturalize themselves and incorporate new arrivals to help execute dominant projects. Additionally, given the impact that U.S. and European media have on the rest of the world, it means a great deal of intellectual, interdisciplinary, or cross-disciplinary work, advancing historical knowledge consistently. For me, as a scholar of Caribbean origin who has witnessed or participated in some of the struggles for full participation of African Americans, it also means not being satisfied with the short-term gains of social movements and instead confronting the fact that these are also at times easily taken away, as is the case now. The logic of permanent revolution has some applicability. By these means, one can adopt a posture of constant vigilance to race-based representations, politics, policy, the media, culture, and the academy as they reassert themselves, sometimes wearing different masks.

11

CIRCULATIONS
Caribbean Political Activism

The work of a generation of Caribbean critical thinkers and activists provides us with an amazing body of material for understanding how they navigated international locations while always thinking about the Caribbean and related experiences in global context. In many discussions of issues related to the "black radical tradition," the question of what generated or produced the range of radical intellectual activists from the Caribbean—the number far exceeding, proportionately, the relative small size of the Caribbean—persists. Glissant, in responding to this question, suggests that one experiences a range of challenges and their resonances in small countries before they move to larger ones—from the archipelagoes to the continents (2010). For C. L. R. James, as discussed in an earlier chapter, it was/is the visible fissures in Caribbean societies themselves that create/created certain conditions and therefore a consciousness of resistance.

This chapter explores what I see as circulations among a group of definable Caribbean activists who widened Caribbean space in international encounters. It examines the movements of a selection of the most visibly representative figures largely from the Anglophone Caribbean in the formative period of black activism leading up to the Black Power period of the 1970s. In pursuing my earlier work on Claudia Jones focusing largely on the 1930s–1950s, I was able to see some patterns emerging in the surrounding intellectuals and activists with whom her work intersected and intersects, that is, the African American activists in the U.S. context and the larger Caribbean and Pan-African and international contexts. Claudia Jones's Caribbean left politics, I show in my earlier work (*Left of Karl Marx*), addresses this question of how to "remake" inherited political positions for usability in black communities. Whereas in the United States she studied and raised issues of class, race, and gender and the particular condition of black women, within formal CPUSA contexts, in the United Kingdom she moved consistently to more practical applications at the level of community building.

One of the places where one finds some definition and articulation of a specific Caribbean left is Brian Meeks's concluding essay to his *Narratives of Resistance:* "The Caribbean Left at Century's End" (2000). However, the Caribbean left that is Brian Meeks's subject is the post-1970s version locatable with people like Walter Rodney, Maurice Bishop, and his colleagues (some of whom later became adversaries) and others in the eastern Caribbean who attempted to implement forms of left ideology into political machinery in the Caribbean state itself and whom Meeks identifies as defeated in this process. There is enough material now perhaps to study the relationships between generations of Caribbean left thinkers at the intellectual and theoretical level, not always reducible to a Marxist-Leninist framing.

Cheryl Higashida, in *Black Internationalist Feminism: Women Writers of the Black Left, 1945–1995* (2011), has an interesting definition on this point. She indicates, "I use 'Left' to designate Communist and Communist-affiliated individuals and groups. I use 'left' to refer to the broader spectrum of radical movements beyond the Communist Party" (177). For her the distinction that she makes via the use of lowercase or uppercase letter was critical in the naming for her to signal "the Communist Left's importance to these writers and to their Black internationalist feminism" (177–78). In my own sense, the designation between capitals is not as significant in identifying a political continuum along which several versions of radical politics that critique capitalist systems of domination as they are manifested through other modalities such as class, race, gender, sexuality. In my reading, Marxism is not the leftmost pole of articulation, as there are many Caribbean activists who studied and worked within the framework of Marxism-Leninism only to find it incapable of meeting the full extent of their realities (*Left of Karl Marx*).

A variety of migratory movements for which the Caribbean has been legendary have also coincided with, or helped to produce, a series of radical political and cultural movements in different locations. These have created diasporic circulations that have been naturalized in Caribbean left practices. So, on the one hand, we have Frantz Fanon (1925–61) from Martinique anatomizing the black and colonial lived reality from France and Algeria and a Pan-Africanist George Padmore from Trinidad (1903–59) insisting on providing a dialectical argument for "Pan-Africanism" or "communism" in the

United States, Europe, and Ghana. Although we know that C. L. R. James offered one of the earliest critiques of state capitalism but always also operated within a Pan-Africanist framework, he would work out of locations at different points in his history, from Europe, the United States, and Trinidad. Sylvia Wynter, born in Cuba and raised in Jamaica, lived for a number of years in the United Kingdom and now makes the United States her residence. She has indicated that Marx was only partially correct in his analysis, so while there is a certain use of Marxist arguments in her work, these have to be complicated with related readings of the larger Western humanist project that has consistently located its abject others as outside of humanity.

I see the Caribbean left, then, not so much as a hardened group of dogmatic Marxists, as Meeks locates them, using the failed Grenada revolution model, or the demise of Walter Rodney, who nonetheless made his own diasporic circulations before his return to Guyana. Rather, the Caribbean left represents a range of intellectual activists, through time, who engage a politics of progressive change from a variety of intersecting political positions. What unites them perhaps is a rejection of conventional oppressive socioeconomic conditions and a critique of forms of colonialism, capitalism, and imperialism, under which the Caribbean labored and the ideas and practices that support newer versions of these oppressions. What unites them as well is a deferral of some progressive realization at the level of practice from which future studies of Caribbean left traditions can learn.

Since in James's view the Haitian Revolution was a radical transatlantic movement to move the world to a progressive place and achieve some of the subsequently identified universal principles of human rights (1948), this is what fails or succeeds as we move through the years. So if the Caribbean is the site of the first major black revolutions against oppression, then there exists an unfulfilled or deferred promise in Haiti's inability to build solid democratic state processes. This deferred promise is articulated in the music or art, in the popular practices, and in the literature as well. Traces of this resistance create a left tradition with many nodal points that refuses to acquiesce fully to domination even in the face of neocolonial state tendencies. If these neocolonial conditions have morphed into new forms of economic colonizations, then the critique of that deferral remains valid.

I want to assert here that Caribbean left traditions are varied, but they are consistently operating from three or four assumptions, organized around these themes: (1) that Caribbean people's full identity has a diasporic nature, the first of which then generates Pan-Africanism as a political philosophy; (2) that Caribbean political and intellectual identity moving consistently toward that realization has sought articulations and intellectual explanations from more organized philosophical places like Marxism-Leninism; (3) that this Caribbean left tradition also has an explicit feminist component that often remains unaccounted for in the larger political articulations; and (4) that Caribbean left traditions view the transatlantic within a series of transoceanic passages that allow the practice of that activism and the other three positions to have currency.

Caribbean Circulations

While the discourse of diaspora has become a popular academic consideration in the late twentieth century and into the twenty-first century, the histories of migration and the consequent diaspora creation have always been significantly central to the definitions of Caribbean identity. I have developed some of these issues more fully in previous work. The argument is that the Caribbean now navigates between the longer historical diaspora and the more recent Caribbean diaspora created in the pre- and postindependence migrations. Stokely Carmichael's narration of a family history of intra-Caribbean migrations on both ends, as we have shown, is illustrative of a series of movements around the Caribbean and then to the United States. He, of course, ends up in Guinea, West Africa, technically completing the migratory circuit deliberately but not without a series of diasporic circulations and sojourns in different locations. These diasporic circulations I see as typifying Caribbean left activist identity. But more deliberately in the Kwame Toure narrative is an awareness of intersecting or overlapping diaspora—the African and the Caribbean, but also the African American. About his activist work and time in Mississippi he says:

> My ancestral stories had a calypso rhythm, an island accent, not a blues beat. The south wasn't my old country, so I thought. So why was I engulfed by an almost nostalgic sense of recognition and homecoming? The place neither looked, sounded, nor really even felt like the Trinidad of my childhood, but I sure felt very strongly that I'd come home, I could feel it. But I couldn't explain it. (277)

The assumption of a series of homes in which one can find recognition and belonging then can create nostalgia, as this Caribbean diasporic activist suggests. He clarifies this later when he says: "The first time I heard anyone else try to describe that exact feeling of recognition was Mrs. [Fannie Lou] Hamer, some years later when she came back from Guinea. And guess what?

My second time having that same feeling as strong was four years later when I first was to visit Guinea myself" (278).

Caribbean identity, according to Dionne Brand (*A Map to the Door of No Return*), is one that has to be ready for continuous self-invention. The problematic framing of Manning Marable's *Malcolm X: A Life of Reinvention* (2011), notwithstanding, one also has an even greater importance of him being in part a product of Caribbean circulations in Jan Carew's *Ghosts in Our Blood* (1994) in which his Garveyite African American father meets his mother through political activism. Thus, Malcolm X can also be read as a Caribbean American activist, with clear memories of a Grenadian mother and connections with a Caribbean family. It is for me significant that Lara Putnam's *Radical Moves* (2013) begins with the mother of Malcolm X, whom Jan Carew and Manning Marable identify as a Grenadian woman who migrated to Montreal and then to Philadelphia and ended up in Lansing, Michigan, having married along the way a fellow Garveyite. But for me it is additionally important because Louise Little has often been lost to the ascendancy of her famous son. That Malcolm X is of Caribbean and African American ancestry and represents one of the logical outcomes of what Putnam defines as the circum-Caribbean migratory sphere is a historical given that this work captures. The version of Pan-Africanism that Malcolm X ends up producing has several precedents and is no longer an unusual outcome. One can study these Caribbean circulations for political activism from a few angles.

Caribbean Pan-Africanist Visions

From Sylvester Williams's first Pan-African Conference in 1900 to the Garvey movement's successful mobilization of Black racial unity within working-class communities in the Caribbean, the United States and Latin America, the Pacific, and Europe, to Bob Marley and the lyrics of Rastafari, iconic diasporan Caribbean political actors created a political movement to challenge a range of colonial practices and reclaim human agency. Thus, by mid-century, George Padmore, also of Trinidad, as Malcolm Nurse, had claimed Pan-Africanism as an independent theoretical political position. Padmore provides the link for understanding how a number of those who followed were able to create ideological linkages between political positions.

Marcus Garvey's diasporic circulations are now legendary, from his travels through the Caribbean and Central America to across the United States and finally to England. Still, Padmore remains significant as the major mid-twentieth-century practicing Pan-Africanist organizer who also lived a certain diasporic circulation. Born in Trinidad, Padmore in 1924 departed for the United States at twenty-one and headed for medical school at Fisk University but ended up nonetheless an activist in Harlem, where he edited a newspaper, the *Negro Champion* (later known as the *Liberator*). He joined the Communist Party in 1927 and began contributing articles to the *Daily Worker* in New York.

Padmore presents one model of a series of diasporic circulations, though he died at fifty-nine before completing fully all his projects. He lived in Russia for a time and was appointed head of the International Trade Union Committee of Negro Workers, which was the arm of the Red International of Labor Unions, or Profintern, and which organized an international conference of Negro workers in July 1930 in Germany. Ideological differences led to Padmore's disillusionment with communism, as it had several other activists before him, and in 1935, Padmore moved to London, England, where he met his childhood friend and fellow Trinidadian C. L. R. James. Toward the end of his life, he would live in Ghana and assist Nkrumah in the Ghanaian leader's initial stages of organizing a newly independent nation.

Still, one can study Padmore's particular pattern of developing and maintaining a series of other political relationships that allowed for the advancement of a number of intellectual projects. His relationship with James is but one of these, as was a series of other associations and projects such as a career as a journalist who published articles on self-government, racism, imperialism, and trade unionism in such working-class and Black publications as the *Crisis, Chicago Defender, Baltimore Afro-American, Clarion, Vanguard*, and *People*.

Padmore would later be the founding presence behind Nkrumah's Bureau of African Affairs, which now is the George Padmore Library in Accra, and a major architect of the development of Ghana's Pan-Africanist framework. But there is also a Padmore association with the first wife of Marcus Garvey, Amy Ashwood Garvey, who would remain the connecting link for a series of political movements.

The political example Padmore provided was also in the creation of networks that could be navigated subsequently. When Claudia Jones indicates that she was most impressed by the interpretation of the reasons behind the Italian invasion of Ethiopia by Mussolini, we understand the sources behind the clarity of the analysis with which she was impressed. In London, Padmore, James, and Amy Ashwood Garvey would be part of the organization that founded the International African Friends of Abyssinia and the International African Services Bureau to provide support for Ethiopia, including the circulation of accurate information. Additionally, Padmore, along with Amy Ashwood Garvey and C. L. R. James, would be among the organizers behind the 1945 Manchester Pan-African conference that charted the decolonization movements around the world. One can therefore see significant connections in terms of journalism, activism, Pan-Africanism, and community organizing and development of ideological leadership.

Some would argue that C. L. R. James best typifies Caribbean Pan-Africanist and diasporic circulations, with his various U.S. activist and teaching sojourns, deportation and returns, willingness to return to work with Eric E. Williams and the Peoples National Movement, but also the various unions such as the Oilfield Workers Union in Trinidad that organized his funeral in Trinidad, his extended periods in the United Kingdom, and his influence on figures like Walter Rodney in a subsequent generation. His political relationships with Padmore as with Amy Ashwood Garvey and his influence on Kwame Nkrumah also provide some other connections. But much work has been done on James as a political intellectual for whom the diaspora had become an important site for the production of the ideas of nationalism and socialism that were so important to the postwar decolonization movement in the Caribbean.

So in defining Caribbean Pan-Africanism as a left tradition, one can identify as well a variety of strands, from the early work of Sylvester Williams to the Garvey movement; the work of Padmore to Stokely Carmichael; the roots reggae tradition of Peter Tosh, Bob Marley, and the Wailers; Black Power calypso in Trinidad; and so on. Although dogmatic Marxists may reject Pan-Africanism as a left tradition, one would have to go back theoretically to Padmore for some responses, as Padmore in one of his last published documents would define the need for an equally developed movement that had its own political and structural orientation that held the advance of black communities as primary. Pan-Africanism as a particular claim of political membership for black people across the African diaspora asserts the right to access, if not return, to an ancestral homeland but also the right to claim a common identity from a series of dispersed locations, even if this remains an ideological position. This is where African diaspora practice (Edwards) has some tangible meaning, as a great deal of Pan-Africanism was initiated in the diaspora but operated not necessarily on the principle of a flattened and permanent return but rather a series of diasporic circulations as one's communities existed in multiple locations. As we have shown, these Caribbean diasporic movements were international, with the U.S. and African American struggle being but one of the critical compass points. If one thinks of Claude McKay, then, we see the same series of constructed "homes" in a Padmore or Kwame Toure or Amy Ashwood Garvey and also a series of diasporic circulations with a parallel sense of participating critically in each of these places.

Stokely Carmichael/Kwame Toure, who saw his relations and homes as varied, was not able to achieve a return to his childhood home in Trinidad until close to the end of his life, but by then he had lived a series of diasporic activist circulations. Mississippi was as much home as was the Bronx or Conakry, Guinea. This is what explains that nostalgia that he describes.

Caribbean Applications of Socialism

Caribbean political and intellectual identity moved consistently toward a critique of that difficult history out of which the Caribbean was created. As a result, its major thinkers have sought articulations and explanations from more organized intellectual philosophies like Marxism-Leninism. Winston James has already challenged in his postscript "Harold Cruse and the West Indians: Critical Remarks on the Crisis of the Negro Intellectual," in *Holding Aloft the Banner of Ethiopia: Caribbean Radicalism in Early Twentieth Century America,* a number of Cruse's assertions on the Caribbean intellectuals, finding them either inaccurate, wrong, misinterpreted, or misread (284).

It is important to note, then, that several major black socialists and communists (some of them Caribbean) would leave the organized Socialist or Communist Party, finding them therefore not radical enough for the kind of work that needed to be done to liberate black communities. Hubert Harrison is definitely one of these figures—clearly an active socialist formerly in the Socialist Party, which would become the Communist Party USA by 1919. Harrison is identified as writing a review that challenged the leading Marxist theoretician of the time. According to Perry, "Harrison's review showed clearly that he had a deep and subtle understanding of Marxism. [But] He was neither blindly dogmatic nor rigidly mechanical" (197).

Thus, there were several very active examples of black communist men and women from the Caribbean and United States who had visible political identities. In this context, Claudia Jones was not a lone, singular figure, or unusual. What marks her instead is that she became both an *organizer* and a leading *theoretician* within the party up to 1955. In assessing the life and work of Claudia Jones, Ricky Cambridge in the afterword to *Beyond Containment* (2011) indicates that Jones's positions engaged the following: the conventional Marxist theory of history, the Leninist theory of imperialism, the national question, and the role of black workers as autonomous catalysts in the labor movement.

The left, which is a position that Claudia Jones occupied, was also at the level of progressive praxis a necessary informed political analysis that intersected with a range of race, gender, and class positions. Though she consistently identified Marxism-Leninism as her central ideological and orienting politics, she would account as well for gender and race, for black communities in migration, for Carnival and Caribbean culture. In the end, these were precisely the sites of community transformation and conceptual formulation of the Claudia Jones legacy, a politics that advanced beyond the limitations of Marxism.

Additionally, one can see the impact of her diasporic circulations, from the Caribbean to the United Kingdom and later on travel to Russia and China, but also in the re-creation of several homes—in Trinidad, London, and New York. In the London context, the transatlantic relationships remain strong in a series of letters back to friends in the United States, in the organizing of a parallel March on Washington, protests against apartheid, and the formation of Caribbean diasporic institutions (newspapers and Carnival). Her writings, such as her essays "American Imperialism and the British West Indies" and "The Caribbean Community in Britain" and of course the journalism and editorial work in the *West Indian Gazette and Afro-Asian Caribbean News,* maintained these intellectual and creative connections.

What one gets with a Claudia Jones, then, is the marrying of certain aspects of theoretical Marxism with a practical application. Particularly relevant for Jones would be the aspect of Marxism that detailed support for workers' struggles and the critique of capitalism, the thinking through one's reality and social condition from an informed analytical position with the knowledge of class relations, and the logic of an international workers' mass movement. From Lenin she would apply the critique of imperialism, from feminism the location of women in these various class relations, and from African American politics the critique of racism.

The range of Caribbean diasporic left activists who navigated similar ground, embraced socialist principles, and intersected with a critique of racism is worth reconsidering. The activity of leftist union organizers and thinkers from the Caribbean like Richard Hart, George Bowrin, and John la Rose would resonate in different ways, with La Rose carrying forward into recent times some of the intent of that earlier political activity also, in the creation of usable institutions like the Black and Third World Book Fair and the New Beacon Books and the George Padmore Institute. La Rose would consistently always identify with the Caribbean diasporic left through a range of intellectual projects and community-support mechanisms.

A more recent version is Stuart Hall, whose New Left approach provided the framework for developing the field of cultural studies in Birmingham that has become now an intellectual field worldwide. In the epilogue to the special issue of *Caribbean Reasonings* on the thought of Stuart Hall (2007), "Through the Prism of an Intellectual Life," he identifies the ideas that accompanied his diasporic circulation, informed by a Caribbean historical background, left politics, and awareness of racial diasporic discourses in Britain and the United States.

Claiming Caribbean Feminism

Any claiming of an explicit Caribbean feminism as also a left discourse is best done first through women like Amy Ashwood Garvey, who explicitly identified herself in these terms. The articulation of a Caribbean feminism has been able to be captured through the works of some of the thinkers who managed these linkages and some of the contemporary scholars who have done the necessary work of recovery. Claudia Jones had reasserted publicly the place of the intellect for black women, in "Speech to the Court" in 1953: "You dare not, gentlemen of the prosecution, assert that Negro women can think, and speak and write!" This assertion has crucial meaning as we "trace" the Black and Caribbean radical intellectual traditions. It signifies a claim for black women's contribution to political work—thinking, speaking, and writing—and thus to intellectual analysis of their locations in society.

The feminist critique of left politics had been that, "within Marxism, the concept of gender has long been treated as the by-product of changing economic structures; gender has no independent analytic status of its own." Sylvia Wynter's critique of what transpired asserted that "in the wake of the sixties, women activists had ceased the earlier 'echoing' of Marxist thought and had redefined the Woman Question into an issue that was specific to their own concerns, rather than being, as before a subset of what might be called the Labor Issue." For her, though, it was always the "multiple movements related to these questions that had most forcibly erupted in concrete political and social struggles all over the globe" ("Unsettling" 312). It was those multiple movements, then, that Marxist-feminists in the pre-1960s period, such as the time in which Claudia Jones worked, that attempted to foreground the positions of working-class and black women.

The point is that there is no longer an accepted assumption of a static sense of gender in scholarship. Indeed, the nature of all recent work in black feminist scholarship is its addressing of the nature of power intersectionally, that is, not gender itself as a "primary way of signifying relationships of power" (J. Scott 1067).

A range of active left women is beginning to be revealed by new scholarship such as Dayo Gore's *Radicalism at the Crossroads: African American Women Activists in the Cold War* (2011). At a time identified with domesticity for women, black left women, we learn, "traveled extensively for their activism. . . . Their mobility, coupled with their organizing experience and their internationalist politics, helped to solidify their contributions as leaders and strategists with national and transnational reach" (10). Some of these include Williana Jones Burroughs, a teacher, union activist, and Communist, who spent some time in the Soviet Union in the 1920s and became active as a left activist through the American Negro Labor Committee in 1926 with which Padmore is identified in the same period. Louise Thompson Patterson, on whose work Erik McDuffie (2011) provides good readings, is also a central figure in these discussions. LaShawn Harris in "Running with the Reds" also identified Bonita Williams, a Caribbean American activist who published poetry and was also an eloquent orator. According to Harris, "Williams's passion for and commitment to civil rights was demonstrated by her affiliation with both leftist and black liberation organizations. . . . [D]uring the 1930s Williams worked closely with other Harlem CP activists such as Richard B. Moore and Maude White." Grace Campbell (1882–1943) as well as "British Guiana–born office worker and communist, Hermie Dumont Huiswoud" (2) are also identified in Joyce Moore Turner's *Caribbean Crusaders and the Harlem Renaissance*. Grace Campbell, who had moved from Washington, D.C., in 1905 and is identified as from Georgia, originally the daughter of a Jamaican father and an African American mother, is identified as the sole woman member in the leadership of the African Blood Brotherhood and had an "unwavering dedication to the socialist cause" (77–78). Claudia Jones also identifies several of these women in her various essays included in *Beyond Containment*. The point, though, is that there were a range of active left women doing organizational work in some of the same communities in the United States ahead of or at the same time as Claudia Jones.

Still, Amy Ashwood Garvey is perhaps best to bring these Caribbean circulations into full view, as she epitomizes these diasporic movements with a Pan-Africanist-feminist framework. Her work with Claudia Jones on the West Indian Workers and Students Association led to the development of the

West Indian Gazette in 1958 and, following the Notting Hill and Nottingham racist riots in 1958, an Association for the Advancement of Negro People, a short-lived organization using the logic of the NAACP with which Claudia would work while it lasted. Tony Martin also reports that Amy Ashwood Garvey complied with Jones's request for an essay on Ghana for the premier issue of the *West Indian Gazette*. "Jones particularly desired Amy's comments on federation and possible independence for the Caribbean and how (if at all) Ghanaians view[ed] this new federation within the context of Nkrumah's plan for a Pan-African Federation" (272).

Amy Ashwood Garvey clearly had tremendous Pan-African credentials, though, and would never become a communist, while many of her friends were active members. She would self-identify as a feminist. The range of activities that Martin reports shows her as performing the kind of political diasporic circulations that this chapter argues typifies Caribbean activists of her period: "She participated in the activities of the left-leaning Council on African Affairs, which had had its genesis in part with the famous actor Paul Robeson in 1937 in England. Amy was present on April 14, 1944, at the council's conference on 'Africa—New Perspectives,' held at its offices at 23 W. 26th Street in New York City. Among the participants were Robeson, Max Yergan, a co-founder, and Ben Davis, a prominent African American Communist Party member (and a friend of Claudia). Also present was Kwame Nkrumah" (170–71).

Since, in her lifetime, she interacted politically with a range of activists across the African world, Amy Ashwood Garvey, then, has to be reconsidered as a pivotal figure in any understanding of Caribbean left diasporic circulations, never a communist but a self-identified Pan-Africanist feminist. Her travel to Africa led to her drafting of the outline of work on the African woman, which is included as an appendix in the Tony Martin biography as the Mother Africa series (238). From this vantage point, it seemed to be the first stirrings of a phenomenal intellectual project that was to include several volumes, which perhaps could not have been realizable under her conditions. Indeed, a similar project, *Women Writing Africa,* of the Feminist Press has required for close to twenty years a team that came from all those regions of the African continent and the diaspora and numerous journeys, conferences, and collection efforts on behalf of the general editors in order to be completed.

Of further significance to this chapter's theme of circulations is her travel through the Caribbean, in the late 1950s and '60s, encouraging and advancing the work of a number of women's organizations in Barbados and Trinidad and

Tobago and speaking at an event in the Himalaya Club in San Juan, which my mother and aunt attended. Amy Ashwood Garvey practiced as well the diasporic political circulation that Brent Hayes Edwards identifies for Padmore and his work with Garane Kouyate in West Africa. It may be worth a closing comment that in a subsequent generation, Audre Lorde would have a similar pattern, as her work in the United States and Germany, South Africa and the Caribbean, follows a similar set of diasporic movements. Recent work on Audre Lorde is significant and also much needed, for Lorde perhaps best carried forward the praxis of black internationalist feminism and its logic of circulations. Also of Caribbean descent, born in New York, Lorde nevertheless finds her sense of identity in reclaiming her Caribbean *Zami* (woman loving) heritage. For Higashida, "Lorde's nationalist internationalism positions her ideologically and historically as a descendant of the postwar Black Left.... Lorde's writing displays a Marxist, pan-Africanist, and feminist worldview that her later years reprised the Black internationalist feminism of Claudia Jones [who] challenged monadic, androcentric formulations of race by accounting for the triple burden of Black working-class women . . . under U.S. imperialism" (157). This is an important observation, as it creates a series of lineages into which Audre Lorde's work fits beyond the popular definition of black lesbian, a point her partner, Gloria Joseph, consistently asserts.

Transoceanic Movements

Migration studies reveal that none of these flows of people that create diasporas are accidental but are all related to larger forces like enslavement that created the initial transatlantic traffic and also created the conditions for Europe's and America's capitalist expansion: colonialism and neocolonialism and underdevelopment, immigration legislation, the push and pull of transnational labor and migration flows, but also, as we see, intellectual, cultural, and political linkages and a basic human desire for movement. The logic of Rastafari that engaged the project of "re-semanticizing blackness," as Wynter calls it, summarizes the sense of inequality of vision, exchange, politics, location, but also resistance. One can identify, therefore, circulations of people, forms, ideas, movements.

One of the telegrams that Claudia Jones received as she left the United States said: "What is an ocean between us; we know how to build bridges." A brief conversation with Charlene Mitchell in 2009 revealed that Mitchell would meet Claudia Jones in London several times after her departure from the United States when she herself made transoceanic voyages, making political linkages that advanced a subsequent generation of intellectual and political work, including that of Angela Davis. Relatedly, Dayo Gore reveals that Vicky Ama Gavin, who was in the CPUSA around the time of Claudia Jones, lived as part of the expatriate community in Ghana that welcomed Malcolm X during his visit there, maintained her activist work, and was able to return home and end her days in the United States (*Want to Start a Revolution?* [2009], *Radicalism at the Crossroads* [2011]).

Significantly, these diasporic circulations were for political connections, knowledge sharing, and organizing. If there are any circulations today, they are perhaps minus the political urgency of an earlier time and remain perhaps at the level of intellectual or cultural exchange or are even Internet social networking. Still, in the final analysis, then, any revisions of transatlantic activism remain incomplete until they make room for more comprehensive and inclusive representations, but also the logic of mobility outside of singular, unitary locations of dominance and a much-broadened reading of the Atlantic beyond the North Atlantic, which I see as a derivative of NATO, and therefore essentially a military formation. A transoceanic framework actively engages multiple connections with the African continent as well as Central and South Americas and even Indian Ocean connections and so provides a more dynamic set of readings of Caribbean diasporic circulations.

Circulations do not presuppose neat returns to a beginning point, but posit a level of engagement that accounts for a series of transnational movement of ideas, if not bodies. The Caribbean left has been clearly active in both of these regards. Because the two pathways that Claudia Jones identified for the Caribbean in 1964—the still-developing Cuban model and the neocolonies heavily mortgaged to various imperialisms—have not been radically altered, the visible fault lines remain. One can take the position, then, that these are still ongoing processes that would therefore never accept unconditioned or permanent deferral and that therefore radiate through what I call Caribbean space in multiple directions.

12

MY FATHER DIED A SECOND TIME

Word that my father had died a second time came to me one sunny morning in Miami about a week after I had returned from a semester-long stay in Trinidad. This time, it was from a sister who gave me particulars about the funeral. Since I had just returned from Trinidad, I contemplated whether I could make a second trip to the Caribbean. After all, I had spent my whole life knowing from my mother that my father had already died. But this death was the real thing, it seemed.

When I first saw my father alive, after his first death, it was in a beautiful little village past Grenville called Paraclete. He sat in a clean white shirt striped with gray and wore gray pants, this seventyish man, and contemplated me with a smile of recognition and reassurance. From time to time, I would catch him staring at me as he inhaled a cigarette. He kept repeating that he knew I would find him one day and that he had been waiting for this moment. From his telling, it was my mother who kept him at bay. But my mother is dead now too and cannot confirm or deny.

But I have witnessed this narrative in friends and relatives—a woman who decides to move on and raise her children alone or with extended family, moving rapidly past a recalcitrant or playing man. And according to African women friends who are scholars of African gender relations, there is a recognizable African matrilineal family pattern that takes over in these cases, in which maternal uncles assume responsibility for children. So this man who was indeed my father had always told his other children, especially on those nights when he had had a couple drinks, that there was a daughter, Carole, in Trinidad. One of his sons, a brother, Leroy, told me later that he had set out to find me once, but by then we had migrated to the United States. A sister who up until she met me assumed eldest rights in the family was a superintendent of police in Grenada and when we met had taken me to dinner and actually was the conduit for all subsequent encounters with family. But before her, I had been directed by family in Trinidad to a cousin, Carl, who I discovered was a competitive sailor in Caribbean boat races. We talked by phone first, and I remember through the haze of actually making a connection late one Miami evening that he kept saying that he did not think my father was dead, that some of his uncles had gone to England and returned. Incredulously, in our first conversation, I dismissed any connecting arguments, as my father was dead and I was looking for extended family connections such as Carl was. Finally, we met, and Carl, whom I liked instinctively, as his name was so close to mine and he was a handsome-looking young man, took me for dinner and drinks in some of the clubs in Grenville, showing me off to his friends as his visiting cousin. My newly acquired sister, though, once we met, swore me to permanent sisterhood at dinner in a restaurant overlooking a beautiful Caribbean bay in Grenada.

As old as I was, I had been initially afraid to meet them, telling Carl that I doubted they would want to know who I was. A sudden shyness at the moment of possible reconnection overtook me until the next evening, when I received a phone call I suppose I had waited for my entire life: "My name is Frank and I am your father." I had always known the name and during my teenage years had even played with naming myself "Franka," thinking it a cute name that one of my Indian girl friends had.

I never met him that time, as I had to leave the next day and had been there on a business matter but returned determinedly a few months later and, after taking care of some professional matters, met my sister, functioning as family elder, in the hotel lobby, as planned. A waiting police car and with a uniformed police driver, which under other circumstances would be cause for alarm but this time was more like having diplomatic police escort service, sped us through winding roads of the rain forest as though we were dignitaries, to this village where I was to meet what had been up until this time a dead man.

As we traveled and the rain-forest landscape of that part of Grenada unfolded, childhood memories returned. All the incompletely closed answers to who was my father from the time I could ask those questions seriously of my mother and aunt, and were met with the line that my father was dead, now seemed to reopen themselves. It seemed that one of my father's friends had told my mother that he had died in a fire, and this provided her with an easy way to silence my questions.

I would learn later that he had indeed died. Like putting together pieces in a jigsaw puzzle, my father explained one day when we had a long conversation in a hotel's outdoor porch overlooking the beautiful Grand Anse Bay that he was the surviving brother of twins. His twin brother, he reported, had died in a fire. It seems that this piece of information wittingly or unwittingly had nevertheless conveniently been omitted somewhere. Along the way, I learned from him that some of his siblings and their mother had made the journey to England, that one of his brothers remained there, that my grandmother Maude on my father's side was half–Carib Indian and half-African and lived in London until she died as an old woman and on many of my journeys to London perhaps I could have met her, given the date of her death that he identified.

Still, my sense of a Caribbean identity was further confirmed in this knowledge, as is the information that Caribs in Grenada had fought to the death against Europe. "Le morne de Sauteurs," or Leapers' Hill, still embodies the resistance to domination that is inscribed on plaques on this historical site in northern Grenada where Caribs after fighting back reached the limits of their physical resistance and jumped into the Caribbean Sea rather than live as enslaved or conquered people.

On another journey to Grenada, this time at my sister's house in St. Georges, I met one of my father's brothers who still lives in London and who was paying his yearly visit home. Happy to meet me and an activist London friend, Ricky Cambridge, he relayed several stories of my father and his many youthful escapades with women, concluding with, "But I was always disappointed with how he treated the schoolteacher." A point of recognition as in the story of the *griot* of Alex Haley's *Roots* or in Amy Ashwood's story of finding her village in Ghana triggered an amazing emotion and a sense of completion. "But that was my mother!" I exclaimed. Later, a few years before her passing, when I showed my mother a photograph I had taken of my father, her resigned response was: "He used to be taller!"

I would see my father many times after that in St. Georges or Paraclete. In Grenville I was able to walk the streets with him as he proudly showed off his daughter to neighbors and friends. People knew him in the community and hailed him Caribbean style: "Bridge!" On one occasion, while I worked on a project we were running for children in the country school where one of my sisters was a teacher and is now the principal, he found a vantage point to study me from a distance as I worked and walked with friends and children at the school. I learned too that he would always go down to the school to help repair benches and desks or whatever was needed from time to time.

Another time, he asked me if I had a photograph of my mother. I carried one with me the next time I visited. It was, of course, of a now much older woman than the one he had left. Still, he gently kissed the photograph, placed it carefully in his shirt pocket, and smiled briefly, perhaps in recognition of an older memory.

In Paraclete, which I learned means "Holy Ghost," on another visit, he took me to meet a seventyish Caribbean woman who lived down the street from where his wife and children lived and with whom he stayed sometimes. Dressed in a loose Caribbean house dress, this cinnamon-colored woman wore huge gold earrings and had her braided hair rolled into circular bumps, now fashionable as Nubian knots but also a convenient way to prepare the hair when not going out. She had entreated me sweetly over a Caribbean fruit drink: "Don't be hard on your father. He always talked about you. Try to understand him. He is a good man!" Caribbean polygamy alive and well and my father a diehard practitioner!

The entire village seemed to know that I was his daughter when I first arrived. It felt then like a scene from Toni Morrison's *Song of Solomon* when the Solomon-Suleyman connection was made. People were quick to point out family characteristics, and people could identify whom I looked like whenever I walked the street. One day I met one of my sisters, the village schoolteacher, and for some reason we were wearing the exact color of mint-green blouses. This was my village too, and I felt I could always return; sisters, brothers, and nephews of all sorts erupted from the neighborhood to meet a long-lost sister or auntie, and some even bore striking resemblance to my daughters.

But my father did die this time. He had spent a few days ill at home with pneumonia and refused to go to the hospital, as he voiced his feeling that he would never come out alive from the local hospital if he did. In the end, he was hospitalized and as he imagined died there a few days later.

I did not go to the funeral. I did not feel sad, only a sense of years that could not be recovered but the security of having the final piece in a jigsaw puzzle finally put in place and the picture finally completed. Still, I would have liked to have known him as a younger man. I learned from a variety of meetings with him that he was vegetarian, naturally as is one of my daughters, and that this is a Carib trait, I gather, that he liked Carnival and Caribbean rum whenever he could get it, and obviously that he liked women. But my father had already died years before, and having buried my mother a year or so before, I did not need then another funeral.

13

POSTSCRIPT
Escape Routes

Yes, the springtime needed you.
Many a star was waiting for your eyes only.
—"Bop: The North Star," from *Open Interval,*
by Lyrae Van Clief-Stefanon

Underground Railroads

I cross back and forth between Ithaca, Binghamton, or Elmira in different seasons. Along the way from Ithaca to Binghamton, there is a city called Caroline. I smile each time I pass there and wondered how it would have been to have such an address as Caroline, New York. Sometimes it is a riotous fall-colored landscape that dazzles the senses. Sometimes it is a somber gray in any given month, or a beautifully vibrant and green spring, or the whiteness of open fields of winter landscapes.

I drove from New York City once after not having been here a long time, and it was spring and the water against the green made this a gorgeous landscape as one passes through the Delaware Water Gap. A certain majesty of rock faces against the water that seemed sculpted at another time presents a breathtaking landscape. The green on either side of the highway where there are no houses makes one think of the way the Native peoples who lived here would have erected their communities.

A sense of nostalgia washed over me and remained as I drove into Ithaca and saw the familiar landmarks. After living in Miami with its even temperature and flattened landscape, I feel a sense that I had actually missed this part of the country and its seasons, that this was still familiar territory. I feel I can embody the meaning of Harriet, and I can leave and return again.

The university etched against the hills, the cute little town in the center presents a pleasing contrast. The university president's office is decorated in pure white, sparkling clean, as is his also crisp white laundered shirt. Affably, he recounts his experience of being Jewish descended to three faculty members, my two colleagues and I. He finally gets to his point that the day that Africana was announced as being merged into Arts and Sciences was one of the happiest days of his life. We counter that it was for us one of the saddest days of our lives. Our students were traumatized a few days before exams in December. We have entered the twilight zone!

The provost sits stone-faced and Boer-like as he announced his decision as a done deal. Professors who had given more than thirty years to the institution remain shocked. One cried! Another looked depressed, as this was his retirement year. One grins! One makes faces! One doesn't know what to do! Some are visibly angry! Twilight zone!

I head to the Ithaca Airport at 5:00 a.m., making my way in the darkness to the airport to catch a 6:00 a.m. flight while snowflakes lightly begin to fall. But I know I am safe as it is just minutes away, and I arrive in time to make my flight, check in successfully, and make it easily this time through the TSA security screening. But for some reason, the flight never leaves at 6:00 a.m. It is delayed in earnest now, and the snow begins a much-steadier pace. The people around me are panicked as they walk around and check with the desk from time to time. An intercom announces a 7:00 a.m. departure and then an 8:00 a.m., and now the snow is really falling as a voice indicates that now they have to wait for clearance from the local weather center. The snow is really falling with more intensity now, and for a while we are all captured in a small airport, at the mercy of weather and recalcitrant personnel.

That sensation of twilightness permeates as the whiteness outside begins to cover everything: small planes, airport paraphernalia, trucks, and the trees, and all is lost in a sea of whiteness. At 11:00 a.m., we are given vouchers for a sandwich and a drink in the tiny greasy deli; we are told that the flight is not leaving until much later that evening once the weather clears. I report to my hosts in Texas where I am scheduled to speak that evening that this does not look good. They agree to cancel my presentation. I realize that nothing will leave that airport today. At 2:00 p.m., I check for the last time with the airport personnel, who recommend that I try tomorrow.

I make my way to my car and use a shovel to dig it out of the snow and return to my apartment, quietly musing to myself about being marooned in upstate New York. I grab something to eat and settle in for an evening of depressed and mindless television watching. The next morning is sunny, though, and the snow glistens through the trees. I return to the airport early, but there is the same crowd there from the day before, and they are not happy, all trying to get on the same flight and competing with the new arrivals who are in fact scheduled for that morning's flight. I make a quick decision that this does not look good and decide to drive to Philadelphia instead and board a plane there for a more favorable location. This is the reunion week at my Maryland university, and I had planned to be there on my way back from Texas.

Now, I am in Maryland again, and it is 2011. A friend meets me at the airport, and we revisit and relearn the community as we drive to places that we would have walked to years ago. We return to what was the women's dormitory, the site for the launching of many incomplete encounters. We walk the same pathways, but the buildings now are used differently. We view a town that not too long ago carried all the visible markers of segregation. Familiar faces are now etched with age and worry lines, but the smiles are the same even if the hair has become gray. They are welcoming faces of people whom you realize you have known since you were eighteen or nineteen. It is easy to feel comfortable now, as age has brought reason, calmness, and evenness, but also a sense of nostalgia for what could have been. Still, I am assured that I made at least 90 percent right decisions along the way.

Today again a fog hung over Ithaca, blocking all flights from entering or leaving until high noon. Farther south, one of the biggest floods in years had inundated the streets of small towns from Owego to Endicott. I wonder if there is a link. Eventually, planes begin to fly in and out, and as ours leaves, the pilot announces that the fog was hovering only over Ithaca; the sun was shining everywhere else. Escape routes can be obliterated from those who can't see, but they are always there.

The underground railroad works both ways, as Zora Neale Hurston revealed in her work and being. Driving through central Florida to get to Sanford, which is just north of Orlando and Eatonville, I imagine Zora on some of these roads in her car driving to a fieldwork site. A turtle makes its way slowly but surely to the other side of the highway. I look back in my rearview mirror to see if he can make it before the upcoming SUV. Fort Myers and Belle Glade have Caribbean-style sugar plantations and orange groves in their landscape. This means that workers of various sorts are still there. I learn on visiting a cousin who had moved there in retirement from

Brooklyn that there was even a place called "Nigger Town" a few miles away that the community wanted to rename but were fighting about what a new name would be. Sanford too has now become forever linked to the senseless shooting of a young Trayvon.

The turtle is almost to the grass now and will make it for sure.

* * *

My cousin, the same one of the encounter my mother described in which her dead lover would return, ended her years in Lake Placid, Florida, and was buried in that community. I visited her a few times toward the end of her life, and she would try to maintain still an older set of courtesies but also family-ness, insisting on making a meal for me and a friend, Leo, and giving me foodstuffs from her refrigerator to take home even though I did not need them; I took small cartons of applesauce out of courtesy. I wished I could but would never have dared to ask her about that episode, though she was the kind who would not have hesitated to provide additional detail. I missed my mother's interventions, as she would have had the right cues for such a conversation. At her viewing after she died, there was something incongruous in how she was laid out in a small and humble funeral home that seemed to have been somebody's house, across the railroad tracks, and away from all the Caribbean family trappings that would have ensured her a classier home going. Still, here she had community, and they came out the next day to bid farewell.

I think of my mother's home going and the fact that she was determined to return to the Caribbean and pass her last days here. Her church, her friends, he family and neighbors in the end provided her a beautiful exit. Different choices, certainly! And so it was that my mother lay regally adorned in a white African dress trimmed with green and gold that I had bought in Ghana, with a head wrap to match that she kept in a drawer and never could find the occasion to wear. A bouquet of yellow flowers brought by one of her helpers was arranged bridal style between her now still hands. The presiding ministers and organist in the A.M.E church we attended would make their characteristic mistakes at times, one lay minister calling out the wrong hymn on one occasion and the other correcting him just as I remembered witnessing when my aunt was the organist. But it was home and just as I remembered, those folksy services in which one can be called on to speak without preparation, to address the church with a few words, especially if visiting from abroad and where protocols in certain high churches were broken all the time.

Generations move in different directions as they navigate the space of the Americas, North and South and in between.

Sanford, Florida, is a little sleepy town to which the auto train arrives and from which it departs. But there is a great deal of history of southern racism as the film 42 on Jackie Robinson revealed. At a service station in Sanford, after we missed the train once, my co-pilot and I decided to take on Highway 95 to New York. A young black man in his thirties approached us at a service station with: "Where you from?" When he learned we were from Miami, he said: "Don't stay here. There is nothing good here for a black man." Prophetic words indeed given recent events. An oracle foreshadowing a troubled future, he disappeared down the road into another twilight space between realities. For those passing through, Sanford is a small country town near Disney World surrounded by marshes, dirt roads off main roadways which go off frighteningly in the distance. For those living there it is a place where one learns to protect oneself from danger one can walk into if a stranger. I see myself retracing the paths of several others who have made these North-South/South-North journeys throughout the years.

We travel again by train this time to attend a funeral. My brother, it seems, gave birth to me again, making his departure suddenly on my birthday. He would always tell stories to friends in my presence and much to my embarrassment but pleasure of the day that I was born and of his trailing of the nurse around the house to ensure that she would not take what was now his baby away. But on that day, there was a tragic call through tears at the other end of the phone from a nephew to open a day that was going to be a glorious one with news I did not want to hear. Trying to help somebody lift a heavy suitcase or something had rendered him with a lingering pain, lethargy, and debilitation. A journey by plane to Baltimore at the end of the week with a wife, who checked him into a hospital and then headed off for Texas, produced the news the next morning that my brother had "coded." So many unanswered questions remain. She had disappeared for the entire day, as many tried to reach her by cell phones that produced no connection. So now here he was lying in state, a wax figure, it seems now. A mocking and empty, sad laughter comes from one cousin who no doubt is in shock herself. A widowed wife seemed to have already anticipated her performance of this ending as my brother lies unmoving, his mouth formed as in a position just ready to mouth some additional words now that would never be heard. A rapid exit! An early checkout! Another twilight zone and an escape route with no return!

*　*　*

At one of the southernmost points of Miami, called Cape Florida, there is a state park. Here one can sit on a beach as one witnesses Caribbean-bound planes flying above or see cruise ships in the distance. My friend Linda and I love this vantage point. We go in and out of the water, sometimes as warm almost as a bathtub, catch up on each other's lives and our children's latest escapades, successes, or troubles. A few year earlier, a visit here for a more official reason of the city's recognition of the historic importance of this place indicated that Cape Florida was an Underground Railroad departure point for those who had reached the edge of their flight from enslavement in the United States. There is a marker here for a group of more than two hundred African Americans who were identified as departing for the Bahamas to escape slavery in the United States. The Underground Railroad moved southward in this context as it did from South Carolina to Fort Mose following the Stono Rebellion in 1739 and created an "Afrodigenous" community around St. Augustine, Florida. Escape routes took Africans to Florida and the Bahamas. Bimini is only forty-eight miles from Key West. And there is also a Bahama Village in the southernmost Keys and an African burial site along the way and into the Keys. Pirates of the Caribbean frequented the Keys and the rest of the Caribbean. And new pirates have started to reappear. Cuba had similar iconic status, then as it does now. While Little Havana freezes into a moment in time just before the 1960s and old men play dominoes in a public park, Little Haiti in Miami makes itself another Caribbean Space.

Harriet Tubman identified the necessity of movement and the transgression of borders as fundamental and critical. And while she is known more for her work liberating Africans from the Maryland area to points north, she also had the leading role in the Combahee River Raid in South Carolina, liberating about eight hundred Africans in 1863 during the Civil War. At the one-hundred-year anniversary of Harriet Tubman's passing in 2013, I attended a church service in Auburn and visited her grave site there, my way to acknowledge the living reality of Harriet—the expectation of an elsewhere that would have to be better than enslavement and a determination to see mobility as essential.

Timbuctoo in the Adirondacks or Africa Road in Vestal have escaped but recoverable historical meaning beyond the emptiness of a street sign. And upstate New York is also a place of waterfalls—natural beauty perched over dangerous gorges. And one always has a choice of the kind of life one leads . . . complacency or challenge, containment or movement.

So I too travel again south—south, to the end of the United States and look over the edge where sunsets are magnificent and unimpeded. The water beckons. Cuba—ninety miles south. Caribbean Space!

BIBLIOGRAPHY

Abiodun, Rowland. "Understanding Yoruba Art and Aesthetics: The Concept of *Àsé*." *African Arts/Arts d'Afrique* (UCLA) (1994).

Adisa, Opal Palmer. *Caribbean Passion*. Leeds: Peepal Tree Press, 2004.

Adisa, Opal Palmer, and Donna Weir-Soley, eds. *Caribbean Erotic: Poetry, Prose & Essays*. Leeds: Peepal Tree Press, 2011.

Afolabi, Niyi. *Afro-Brazilians: Cultural Production in a Racial Democracy*. Rochester, N.Y.: University of Rochester Press, 2009.

Aidoo, Ama Ata. *The Dilemma of a Ghost and Anowa*. London: Longman, 1995.

Aldana, Ligia S. "Blackness, Music, and (National/Diasporic) Identity in the Colombian Caribbean." In *Let Spirit Speak: Cultural Journeys through the African Diaspora,* edited by Vanessa K. Valdes, 39–50. Albany: State University of New York Press, 2012.

Alexander, Michelle. *The New Jim Crow: Mass Incarceration in the Age of Colorblindness*. New York: New Press, 2012.

Althusser, Louis. *Philosophy of the Encounter: Later Writings, 1978–1987*. Edited by François Matheron and Oliver Corpet. London: Verso, 2006.

Alves, Miriam, ed. *Enfim Nós/Finally Us: Contemporary Black Brazilian Women Writers*. Pueblo, Colo.: Three Continents/Passeggiata Press, 1995.

———. "Mulheres Negras Escritoras Brasileiras: A Magia da Força Ancestral Escre-Vindo." Unpublished manuscript.

Appadurai, Arjun. "Disjuncture and Difference in the Global Cultural Economy." *Public Culture* 2, no. 2 (1990): 1–24.

Auguiste, Reece. *Twilight City*. London: Black Audio Film Collective for Channel 4, 1989.

Baker, Ella, and Marvel Cooke. "The Bronx Slave Market." *Crisis* 42 (November 1935): 330–31, 340.

Baker, Houston. *Betrayal: How Black Intellectuals Have Abandoned the Ideals of the Civil Rights Era.* New York: Columbia University Press, 2008.

———. *Blues, Ideology, and Afro-American Literature: A Vernacular Theory.* Chicago: University of Chicago Press, 1987.

———, ed. *Workings of the Spirit: The Poetics of Afro-American Women's Writing.* Chicago: University of Chicago Press, 1993.

Ball, Jared, and Todd Steven Burroughs, eds. *A Lie of Reinvention: Correcting Manning Marable's Malcolm X.* Silver Springs, Md.: Black Classics Press, 2012.

Baptiste, Fitzroy, and Rupert Lewis, eds. *George Padmore: Pan-African Revolutionary.* Caribbean Reasonings Series. Kingston, Jamaica: Ian Randle, 2006.

Barnes, Natasha. *Cultural Conundrums: Gender, Race, Nation, and the Making of Caribbean Cultural Politics.* Ann Arbor: University of Michigan Press, 2006.

———. "Face of the Nation: Race, Nationalisms, and Identities in Jamaican Beauty Pageants." In *Daughters of Caliban: Caribbean Women in the Twentieth Century,* edited by Consuelo Lopez-Springfield, 285–305. Bloomington: Indiana University Press, 1997.

Barrera, Mario. *Race and Class in the Southwest: A Theory of Racial Inequality.* Notre Dame, Ind.: University of Notre Dame Press, 1989.

Beckles, Hilary. "The Hate and the Quake." Caribbean Studies Association, 2010. http://www.csa.com.

Beckles, Hilary, and Verene Shepherd. *Caribbean Freedom: Economy and Society from Emancipation to the Present.* Princeton, N.J.: Marcus Wiener, 1996.

———. *Freedoms Won: Caribbean Emancipations, Ethnicities, and Nationhood.* Cambridge: Cambridge University Press, 2007.

Bell, Beverly, ed. *Walking on Fire: Haitian Women's Stories of Survival and Resistance.* Ithaca, N.Y.: Cornell University Press, 2001.

Benitez-Rojo, Antonio. *The Repeating Island: The Caribbean and Postmodern Perspective.* 1992. Reprint, Durham, N.C.: Duke University Press, 1997.

Black, Stephanie. *Life and Debt.* Tuff Gong Pictures, 2001.

Boyce Davies, Carole. "African Diaspora Memory and LeRoy Clarke's Aesthetic of the Shadow." In *LeRoy at 70: The Art, the Poetry, the Man,* 44–69. Trinidad and Tobago: UNESCO National Commission, 2011.

———. *Black Women, Writing, and Identity: Migrations of the Subject.* London: Routledge, 1994.

———, ed. *Claudia Jones: Beyond Containment.* Banbury, Oxfordshire, England: Ayebia Clarke, 2011.

———. "From Masquerade to Maskarade: Sylvia Wynter and the Re-humanizing Project." In *Yours in the Intellectual Struggle: On Sylvia Wynter and the Realization of the Living,* edited by Katherine McKittrick. Durham, N.C.: Duke University Press, in press.

———. "Haiti, I Can See Your Halo: Migration, Landscape, and Nation in Danticat's Diaspora." *JALA: Journal of the African Literature Association* (Spring 2011): 87–100.

————. Introduction to *Encyclopedia of the African Diaspora: Origins, Experiences, and Culture,* 1: xxxi–lviii. Santa Barbara, Calif.: ABC-CLIO, 2008.

————. *Left of Karl Marx: The Political Life of Black Communist Claudia Jones.* Durham, N.C.: Duke University Press, 2008.

————, ed. *Moving beyond Boundaries: International Dimensions of Black Women's Writing and Black Women's Diasporas.* Vol. 2. New York: New York University Press, 1994.

————. "The Politics of African Identification in Trinidad Calypso." *Studies in Popular Culture* 8, no. 2 (1985): 77–94.

————. "Triply Diasporized: Literary Pathways of Caribbean Migration and Diaspora." In *Routledge Companion to Caribbean Literature,* edited by Michael Bucknor and Allison Donnell, 508–16. London: Routledge, 2011.

Boyce Davies, Carole, and Elaine Savory Fido, eds. *Out of the Kumbla: Caribbean Women and Literature.* Trenton, N.J.: Africa World Press, 1990.

Boyce Davies, Carole, and Monica Jardine. "Caribbean Migrations and Identities." In *Sage Handbook of Identities,* edited by Chandra Mohanty and Margaret Wetherell, 437–54. London: Sage, 2010.

Boyce Davies, Carole, and Babacar M'bow. "Toward African Diaspora Citizenship: Politicising an Existing Geography." In *Black Geographies and the Politics of Place,* edited by Katherine McKittrick and Clyde Woods, 14–45. Cambridge, Mass.: South End Press, 2007.

Braga, Julio. "Candomblé: Força e resistência." *Afro-Asia: Publicação do Centro Afro-Orientais da Universidade Federal da Bahia* 15 (1992).

Brand, Dionne. *In Another Place, Not Here.* Toronto: Alfred A. Knopf, 1997.

————. *A Map to the Door of No Return: Notes to Belonging.* Toronto: Vintage, 2001.

Brathwaite, Kamau. *The Arrivants: A New World Trilogy.* Oxford: Oxford University Press, 1967.

————. *Middle Passages.* New York: New Directions, 1993.

Bryce, Jane, ed. *Caribbean Dispatches: Beyond the Tourist Dream.* Oxford: Macmillan Caribbean, 2006.

Cambridge, Alrick X. "When Socialist Values Harmonize with the Human Desire for Liberation: Assessing Claudia Jones' Politics." Afterword to *Claudia Jones: Beyond Containment,* 207–20. Banbury, UK: Ayebia, 2011.

Carew, Jan. *Ghosts in Our Blood: With Malcolm X in Africa, England, and the Caribbean.* Chicago: Lawrence Hill Books, 1994.

Carmichael, Stokely, with Michael Thelwell. *Ready for Revolution: The Life and Struggles of Stokely Carmichael.* New York: Scribner, 2003.

Carpentier, Alejo. "On the Marvelous Real in America." In *The Kingdom of This World: A Novel.* 1949. Reprint, New York: Farrar, Straus, and Giroux, 1989.

Carter, Thomas F. "Absence Makes the State Grow Stronger: Preliminary Thoughts on Revolutionary Space, Spectacle, and State Legitimacy." In *Cuban Intersections of Literary and Urban Spaces,* edited by Carlos Riobo, 49–65. Albany: State University of New York Press, 2011.

Centre for Contemporary Cultural Studies, University of Birmingham. *The Empire Strikes Back: Race and Racism in '70s Britain*. New York: Routledge, 1982.

Césaire, Aimé. *Discourse on Colonialism*. New York: Monthly Review Press, 1955.

Chamberlain, Mary, ed. *Caribbean Migration, Globalised Identities*. London: Routledge, 1998.

Chisholm, Shirley. *Unbought and Unbossed*. 1970. Reprint, New York: Houghton Mifflin, 2010.

Cianci, Giovanni, Caroline Patey, and Sara Sullam, eds. *Transits: The Nomadic Geographies of Anglo-American Modernism*. Oxford: Peter Lang, 2010.

Clarke, Austin. *Pig Tails 'n Breadfruit: A Culinary Memoir*. New York: New Press, 2000.

Clarke, LeRoy. *De Distance Is Here: The El Tucuche Epic, 1984–2007*. Port of Spain: University of Trinidad and Tobago Press, 2007.

Coiner, Constance, with Diane Hume George, eds. *The Family Track: Keeping Your Faculties while You Mentor, Nurture, Teach, and Serve*. Urbana: University of Illinois Press, 1998.

Colina, Paulino, ed. *Axé: Antologia da Poesia Negra Contemporânea Brasileira*. São Paulo: Global, 1982.

Cooper, Carolyn. "Caribbean Fashion Week: Remodelling Beauty in 'Out of Many One' Jamaica." *Fashion Theory* 14, no. 3 (2010): 387–404.

Craig-James, Susan. *The Changing Society of Tobago, 1838–1938: A Fractured Whole*. Vol. 1, *1838–1900*. Vol. 2, *1900–1938*. Trinidad and Tobago: Cornerstone, 2008.

Crichlow, Michaeline, and Patricia Northover, eds. *Race, Space, Place: The Making and Unmaking of Freedoms in the Atlantic World*. Beverly Hills, Calif.: Sage, 2009.

———. "Rethinking the Mangrove of Caribbean Space and Time." *Social and Economic Studies* 61, no. 4 (2012): 216–28.

Cruz, Angie. *Let It Rain Coffee*. New York: Simon and Schuster, 2005.

Cury, Cristiane Abdon, and Sueli Carneiro. "O Poder feminino no Culto aos Orixás." *Revista de Cultura Vozes* 84, no. 2 (1990): 157–79.

D'Aguiar, Fred. *Continental Shelf*. Manchester: Carcanet Press, 2011.

Dalleo, Raphael. *Caribbean Literature and the Public Sphere: From the Plantation to the Postcolonial*. Charlottesville: University Press of Virginia, 2011.

Damas, Leon. *Pigments—Névralgies*. Paris: Presence Africaine, 2001.

Danticat, Edwidge. *After the Dance: A Walk through Carnival in Jacmel, Haiti*. New York: Crown Books, 2002.

———. *Behind the Mountains*. New York: Scholastic Books, 2004.

———. *Breath, Eyes, Memory*. New York: Vintage, 1994.

———. *Brother, I'm Dying*. New York: Alfred A. Knopf, 2007.

———, ed. *The Butterfly's Way: Voices from the Haitian Dyaspora in the United States*. New York: Soho Press, 2003.

———. "Children of the Sea." In *Krik? Krak!* New York: Knopf/Doubleday, 1996.

———. *Create Dangerously: The Immigrant Artist at Work*. New York: Vintage, 2011.

————. *The Dew Breaker.* London: Vintage, 2005.

————. *The Farming of Bones.* London: Penguin, 1999.

————. "Ghosts." *New Yorker,* November 2008. http://www.newyorker.com/fiction/features/2008/11/24/081124fi_fiction_danticat.

————. "We Are Ugly, but We Are Here." *Caribbean Writer* 10 (1996).

Dash, Michael. *The Other America: Caribbean Literature in a New World Context.* Charlottesville: University Press of Virginia, 1998.

da Silva, Benedita. *Benedita da Silva: An Afro-Brazilian Woman's Story of Politics and Love.* Oakland, Calif.: Food First Books, 1997.

Davis, Arthur P., J. Saunders Redding, and Joyce Ann Joyce eds. *The New Cavalcade: African American Writing from 1760 to the Present.* Washington, D.C.: Howard University Press, 1992.

de Almeida, Lino. "Religion, Culture, and Revolution in the African Diaspora." Global Yoruba Conference, Florida International University, 1999. Unpublished paper in author's possession.

DeLoughrey, Elizabeth. *Routes and Roots: Navigating Caribbean and Pacific Island Literatures.* Honolulu: University of Hawaii Press, 2010.

Diawara, Manthia. "Conversation with Edouard Glissant aboard the *Queen Mary II* (August, 2009)." In *Afro Modern: Journeys through the Black Atlantic,* edited by Tanya Barson and Peter Gorschluter, 58–64. Liverpool: Tate Liverpool, 2010.

Diaz, Junot. *Drown.* New York: Riverhead Books, 1996.

do Nascimento, Abdias. "O Quilombismo: Uma Alternativa Politica Afro-Brasileira." In *Carta' 13: Falas, Reflexoes, Memorias.* Brasília: Gabinete do Senador Darcy Ribeiro, 1994.

Douglas, Marcia. *Notes from a Writer's Book of Cures and Spells.* Leeds: Peepal Tree Press, 2005.

Dunkley, Daive A., ed. *Readings in Caribbean History and Culture.* Lanham, Md.: Lexington Books, 2011.

Edmondson, Belinda. *Caribbean Middlebrow: Leisure, Culture, and the Middle Class.* Ithaca, N.Y.: Cornell University Press, 2009.

————. "Public Spectacles: Caribbean Women and the Politics of Public Performance." *Small Axe* 13 (2005).

Edwards, Brent Hayes. *The Practice of Diaspora: Literature, Translation, and the Rise of Black Internationalism.* Cambridge, Mass.: Harvard University Press, 2003.

Eells, Josh. "Rihanna: Queen of Pain." *Rolling Stone,* April 24, 2011, 40–45, 80.

Elder, J. D. "Towards a Caribbean Aesthetic." In *LeRoy Clarke: Of Flesh and Salt and Wind and Current, a Retrospective,* edited by Caroline C. Ravello, 166–70. Port of Spain, Trinidad and Tobago: National Museum and Art Gallery, 2003.

Erikson, Erik H. "Inner and Outer Space: Reflections on Womanhood." *Daedalus* 93, no. 2 (1964): 582–606.

Eshun, Kodwo. "Twilight City: Outline for an Archaeopsychic Geography of New London." *Wasafiri* 19, no. 43 (2004): 7–13.

Fanon, Frantz. *Black Skin, White Masks*. 1952. New York: Grove, 2008.

———. *The Wretched of the Earth*. 1963. New York: Grove, 2005.

Figueroa, Mark. "Migration and Remittances: Typologies and Motivations." In *Freedom and Constraint in Caribbean Migration and Diaspora,* edited by Elizabeth Thomas-Hope, 235–57. Kingston and Miami: Ian Randle, 2009.

Fox, Margalit. "Rosa Guy, 89, Author of Forthright Novels for Young People, Dies." *New York Times,* June 7, 2012, A25.

Fulani, Ifeona, ed. *Archipelagos of Sound: Transnational Caribbeanities, Women, and Music*. Kingston, Jamaica: University of the West Indies Press, 2012.

Garcia, Cristina. *Dreaming in Cuban*. New York: Alfred A. Knopf, 1992.

Giddings, Paula. *When and Where I Enter*. New York: Bantam, 1984.

Gilroy, Beryl. *Black Teacher*. 1976. Reprint, London: Bogle l'Ouverture Press, 1994.

———. *Frangipani House*. 1982. Reprint, London: Heinemann, 1986.

———. *Gather the Faces*. Leeds: Peepal Tree Press, 2001.

———. *In Praise of Love and Children*. Leeds: Peepal Tree Press, 2002.

Girvan, Norman. "Creating and Recreating the Caribbean." In *Contending with Destiny: The Caribbean in the 21st Century,* edited by Kenneth Hall and Denis Benn, 31–36. Mona, Jamaica: Ian Randle, 2000.

———. "Reinterpreting the Caribbean." In *New Caribbean Thought: A Reader,* edited by Brian Meeks and Folke Lindahl, 3–22. Jamaica, Barbados, Trinidad and Tobago: University of the West Indies Press, 2001.

Glave, Thomas, ed. "He Who Would Have Become 'Joshua,' 1791." In *The Torturer's Wife*. San Francisco: City Lights, 2009.

———. *Our Caribbean: A Gathering of Lesbian and Gay Writing from the Antilles*. Durham, N.C.: Duke University Press, 2008.

Glissant, Edouard. *Caribbean Discourse: Selected Essays*. 1989. Charlottesville: University Press of Virginia, 1999.

———. *Poetics of Relation*. Ann Arbor: University of Michigan Press, 1997.

Goodison, Lorna. *By Love Possessed: Stories*. New York: Amistad, 2012.

———. *From Harvey River: A Memoir of My Mother and Her Island*. New York: Amistad, 2008.

———. *Travelling Mercies*. Kingston, Jamaica: Ian Randle, 2001.

Gore, Dayo. "From Communist Politics to Black Power: The Visionary Politics and Transnational Solidarities of Victoria Vicky Ama Gavin." In *Want to Start a Revolution? Radical Women in the Black Freedom Struggle*. New York: New York University Press, 2009.

———. *Radicalism at the Crossroads: African American Women Activists in the Cold War*. New York: New York University Press, 2011.

Gore, Dayo, Jeanne Theoharis, and Komozi Woodard, eds. *Want to Start a Revolution? Radical Women in the Black Freedom Struggle*. New York: New York University Press, 2009.

Goulbourne, Harry, and Mary Chamberlain, eds. *Caribbean Families and the Trans-Atlantic World*. Warwick University Caribbean Studies. London: Macmillan, 2001.

Greene, Brian. *The Hidden Reality: Parallel Universes and the Deep Laws of the Cosmos.* New York: Alfred A. Knopf, 2011.

Griffith, Ivelaw Lloyd. "Drugs and Crime as Problems without Passports in the Caribbean: How Secure Is Security and How Sovereign Is Sovereignty." Thirteenth Annual Eric E. Williams Memorial Lecture, Florida International University, October 28, 2011.

———. *Drugs and Security in the Caribbean: Sovereignty under Siege.* University Park: Pennsylvania State University Press, 1997.

Haile, Reesom. *We Invented the Wheel.* Translated by Charles Cantalupo. Trenton, N.J.: Red Sea Press, 2002.

Hall, Stuart. "Cultural Identity and Cinematic Representation." In *Ex-Iles: Essays on Caribbean Cinema,* edited by Mbye Cham, 220–36. Trenton, N.J.: Africa World Press, 1992.

———. "Race, Articulation, and Societies Structured in Dominance." In *Sociological Theories: Race and Colonialism,* 305–45. Paris and London: UNESCO, 1980.

———. "Thinking about Thinking." Afterword to *Culture, Politics, Race, and Diaspora: The Thought of Stuart Hall,* edited by Brian Meeks. Caribbean Reasonings Series. Kingston, Jamaica: Ian Randle, 2007.

———. "Thinking the Diaspora: Home-Thoughts from Abroad." *Small Axe* 6 (September 1999): 1–18.

———. "What Is This 'Black' in Black Popular Culture?" In *Black Popular Culture,* edited by Gina Dent and Michelle Wallace, 21–33. Seattle: Bay Press, 1992.

Halperin, Shirley. "Meet the Real Nicki Minaj." *Cosmopolitan,* November 2011, 31–35.

Hardt, Michael, and Antonio Negri. *Empire.* 2000. Reprint, Cambridge: Cambridge University Press, 2004.

Harris, Cheryl. "Whiteness as Property." *Harvard Law Review* 106, no. 8 (1993): 1707–91.

Harris, Lashawn. "Running with the Reds: African American Women and the Communist Party during the Great Depression." *Journal of African American History* 94, no. 19 (2009): 21–43.

Harris, Wilson. *The Womb of Space: The Cross-Cultural Imagination.* Westport, Conn.: Greenwood Press, 1983.

Harvey, David. *Spaces of Hope.* Berkeley: University of California Press, 2000.

Hayden, Delores. *The Power of Place: Urban Landscapes as Public History.* Boston: MIT Press, 1997.

Henderson, Stephen. *Understanding the New Black Poetry: Black Speech and Black Music as Poetic References.* New York: William Morrow, 1973.

Hernandez i Marti, Gil-Manuel. "The Deterritorialization of Cultural Heritage in a Globalized Modernity." http://www.llull.cat/rec_transfer/webt1/transfer01_foco4.pdf.

Higashida, Cheryl. *Black Internationalist Feminism: Women Writers of the Black Left, 1945–1995.* Urbana: University of Illinois Press, 2011.

Hill, Anita. *Reimagining Equality: Stories of Gender, Race, and Finding Home.* Boston: Beacon Press, 2011.

———. *Speaking Truth to Power*. New York: Anchor, 1998.

Hudson, Brian. "Caribbean Migration: Motivation and Choice of Destination in West Indian Literature." In *Small Worlds, Global Lives: Islands and Migration,* edited by Russell Kini and John Connell. London and New York: Pinter, 1999.

Hull, Gloria T., Patricia Bell-Scott, and Barbara Smith. *All the Women Are White, All the Blacks Are Men, but Some of Us Are Brave*. New York: Feminist Press, 1982.

Hurston, Zora Neale. *Tell My Horse: Voodoo and Life in Haiti and Jamaica*. New York: Harper Perennial, 2008.

Inikori, Joseph E. "The Slave Trade and the Atlantic Economies, 1451–1870." In *Caribbean Slavery in the Atlantic World: A Student Reader,* edited by Hilary McD. Beckles and Verene A. Shepherd, 290–308. Kingston, Jamaica: Ian Randle, 2000.

Jackson, Shona. *Creole Indigeneity: Between Myth and Nation in the Caribbean*. Minneapolis: University of Minnesota Press, 2012.

James, C. L. R. *The Black Jacobins: Toussaint L'Ouverture and the San Domingo Revolution*. New York: Vintage, 1989.

James, Winston. *Holding Aloft the Banner of Ethiopia: Caribbean Radicalism in Early Twentieth Century America*. London: Verso, 1999.

James, Winston, and Clive Harris. *Inside Babylon: The Caribbean Diaspora in Britain*. London: Verso, 1993.

James, Winston, and Claude McKay. *A Fierce Hatred of Injustice: Claude McKay's Jamaican Poetry of Rebellion*. London: Verso, 2001.

Jardine, Monica. "Caribbean Migrations: The Caribbean Diaspora." In *Encyclopedia of the African Diaspora,* 270–87. Oxford and Santa Barbara, Calif.: ABC-CLIO, 2008.

Jarrett-Macauley, Delia. *The Life of Una Marson, 1905–1965*. 1998. Reprint, Manchester: Manchester University Press, 2010.

Jones, Claudia. "American Imperialism and the British West Indies." In *Claudia Jones: Beyond Containment,* edited by Carole Boyce Davies, 156–65. Banbury, UK: Ayebia, 2011.

———. "The Caribbean Community in Britain." *Freedomways* (Summer 1964): 340–57.

Josephs, Kelly Baker. "Versions of X/Self: Kamau Brathwaite's Caribbean Discourse." *Anthurium: A Caribbean Studies Journal* 1, no. 1 (2003): 1–12.

Julien, Isaac, and Kobena Mercer. *Brother to Brother: New Writings by Black Gay Men*. Edited by Essex Hemphill. 1991. Reprint, Washington, D.C.: RedBone Press, 2007.

Kammem, Carol. Review of *Part and Apart: Black Students at Cornell University, 1865–1945. Cornell Chronicle,* May 28, 2009.

Kelley, Robin D. G. "But a Local Phase of a World Problem: Black History's Global Vision, 1883–1950." *Journal of American History* 86, no. 3 (1999): 1045–77.

Kincaid, Jamaica. *Annie John*. 1985. Reprint, New York: Farrar, Straus, and Giroux, 1997.

———. *Lucy: A Novel*. 1990. Reprint, New York: Farrar, Straus, and Giroux, 2002.

———. *My Garden Book*. New York: Farrar, Straus, and Giroux, 1999.

———. *See Now Then: A Novel*. New York: Farrar, Straus, and Giroux, 2013.

———. *A Small Place.* New York: Vintage, 1988.

Knight, Franklin W. *The Caribbean: The Genesis of a Fragmented Nationalism.* New York: Oxford University Press, 2012.

Koschar, Rakesh, Richard Fry, and Paul Taylor. "Wealth Gap Rises to Record Highs between Whites, Blacks, and Hispanics." Pew Research Center Social and Demographic Trends. *Pew Report* (July 26, 2011).

Kunjufu, Jawanza. *Countering the Conspiracy to Destroy Black Boys.* 1985. Reprint, Chicago: African American Images, 2004.

Lacy, Karyn. "Black Spaces, Black Places: Strategic Assimilation and Identity Construction in Middle-Class Suburbia." *Ethnic and Racial Studies* 27, no. 6 (2004): 908–30.

Lamming, George. *The Emigrants.* 1954. Reprint, London: Allison and Busby, 1980.

———. *The Pleasures of Exile.* 1960. Reprint, London: Allison & Busby, 1984.

Lazarus, Neil. *Nationalism and Cultural Practice in the Postcolonial World.* Cambridge: Cambridge University Press, 1999.

Lefebvre, Henri. *State, Space, World: Selected Essays.* Edited by Neil Brenner and Stuart Elden. Minneapolis: University of Minnesota Press, 2009.

Lemelle, Sidney, and Robin D. G. Kelley. *Imagining Home: Class, Culture, and Nationalism in the African Diaspora.* London: Verso, 1994.

Lorde, Audre. "Uses of the Erotic: The Erotic as Power." In *Sister Outsider: Essays and Speeches,* 53–59. Trumansburg, N.Y.: Crossing Press, 1984.

———. *Zami: A New Spelling of My Name.* 1982. Trumansburg, N.Y.: Crossing Press, 2011.

Lovelace, Earl. *A Brief Conversion, and Other Stories.* London: Heinemann, 1988.

———. *Is Just a Movie.* Chicago: Haymarket Books, 2012.

Mahabir, Joy. "Poetics of Space in the Worlds of Mahadai Das and Adesh Samaroo." *Anthurium: A Caribbean Studies Journal* 7, nos. 1–2 (2009).

Mahabir, Joy, and Mariam Pirbhai, eds. *Critical Perspectives on Indo-Caribbean Literature.* London: Routledge, 2013.

Makalani, Minkah. *In the Cause of Freedom: Radical Black Internationalism from Harlem to London, 1917–1939.* Chapel Hill: University of North Carolina Press, 2011.

Marable, Manning. *Malcolm X: A Life of Reinvention.* New York: Penguin, 2011.

Marshall, Paule. *Brown Girl, Brownstones.* 1959. Reprint, New York: Feminist Press, 1981.

———. *The Chosen Place, the Timeless People.* 1969. Reprint, New York: Vintage, 1984.

———. *Daughters.* New York: Plume, 1992.

———. *Fisher King.* New York: Scribner, 2001.

———. *Praisesong for the Widow.* New York: Putnam, 1983.

———. *Reena, and Other Stories.* 1983. Reprint, New York: Feminist Press, 1993.

———. *Triangular Road.* New York: Basic Civitas Books, 2009.

Martin, Anthony. *Amy Ashwood Garvey: Pan-Africanist, Feminist, and Mrs. Marcus Garvey No. 1; or, A Tale of Two Amies.* Dover, Mass.: Majority Press, 2007.

Massey, Doreen B. *For Space.* London: Sage, 2005.

Mathurin, Owen. *Henry Sylvester Williams and the Origins of the Pan-African Movement.* West Port, Conn.: Greenwood Press, 1976.

McDuffie, Erik. *Sojourning for Freedom: Black Women, American Communism, and the Making of Black Left Feminism.* Durham, N.C.: Duke University Press, 2011.

McKay, Claude. *Harlem Shadows: The Poems of Claude McKay (1922).* Whitefish, Mont.: Kessinger, 2009.

———. *Home to Harlem.* Northeastern Library of Black Literature. 1928. Reprint, Boston: Northeastern University Press, 1987.

———. *A Long Way from Home.* 1937. Reprint, New Brunswick, N.J.: Rutgers University Press, 2007.

McKittrick, Katherine. "Who Do You Talk to, When a Body's in Trouble? M. Nourbese Philip's (Un)silencing of Black Bodies in the Diaspora." *Social and Cultural Geography* 1, no. 2 (2000): 223–36.

McKittrick, Katherine, and Clyde Woods, eds. *Black Geographies and the Politics of Place.* Toronto: Between the Lines; Cambridge, Mass.: South End Press, 2007.

Meeks, Brian. "The Caribbean Left at Century's End." In *Narratives of Resistance.* Kingston, Jamaica: University of the West Indies Press, 2000.

———, ed. *Culture, Politics, Race, and Diaspora: The Thought of Stuart Hall.* Caribbean Reasonings Series. Kingston, Jamaica: Ian Randle, 2007.

Mehta, Brinda. *Diasporic (Dis)locations: Indo-Caribbean Women Writers Negotiate the Kala Pani.* Kingston, Jamaica: University of the West Indies Press, 2004.

Mies, Maria, Veronika Bennholdt-Thomsen, and Claudia von Werholf. *Women: The Last Colony.* Atlantic Highlands, N.J.: Zed Press, 1988.

Mignolo, Walter. "Delinking: The Rhetoric of Modernity, the Logic of Coloniality, and the Grammar of De-coloniality." *Cultural Studies* 21, no. 2 (2007): 449–514.

Morrison, Toni. *Beloved.* New York: Alfred A. Knopf, 1987.

———. *Playing in the Dark: Whiteness and the Literary Imagination.* New York: Vintage, 1993.

Murphy, Joseph M. *Working the Spirit: Ceremonies of the African Diaspora.* Boston: Beacon Press, 1995.

Nichols, Grace. *I Is a Long Memoried Woman.* London: Karnak House, 1983.

Noguera, Pedro. "Anything but Black: Bringing Politics Back to the Study of Race." Afterword to *Problematizing Blackness: Self-Ethnographies by Black Immigrants to the United States,* edited by Jean Muteba Rahier and Percy Hintzen, 193–200. London: Routledge, 2002.

Nourbese Philip, M. "Dis Place: The Space Between." In *A Genealogy of Resistance, and Other Essays.* Toronto: Mercury Press, 1997.

———. *Frontiers: Selected Essays and Writings on Racism and Culture, 1984–1992.* Toronto: Mercury, 1992.

———. *She Tries Her Tongue: Her Silence Softly Breaks.* Charlottetown, Prince Edward Island, Canada: Ragweed Press, 1989.

————. *Zong.* Middletown, Conn.: Wesleyan University Press; Toronto: Mercury Press, 2008.

Nunez, Elizabeth. *Beyond the Limbo Silence.* New York: One World/Ballantine, 2003.

Nuttall, Sarah, ed. *Beautiful/Ugly: African and Diaspora Aesthetics.* Durham, N.C.: Duke University Press, 2007.

Page, Kezia Ann. *Transnational Negotiations in Caribbean Diasporic Literature: Remitting the Text.* New York: Routledge, 2011.

Paul, Annie, ed. *Caribbean Culture: Soundings on Kamau Brathwaite.* Mona, Jamaica: University of the West Indies Press, 2006.

Perez, Loida Maritza. *Geographies of Home.* London: Penguin, 2000.

Perry, Jeffrey B. *Hubert Harrison: The Voice of Harlem Radicalism, 1883–1918.* New York: Columbia University Press, 2009.

Pessar, Patricia. *Caribbean Circuits.* New York: Center of Migration Studies, 1996.

Phillips, Caryl. *The Atlantic Sound.* London: Faber and Faber, 2000.

————. *The Final Passage.* London: Faber and Faber, 1985.

Pinha, Patricia. "Afro-Aesthetics in Brazil." In *Beautiful/Ugly: African and Diaspora Aesthetics,* edited by Sarah Nuttall, 266–89. Durham, N.C.: Duke University Press, 2006.

Prater, Tzarina T. "Caribbean Spaces, Transatlantic Spirit: Violence and Spiritual Reimaginings in the Caribbean." In *Let Spirit Speak: Cultural Journeys through the African Diaspora,* edited by Vanessa K. Valdes, 77–87. Albany: State University of New York Press, 2012.

Putnam, Lara. *Radical Moves: Caribbean Migrants and the Politics of Race in the Jazz Age.* Chapel Hill: University of North Carolina Press, 2013.

Quijano, Annibal. "Coloniality of Power, Eurocentrism, and Latin America." *Nepantla: Views from the South* 1, no. 3 (2000): 533–80.

Ramchand, Kenneth. *The West Indian Novel and Its Background.* 1970. Reprint, Kingston, Jamaica: Ian Randle, 2004.

Rhys, Jean. *Wide Sargasso Sea.* 1966. Reprint, New York: W. W. Norton, 1992.

Riley, Joan. *The Unbelonging.* 1985. Reprint, London: Trafalgar Square, 1993.

Riley, Joan, and Briar Wood, eds. *Leave to Stay: Stories of Exile and Belonging.* London: Virago, 1996.

Riobó, Carlos. "Cuban Intersections of Writing and Space: Colonial Foundations and Neobaroque *Orígenes.*" In *Cuban Intersections of Literary and Urban Spaces,* 3–21. Albany: State University of New York Press, 2011.

Robinson, Eugene. *Disintegration.* New York: Anchor Books, 2010.

Robinson, Michelle LaVaughn. "Princeton-Educated Blacks and the Black Community." Undergraduate thesis, Princeton University, 1985.

Rodney, Walter. *Walter Rodney Speaks: The Making of an African Intellectual.* Trenton, N.J.: Africa World Press, 1990.

Rojas, Fabio. *From Black Power to Black Studies: How a Radical Social Movement Became an Academic Discipline.* Baltimore: Johns Hopkins University Press, 2010.

Rudder, David. "Haiti, I'm Sorry." 1988.

Santiago, Kelvin. *Subject Peoples*. Albany: State University of New York Press, 1994.

Santos-Febres, Mayra. *Boat People*. San Juan: Ediciones Callejon, 2005.

———. *Sirena Selena: A Novel*. New York: Picador, 2001. [Spanish edition: *Sirena Selena vestida de pena*. Italy: Mondari, 2000 & Punto de Lectura, 2009.]

Sassen, Saskia. *Deciphering the Global: Its Spaces, Scales, and Subjects*. New York: Routledge, 2007.

———. *The Global City*. Princeton, N.J.: Princeton University Press, 2001.

Scher, Philip. W., ed. *Perspectives on the Caribbean: A Reader in Culture, History, and Representation*. Malden, Mass.: Wiley-Blackwell, 2010.

Scott, David. *Conscripts of Modernity: The Tragedy of Colonial Enlightenment*. Durham, N.C.: Duke University Press, 2004.

———. "The Re-enchantment of Humanism: An Interview with Sylvia Wynter." *Small Axe* (2000): 120–207.

———. *Refashioning Futures: Criticism after Postcoloniality*. Princeton, N.J.: Princeton University Press, 1999.

Scott, Joan. "Gender: A Useful Category of Analysis." *American Historical Review* 91, no. 5 (1986): 1053–75.

Selvon, Samuel. *An Island Is a World*. Toronto: TSAR, 1993.

———. *The Lonely Londoners*. 1956. Reprint, London: Penguin, 2006.

Sheller, Mimi. *Citizenship from Below: Erotic Agency and Caribbean Freedom*. Durham, N.C.: Duke University Press, 2012.

———. *Consuming the Caribbean: From Arawaks to Zombies*. London: Routledge, 2003.

Shepherd, Jessica. "14,000 British Professors—but Only 50 Are Black." *Guardian*, May 27 and 30, 2011.

Smartt, Dorothea. "Medusa? Medusa Black!" In *Connecting Medium*. Leeds: Peepal Tree Press, 2001.

———. *Ship Shape*. Leeds: Peepal Tree Press, 2009.

Smedley, Audrey, and Janis Faye Hutchison. *Racism in the Academy: The New Millennium*. American Anthropological Association, 2007. http://www.aaanet.org/cmtes/commissions/Racism-in-the-Academy-New-Millennium.cfm.

Smedley, Audrey, and Brian Smedley. *Race in North America: Origin and Evolution of a Worldview*. Boulder, Colo.: Westview Press, 2011.

Sodré, Muniz. *O terreiro e a cidade: A forma social Afro-brasileiro*. Vol. 1 of *Coleção Negros em libertação: Rio de Janeiro*. Secretaria da Cultura e Turismo, 1988; Salvador: Imago, Fundação Cultural do Estado da Bahia, 2002.

Soja, E. W. *Postmodern Geographies: The Reassertion of Space in Critical Social Theory*. London: Verso, 1989.

———. *Seeking Spatial Justice*. Minneapolis: University of Minnesota Press, 2010.

Springer, Eintou Pearl. *Out of the Shadows*. London: Karia Press, 1986.

Steele, Claude M. *Whistling Vivaldi: How Stereotypes Affect Us and What We Can Do*. New York: W. W. Norton, 2011.

Stephens, Michelle Ann. *Black Empire: The Masculine Global Imaginary of Caribbean Intellectuals in the United States, 1914–1962.* Durham, N.C.: Duke University Press, 2005.

Tanker, Andre. "I Went Away" (1970). On *Andre Tanker's Greatest Hits* (2008).

Teelucksingh, Jerome. *Caribbean Liberators: Bold, Brilliant, and Black Personalities and Organizations, 1900–1989.* Bethesda, Md.: Academica Press, 2012.

Thompson, Robert Farris. *Flash of the Spirit: African & Afro-American Art & Philosophy.* New York: Vintage, 1984.

Tinsley, Omise'eke Natasha. *Thiefing Sugar: Eroticism between Women in Caribbean Literature.* Durham, N.C.: Duke University Press, 2010.

Torres-Salliant, Silvio. *Caribbean Poetics: Towards an Aesthetic of West Indian Literature.* Cambridge: Cambridge University Press, 1997.

Turner, Joyce Moore. *Caribbean Crusaders and the Harlem Renaissance.* Urbana: University of Illinois Press, 2005.

Van Clief-Stefanon, Lyrae. "Bop: the North Star." In *Open Interval,* 3. Pittsburgh: University of Pittsburgh Press, 2009.

Vergès, Françoise. "Writing on Water: Peripheries, Flows, Capital, and Struggles in the Indian Ocean." *Positions: East Asia Cultures Critique* 11, no. 1 (2003): 241–57.

Walcott, Derek. "The Antilles: Fragments of Epic Memory." Nobel presentation, 1992.

———. "The Sea Is History." In *Collected Poems, 1948–1984.* New York: Farrar, Straus, and Giroux, 1987.

———. "What the Twilight Says: An Overture." In *Dream on Monkey Mountain, and Other Plays.* New York: Farrar, Straus, and Giroux, 1971.

Warf, B., and S. Arias. *The Spatial Turn: Interdisciplinary Perspectives.* London: Routledge, 2009.

wa Thiong'o, Ngugi. *Globalectics: Theory and the Politics of Knowing.* New York: Columbia University Press, 2012.

Weir, Donna M. "Leaving." *Moving Beyond Boundaries.* Vol. 1 of *International Dimensions of Black Women's Writing,* edited by Carole Boyce Davies and Molara Ogundipe-Leslie. New York: Pluto Press, New York University Press, 1995.

Williams, Eric. *Capitalism and Slavery.* Chapel Hill: University of North Carolina Press, 1944.

———. *From Columbus to Castro: The History of the Caribbean, 1492–1969.* 1970. Reprint, New York: Harper and Row, 1989.

Wolff, Cynthia Griffin. "Erikson's 'Inner Space' Reconsidered." *Massachusetts Review* 20, no. 2 (1979): 355–68.

Wynter, Sylvia. "Jonkonnu in Jamaica: Towards the Interpretation of Folk Dance as a Cultural Process." *Jamaica Journal* (June 1970): 34–48.

———. "Novel and History, Plot and Plantation." *Savacou* 5 (June 1971): 95–102.

———. "One Love—Rhetoric or Reality? Aspects of Afro-Jamaicanism." *Caribbean Studies* 12, no. 3 (1972): 64–97.

————. "On How We Mistook the Map for the Territory and Re-imprisoned Our-selves in Our Unbearable Wrongness of Being, of *Desêtre:* Black Studies toward the Human Project." In *Not Only the Master's Tools: African American Studies in Theory and Practice,* edited by Lewis R. Gordon and Jane Anna Gordon, 107–69. Boulder and London: Paradigm, 2005.

————. "Unsettling the Coloniality of Being/Power/Truth/Freedom: Towards the Hu-man, after Man, Its Overrepresentation—an Argument." *New Centennial Review* 3, no. 3 (2003): 257–337.

INDEX

Abiodun, Rowland, 73

activism and activist groups: Black Power movement, 48, 174–75, 189; Black Student Organizations, 48; and Black Studies, 188; of Caribbean radicals, 202–15; literary, 75–76; and Pan-Africanism, 99, 175–76, 207–9, 213; and socialism, 209–10; women, 211–14

Adisa, Opal Palmer, 157

aerial space, 97–98

aesthetics of Middle Passages, 100–101

afoxés (Carnival groups), 78–79

Africana Center (Cornell Univ.), 188–90, 192

African/Africana Studies programs, 55–56, 183, 189–90, 221

African Americans: in academia, 26–27; alienation of, 136, 165; exploitation of women, 108–9, 124–25; membership in the black community, 62–63; music of, 11, 51, 80, 112, 193; political education of, 47–49; and racism, 148–49, 173–75, 178–81; relationship with Caribbean-Americans, 52; sororities, 50–52; and stereotypes of, 193–99; in upstate NY, 30. *See also* slavery

African American Studies departments, 26–27, 56

African Blood Brotherhood, 212

African Union, 154, 162

"African Women in Defense of Ourselves" statement, 197

Afro-Brazilians, 65–68, 71–72, 75–84

Afro-Caribbeans, 135, 193–99

After the Dance (Danticat), 153

Aidoo, Ama Ata, 59, 224

Alexander, Michelle, 181

Alves, Miriam, 80–81

"American Imperialism and the British West Indies" (Jones), 210

American Negro Labor Committee, 212

Andall, Ella, 79, 82

Anglo-Caribbean literature, 154–56

Annie John (Kincaid), 151

anti-apartheid movement, 77

antiphony, 73

Appadurai, Arjun, 7

Arawaks, 38

archipelagization, 3

Aristide, Jean-Bertrand, 161

art, Caribbean, 163–64, 168, 171–72

àsé (voiced power), 73

ashe/àshé/àxé (spirit), 72–75, 81–82

Association for the Advancement of Negro People, 213

Atlantic Sound, The (Philips), 155

Australia, 38

"Back-Ah-Yard Cabirian" restaurant, 103

Bahamas, 225

"Bahia Girl" (Rudder), 79, 84

Baker, Houston, 74, 191

Barataria, Trinidad and Tobago, 129

CAROLE BOYCE DAVIES is professor of Africana studies and English at Cornell University. Her many works include *Left of Karl Marx: The Political Life of Black Communist Claudia Jones* and *Black Women, Writing and Identity: Migrations of the Subject*. She is the editor of the three-volume *Encyclopedia of the African Diaspora: Origins, Experiences, and Culture* and several other collections in African and Caribbean studies and black women's studies internationally.

The University of Illinois Press
is a founding member of the
Association of American University Presses.

Composed in 10.5/13 Adobe Minion Pro
with Adrianna Extended Pro display
by Lisa Connery
at the University of Illinois Press
Manufactured by Sheridan Books, Inc.

University of Illinois Press
1325 South Oak Street
Champaign, IL 61820-6903
www.press.uillinois.edu